URBAN TOURISM AND DEVELOPMENT IN THE SOCIALIST STATE

New Directions in Tourism Analysis

Series Editors: Kevin Meethan, University of Plymouth
Dimitri Ioannides, Southwest Missouri State University

Although tourism is becoming increasingly popular as both a taught subject and an area for empirical investigation, the theoretical underpinnings of many approaches have tended to be eclectic and somewhat underdeveloped. However, recent developments indicate that the field of tourism studies is beginning to develop in a more theoretically informed manner, but this has not yet been matched by current publications.

The aim of this series is to fill this gap with high quality monographs or edited collections that seek to develop tourism analysis at both theoretical and substantive levels using approaches which are broadly derived from allied social science disciplines such as Sociology, Social Anthropology, Human and Social Geography, and Cultural Studies. As tourism studies covers a wide range of activities and sub fields, certain areas such as Hospitality Management and Business, which are already well provided for, would be excluded. The series will therefore fill a gap in the current overall pattern of publication.

Suggested themes to be covered by the series, either singly or in combintion, include – consumption; cultural change; development; gender; globalisation; political economy; social theory; sustainability.

Also in the series

The Global Tourism System
Scarlett Cornelissen
ISBN 0 7546 4250 X

Performing Tourist Places
Jørgen Ole Bærenholdt, Michael Haldrup, Jonas Larsen and John Urry
ISBN 0 7546 3838 3

The Challenge of Tourism Carrying Capacity Assessment
Edited by Harry Coccossis and Alexandra Mexa
ISBN 0 7546 3569 4

Urban Tourism and Development in the Socialist State
Havana during the 'Special Period'

ANDREA COLANTONIO
Oxford Brookes University, UK

ROBERT B. POTTER
University of Reading, UK

ASHGATE

Andrea Colantonio and Robert B. Potter have asserted their moral right under the Copyright, Designs and Patents Act, 1988, to be identified as the authors of this work.

Published by
Ashgate Publishing Limited
Gower House
Croft Road
Aldershot
Hampshire GU11 3HR
England

Ashgate Publishing Company
Suite 420
101 Cherry Street
Burlington, VT 05401-4405
USA

Ashgate website: http://www.ashgate.com

British Library Cataloguing in Publication Data
Colantonio, Andrea
　　Urban tourism and development in the socialist state :
　　Havana during the 'special period'. - (New directions in
　　tourism analysis)
　　1. Tourism - Cuba - Havana 2. Cuba - Economic conditions -
　　1990- 3. Havana (Cuba) - Economic conditions 4. Cuba -
　　Economic policy
　　I. Title II. Potter, Robert B.
　　338.4'791'09729123

Library of Congress Cataloging-in-Publication Data
Colantonio, Andrea.
　　Urban tourism and development in the socialist state : Havana during the 'special
period' / by Andrea Colantonio and Robert B. Potter.
　　　　p. cm. -- (New directions in tourism analysis)
　　Includes bibliographical references and index.
　　ISBN 0-7546-4739-0
　　1. Tourism--Cuba--Havana. 2. City planning--Cuba--Havana. 3. Havana (Cuba)--
Economic conditions. I. Potter, Robert B. II. Title. III. Series.

　　G155.C9C53 2005
　　338.4'7917291230464--dc22

ISBN 0 7546 4739 0

2005028055

Printed and bound in Great Britain by Antony Rowe Ltd, Chippenham, Wiltshire.

Contents

List of Figures

List of Tables

Preface

This research monograph looks at the re-establishment and redevelopment of the tourism industry in Havana, Cuba since the introduction of the so called 'Special Period' in 1989, following the collapse of State socialism in the USSR and Eastern Europe. Since the early 1990s, the need to look outward to other economies of the developed world has meant that Cuba has specifically targeted tourism as a mechanism for economic growth and development. The research investigates the role played by international tourism in Cuba's institutional and economic restructuring and the country's re-insertion into the capitalist world economy.

To this point, the present study provides the most comprehensive and in-depth analysis of the economic, social, environmental and political realities that have emerged in Cuba as a result of the redevelopment of urban tourism since 1989. The approach adopted in this work focuses on the political economy of urban tourism in Havana, and encompasses the study of the allocation of tourism resources and its impacts, the generation of tourism policy, and the politics of tourism development in Cuba. Along similar lines, the research endeavours to assess the change in planning practices and mechanisms that have been brought about during the Special Period and to identify domestic and foreign stakeholders that are currently involved in the Cuban tourism industry.

Additionally, the research surveys Havana residents' perceptions concerning vital aspects of the current tourism-led development strategy, such as the future of tourism and preferred scenarios for the development of tourism. The residents of Havana have *de facto* become important 'stakeholders' within the tourism industry, whether they want to be or not. Hence, their perceptions should feed through the tourism policy-making process in order to foster real public involvement in governance at the municipal and national levels. This holistic approach to the study of tourism in Havana has not been attempted before and represents a novel approach to the study of Cuban tourism during the Special Period.

The work presented in this volume was carried out as part of Andrea's doctoral research, under the supervision of Rob, during the period October 2001 to January 2005. In respect of the conduct of the work we owe a considerable debt to The University of Reading Endowment Trust Fund (RETF), which on the appointment of Rob to the Chair of Human Geography at Reading, provided a full postgraduate studentship for Andrea. Before the transfer of both Andrea and Rob to Reading, a number of organizations had provided partial support for the research. These included Royal Holloway, University of London, the Developing Areas Research Group (DARG) of the Royal Geographical Society with the Institute of British Geographers, British Airways' Assisting Conservation Programme and the Dudley Stamp Memorial Fund of the Royal Society. In the summer of 2004 the Association for the Study of the Cuban Economy (ASCE) provided Andrea with the funding to enable him to present a paper at their Annual Conference held in Miami.

At the more personal level, Andrea would like to thank his parents and sister for their consistent and unconditional support, which they have given over the last few years. Further appreciation is expressed to a number of individuals who have helped in the conduct of this research. Firstly, Andrea would like to thank a courageous Cuban sociologist for her help in the conduct of the questionnaire survey in Havana's politically controlled research environment. In Havana, several officials at the Institute of Physical Planning, the Ministry of Environment, Science and Technology and the Ministry of Tourism facilitated access to unpublished documents. Both of us would like to express our sincere thanks to Dr Sally Lloyd-Evans and Dr Erlet Cater of the Department of Geography at the University of Reading, for discussing various aspects of the research at various junctures. Likewise, Professor Joseph Scarpaci of the Virginia State Polytechnic and University, made numerous helpful suggestions. Professor Derek Hall and Kate Paice also read and provided valuable comments and suggestions on the manuscript.

Andrea Colantonio
and Rob Potter
August 2005

For my family, Chiara, Bernardo and Frida
AC

PART I
Urban Tourism, Planning and Development

Chapter 1

Introduction, Aims and Objectives

Introduction

The demise of the Socialist bloc in 1989 has engendered structural changes in the economies of socialist countries. In the early 1990s, former socialist Eastern European countries began to abandon centralized planning systems and to embark upon liberalization reforms and outward-oriented development strategies which determined their transition towards a market economy. The institutional reforms promoted in these transitional countries mirrored political models provided by western liberal-capitalist democracies. Economic reforms often envisaged the promotion of export-oriented sectors according to neo-liberal development theories that were embraced by the main economic international organizations such as the World Bank and the International Monetary Fund throughout the 1980s and 1990s.

Other countries belonging to the bloc, such as Cuba and Vietnam, undertook more eclectic paths of institutional and economic restructuring, which aimed at keeping alive their centrally planned forms of economic and political governance. Thus, the outcome of the reforms embarked upon in such countries has been the hybrid transition toward a development model that blends awkwardly socialist planning and market principles. In this new model, political power and decision-making have been retained by the socialist leadership, while newly set up state corporations operate in 'emerging sectors', such as tourism and other non-traditional-exports, under market economy principles. Tourism, which was previously generally considered an unproductive economic sector by socialist governments (see chapter 3), has been rediscovered as a key economic activity by countries such as Cuba which have comparative advantages, including good climate and adequate environmental health conditions. Indeed, in the 1990s tourism has become the new pivot of Cuba's economic development and the main driver of its economic re-insertion into the global economy. As Hall (2001: 96) notes:

> For...Cuba, continuing communism in the post-Soviet era required readjustment from semi-colonial client state status (in relation to the Soviet Union) to an independent status exposed to the rigours of the (capitalist) global economy, of which international tourism is clearly an integral element.

After the collapse of the Soviet bloc in 1989, Castro announced the beginning of a 'Special Period'[1] for the island. In the early 1990s the Cuban government was obliged to promote a series of economic and institutional reforms (that will be assessed in chapters 6 and 10) that in Castro's words were designed to save the revolution and not to transform it. Tourism promotion was therefore identified as a crucial economic tool to avoid the country's total breakdown. Ayala (2001) and Brundenius (2002) identify two main stages to the new tourism development strategy embarked upon in the Special Period. The first one extended from 1990 to 1994, when the development of international tourism was seen mainly as a temporary solution to the growing hard currency gap in the external accounts. The second stage began from 1994 onwards when it became clear that tourism was acquiring a driving role in Cuba's long-term development strategy.

In the early 1990s, however, both the Cuban economic planning system and the tourist industry were not ready to compete with the pre-existing mature Caribbean tourism destinations and new globalizing economic forces. Thirty years of isolation from economic globalization had led to a shortfall of managerial skills among generations of workers in the tourist industry, as well as within the various tourism planning authorities. Moreover, restricted access to financial capital represented an obstacle to financing the quality tourism infrastructures and facilities capable of meeting the ever more sophisticated standards that are required by international tourists.

The Cuban government acted on an *ad hoc* basis and grounded the new international tourism promotion strategy on four measures, which are explored in more detail throughout this monograph. These were: (i) economic and environmental reforms which encompassed *Law 77/1995* that encouraged Foreign Direct Investment (FDI) and *Law 81/1997*, the Law of the Environment, which provided the environmental regulatory framework for the development of new activities; (ii) institutional capacity strengthening which entailed the creation of the Ministry of Tourism and the Ministry of Environment, Science and Technology as well as the development of schools for the consolidation of human resources such as 'Formatur'; (iii) the establishment of State holding companies and tour operators ranging from healthcare to the transport sector and (iv) the establishment in 1996 of 67 'tourist poles' or zones at the national and provincial levels.

Five of these tourist growth poles are to be found in Havana as will be discussed in detail in chapter 3. As a result of the mix of national tourism policies and promotion strategies, Havana experienced a rapid increase in tourist arrivals and has became a major recipient of FDI in the tourism industry since 1989. Several new hotels have been built or refurbished through joint ventures, while others have been built by the Cuban government and contracted out through management agreements with foreign firms. The economic opening up and growth of the external sector have

---

1   The term 'Special Period in time of peace' was introduced by Fidel Castro during a speech in October 1990. Throughout this book the term will be referred to as the Special Period, as commonly accepted in the literature.

determined the embryonic establishment of a small private sector and brought about new 'stakeholders' and civil society groups within Havana's settings. Indeed, tourism has often been regarded as a critical catalyst for social change and political transition in both former and current socialist countries for reasons that will be explored in more depth in chapters 2 and 4.

Aims and Objectives

The main purpose of this book is to examine the nature and the key characteristics of Cuba's transition and to assess the role played by tourism in the country's institutional and economic restructuring. The temporal framework of the analysis is provided by the Special Period while Havana sets the spatial stage for the investigation. A further purpose of this book is to fill a gap on Havana that exists in the literature concerning Latin American cities. In fact, there are few books or journal articles that discuss the main urban issues of contemporary Havana, with the exception of a handful of noteworthy publications (for example Scarpaci *et al.*, 2002; OTH, 2003a; INRH, 1997a; Segre *et al.*, 1981).

It can be argued that today's Havana (and Cuba as a whole) is characterized by two diverging forces that are pulling the city in two different directions. One force is embedded in the Cuban leadership's socialist ideology and is driven by an inward-looking model of development which aims to preserve the social achievements of the 1959 Revolution despite the scarcity of financial resources. The second force is exerted and driven by the global economy and the tourism industry, both of which are pulling Havana into the world market economy and forcing the city to look outward rather than inward. This force, if not adequately managed, risks yielding negative social and environmental outcomes for Havana's environments and its inhabitants.

There are at least two themes that will be directly or indirectly addressed throughout this research. The first one revolves around the in-depth examination of the two forces discussed above and the assessment of the nature of the changes in urban management, tourism planning and urbanization patterns that stem from the economic and institutional reforms of the Special Period. The second theme focuses on the effectiveness of the 1990s reforms and decentralization process in fostering participatory planning and generating the emergence of agents of change and new planning practices that could prove crucial in a post-Castro Cuba.

The key arguments of the book are twofold. The first one maintains that decentralization and the economic reforms of the 1990s are simply recasting vertical models of governance into new forms. Indeed, participatory and bottom-up planning are still absent in Havana and Cuba. Centralized urban governance and obsolete planning practices are becoming increasingly incompatible with new tourism project procedures and need modernizing to prevent negative outcomes. The second argument holds that the current planning, implementation and monitoring of Havana's urban development are not being carried out according to integrated physical and economic criteria that mirror the two diverging forces reviewed above. For example, tourism development plans are made individually, according to economic criteria, by tourism corporations without a holistic approach in accordance with Havana's planning authorities. Indeed, while the latter still devise plans for future urban development, they lack the resources to implement them.

Closely linked to the main aims and arguments of the monograph, there are five specific objectives and an equivalent number of questions that the research endeavours to address. The objectives are:

1. To critically review Havana's past and present urban and tourism development. There is a considerable literature, mostly in Spanish, concerning both the historical development of tourism in Cuba and Havana's urban development. However, the interrelationships between these two fields of investigation have never been incorporated into a single integrated study.
2. To assess the change in planning practices and mechanisms brought about by the Special Period. There is currently scant material providing insightful and in-depth analyses of this topic.
3. To identify domestic and foreign stakeholders that are currently involved in the Cuban tourism industry and appraise how they are contributing to the planning and decision-making process. This objective is entwined with the previous one. Both are of vital importance to understand Cuba's current transitional patterns and to identify recommendations for the future.
4. To demonstrate how the current tourism development strategy is skewed toward meeting tourists' recreational needs whilst neglecting local residents. Current patterns of tourism infrastructure promotion mean the establishment of *urban tourism enclaves* in the form of Havana's best hotels that, in turn, undermine Havana inhabitants' recreational needs.
5. To survey residents' perceptions on the impacts of tourism in their area as a vital source of data and the first crucial step toward participatory planning in Havana. This has never been attempted before in Havana due to the politically controlled research environment in which, both national and foreign researchers are forced to work in Cuba.

Similarly, the five main questions that will be addressed in the study are: to what extent is tourism transforming Havana's main functions and its environmental, economic and social fabrics? Is tourism a major driver of urban environmental and social stresses or is it contributing to the enhancement of Havana's social and environmental assets? What are the changes in urban and tourism planning that stem from the economic and institutional reforms of the Special Period? Are the 1990s reforms and decentralization process effective? Can we talk of participatory planning practices in Havana?

There are important issues, such as the Cuban Diaspora, the USA blockade (*embargo*) and the recent legislation implemented in the USA against Cuba, that have great consequences for Cuba's current transition and its future development model which cannot be studied in depth in this book. For example, it is argued that if the *embargo* was to be lifted, the sheer increase of USA tourists to Cuba could significantly contribute to boosting the country's hard currency revenue, although the social and ideological consequences of this remain to be seen.

Cuba's Hybrid Transition and its Peculiarities

After the demise of socialism, the literature on development studies has increasingly explored the nature of the transition in former socialist states. Harloe (1996) notes how much of this literature has focused on Eastern European countries and developed transitional models and theories, which have identified emerging patterns of urbanization. In Harloe's (1996: 3-4) view the theory of transition has so far endeavoured to answer three main questions:

- What is involved in the transition?
- How it proceeds and how it relates to the previous histories of the societies in which it takes place.
- Does it involve a simple negation of the previous social order or a more complex mixture of rejection and adaptation?

Pickvance (1996) argues that much of mainstream transitional theory has been mistakenly influenced by oversimplified attempts to reject or ignore the significance of persisting legacies of the socialist period. Indeed, the notion that doctrines of neo-liberal economics, developed in the North during the 1980s are simply having a re-run in the East European countries a decade later is fundamentally flawed and should therefore be rejected. In other words, there are important socio-economic and environmental legacies from the socialist era which are playing a crucial role in shaping the transition of many East European former socialist nations. These place-specific legacies cannot be ignored by current transition models.

Thus, the most valuable empirical studies that have tested the validity of transitional theory have concentrated on the study of the nature and effects of privatization in Eastern European countries (see Marcuse, 1996). Such studies have demonstrated the 'path dependent'[2] nature of post-socialist change (Stark, 1992; Szelenyi, 1996). The 'path dependent' concept highlights the constraints exerted by existing institutional resources on actors in the transformation process. Thus, the economic, political and social outcomes of the transition have been contingent on local institutional specificities. In fact, state socialism was not a cross-nationally identical phenomenon. Hence, a uniform analysis of the transition cannot be easily provided. In tourism research, for example, Williams and Baláž (2000) compared the privatization of tourism enterprises in Slovakia and the Czech Republic and highlighted how they have followed different paths depending on privatization

---

2   Harloe (1996) argues that economic historians first used this term which was taken up more widely by sociologists and political scientists who study institutional and organizational change.

methods, changes in tourism demand and the professional skills of the enterprise management.

The analysis of Cuba's hybrid transition does have to take into account several factors which impede easy comparisons with the paths embarked upon by East European countries. These factors are summarized below and will be re-examined in more depth throughout this volume:

- Politically and administratively Cuba is still a socialist country.
- Ideology and the figure of Castro still permeate Cuban politics.
- Centralized and vertical planning characterize decision making.
- There exist several state corporations working in the external sector under market economy principles which participate in numerous joint ventures set up with foreign investors.
- The private sector is still small and no privatization has been carried out so far.
- Civil society movements are absent from Cuban politics or at least not formally acknowledged outside state institutions.
- For the first time in its history Cuba is truly independent. Indeed, after political and economic domination from Spain, the USA and, to lesser extent Russia, the island has been left to stand on its own feet since 1990.

The Selection of Cuba and Havana as Case Studies

There are several reasons why Cuba and its capital were selected as the subject of this research. The first was the geo-political role that Cuba has played and continues playing in the Americas. With an area of 105,006 square kilometres (40,543 square miles) and an estimated population of 11,308,764 in 2004, Cuba is the largest and most Western island of the West Indies, as shown in Figure 1.1. Furthermore, it occupies a strategic location between North and South America and lies on the commercial lanes of most sea travel to all countries in the Caribbean Sea and the Gulf of Mexico.

The island's history spans three principal periods, each of which is characterized by distinct socio-economic and political forms of societal organization: the Spanish Colonial (1492 to 1898), the American Neo-colonial (1898 to 1959) and the Revolutionary (1959 to present). The first period was characterized by a dependent colonial development (see chapter 3), while the second period was grounded on North American capitalism, sharp social stratification and a weak democratic system (see chapter 6). Following the 1959 revolution, Cuba adopted Marxism as its main form of economic and political governance. Broadly speaking, this meant strong central government with indirect citizen participation in policy decisions, a centrally controlled economy, the eradication of social divisions and a more egalitarian society.

By the mid-1970s, the geo-political significance of Cuba's socialist experiment began to unravel as other Caribbean and Latin American countries showed interest in the social achievements of Cuba's revolutionary government. In Jamaica, for example, Michael Manley became a close admirer of Fidel Castro's political ideals. Similarly, the Sandinista government of Nicaragua was inspired and supported by Cuba. This anti-capitalist wave caused concern among USA officials that Marxism could spread to other nearby countries. As a result, in the 1980s, the U.S. administration began numerous covert and open political anti-communism campaigns in Central America. Today, however, only a handful of Latin American countries, such as Venezuela and Brazil, continue to show direct economic and political support for Cuba. Nevertheless, Cuba still represents the last bastion of communism between the USA and Latin America and a direct threat to USA economic and political interest in the region.

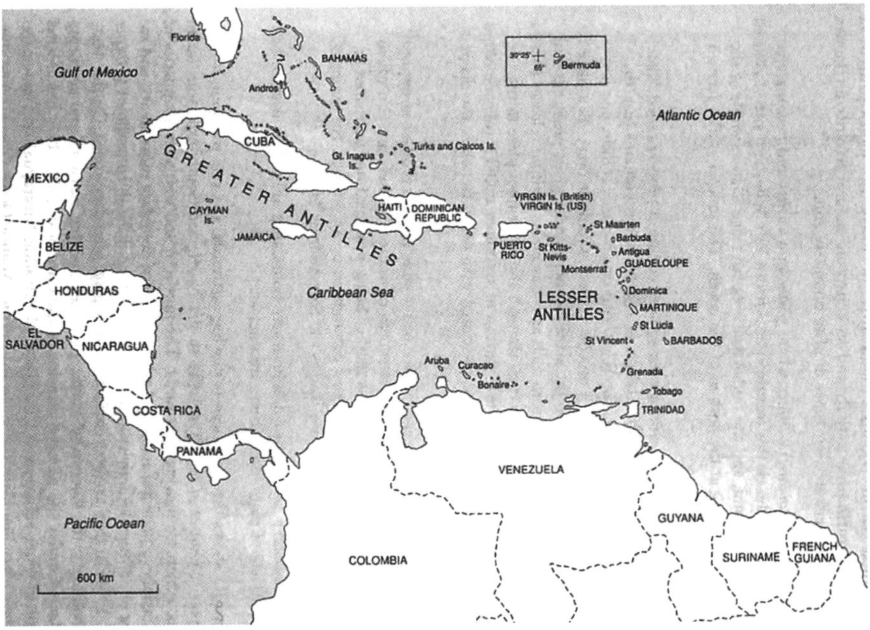

Figure 1.1 Cuba and the Commonwealth Caribbean

(*Source:* Lloyd-Evans, 1994)

Another reason for choosing Cuba lies in the fact that the country provides a *sui generis* case study for the critical evaluation of the transition towards a new socialist development model after the collapse of the Soviet bloc. Cuba has therefore been selected for this investigation as it offers a unique opportunity to formulate a possible 'third way' between market-based and centrally planned forms of economic and political governance. This 'third way' provided by the Cuban context could, at least in theory, set examples of good political governance and successful development models for other less developed countries whose economy relies significantly on the tourism sector.

This book, however, will highlight how there often exists discrepancies between 'good intentions' expressed by socialist governments and their actual translation into reality. Nonetheless, the study of Cuba provides an exceptional prospect to learn lessons about the difficulties, risks and opportunities of implementing tourism-oriented development strategies in the Caribbean and the South as a whole. Indeed, the main challenge faced by countries in which tourism is the pivot of the accumulation of national health consists often of maximizing the economic benefits of the global tourism industry without exacerbating local social and environmental problems.

Havana as a Case Study

Urban tourism in Havana has been pivotal in Cuba's political and economic re-insertion into the world economy. Indeed, since 1989, Havana has experienced a significant increase in tourism development projects and has undergone unique urban change. After forty years of under-investment in urban infrastructure and the curbing of urban development, Havana is slowly regaining its primacy as one of Cuba's, and indeed the Caribbean's, major tourist destinations. Havana's tourist re-development can be seen as a direct outcome of the national economic strategy embarked upon by the Cuban leadership at the beginning of the 1990s, which was grounded on the promotion of tourism.

Although criticisms of the current program of tourism promotion in Havana have not appeared in print, there are many voices within Cuba that pointed out four main areas of concern regarding the city's future. Firstly, at the national level, tourism is engendering regional imbalances in Cuba. This is prompting migration towards national tourist poles and weakening the objectives of national and local physical planning. Secondly, tourism has been the only force responsible for urban development in Havana during the Special Period. Thirdly, Havana is developing along its coastline, as often happens in Caribbean and island cities. In addition, tourist development is prompting diverging environmental and socio-economic conditions within Havana's neighbourhoods and triggering the (re-)emergence of a 'dual city' according to urban development patterns characteristic of the pre-revolutionary period. Lastly, it is argued that the rapid increase of tourist inflows and tourism-oriented facilities is testing Havana's dilapidated urban infrastructural network and prompting old social problems and new economic planning and policy-making issues.

Havana, therefore, represents a fascinating case study allowing the investigation of the key role, risks, opportunities and impacts of tourism development in the implementation of integrated urban and tourism planning in the Caribbean. As noted earlier, Havana and Cuba as a whole have not been exposed to globalizing forces for over thirty years and allow, therefore, a critical analysis of the powerful transforming effects of tourism on urban development and practices of urban governance in socialist countries after socialism. Moreover, Havana is likely to play a central role in Cuba's transition towards a new political and economic path of development in a post-Castro Cuba. It is in Havana that the economic and societal changes brought about by the Special Period are more visible than in the rest of Cuba. Indeed, in rural areas, the Cuban leadership still holds genuine popular support. In this respect, it is worth pointing out how it is not a coincidence that two thirds of the people who leave Cuba by any means possible, including rafts, are from Havana (GDIC, 2002).

Outline of this Book

The book is divided into three main parts. Part I, comprising chapters 1 to 5, addresses the context of the research and reviews the literature concerning urban tourism and development in the socialist State. Further, it establishes the framework for the measurement of specific variables, the data collection and the interpretation of problems which will be tackled throughout the research. The present chapter has set the context of the study by introducing the Special Period and the paradigm shift in Cuba's development model in the 1990s in which great emphasis has been placed on tourism promotion. The chapter has introduced how Havana has been pivotal in the pursuit of this new development strategy and has undergone an important urban change as a result of tourism growth.

Chapter 2 illustrates the methodology of the present work while chapter 3 examines the changing role of tourism within transitional countries and introduces the case study of Cuba. More specifically, chapter 3 compares the conceptualization and the role of tourism in development models of both Western (capitalist) and former and continuing socialist countries. Further, the chapter explores the main political and economic reasons for the intervention of governments in the sector, with a special emphasis on the Cuban context.

The impacts and the planning implications of tourism promotion in urban areas are discussed in chapters 4 and 5. Most specifically, chapter 4 provides a theoretical framework for the study of urban tourism and reviews several approaches to examine tourism in urban areas. Chapter 5 analyses the main economic, environmental and social impacts of tourism. Further, the chapter highlights important differences that exist between cities in the developed and developing worlds and discusses the problems involved with the selection of urban tourism indicators and variables to be used in development planning.

Part II of the book, consisting of chapters 6 to 9, addresses the main hypotheses and arguments used as part of the work. Most specifically, chapter 6 provides an historical account of the importance of tourism as the driving force in Havana's urban expansion, with the exception of the revolutionary period from 1959 to 1990. This chapter is of vital importance in paving the way for the study of the next three chapters which in turn assess the economic, social and environmental effects of tourism on Havana's urban fabric during the Special Period.

The socio-economic impact of tourism development in Havana is critically examined in chapter 7 with a special emphasis on the economic reforms of the 1990s and the significance of the opening up of the economy. The chapter assesses the emergence of civil society groups in Cuba and the re-appearance of old social problems, such as prostitution and crime, which had been virtually eliminated by the revolutionary government. These phenomena are directly and indirectly linked to tourism and the promotion of the external sector.

Chapter 8 examines the environmental impact of tourism on Havana with a special emphasis on the city's infrastructure. The chapter argues that the tourism re-development of the Special Period is responsible for the broad re-emergence of patterns of duality in Havana. Lastly, chapter 9 reports the findings of the survey results on residents' perceptions concerning tourism development in Havana. The survey results are used to test contrasting claims about the impacts of tourism in Havana by advocates of tourism on one side, and critics of the tourism development strategy on the other.

The main planning and policy-making implications that stem from issues identified in Part II are discussed in Part III of the book. This part, made up of chapters 10 and 11, links the empirical findings to the current politics of planning and governance practices in Havana and Cuba as a whole. Thus, chapter 10 discusses the nature of the institutional reforms promoted in Cuba during the Special Period and examines their effectiveness at the local level. Further, it reviews actors and stakeholders involved in Havana's city governance and highlights the importance of tourism planning for the city's urban development. Lastly, chapter 11 presents the main conclusions of the study and suggests some recommendations for both Havana's future urban and tourism development and topics for future research.

Conclusions

In the 1990s, the collapse of the Soviet block promoted the implementation of moderate market-oriented reforms and prompted structural changes in Cuba's economic and centralized planning system. Tourism has become the 'new engine' and driving force of the Cuban economy, replacing the agricultural sector. This book looks at the role, impacts and planning implications of urban tourism in Havana within the new national and local development strategy of Cuba.

The study will yield in-depth evidence on the influence of international tourism on the transitional path of socialist countries in the post-Soviet Union era. Furthermore, the findings of the research will provide valuable insights concerning the correlation between globalizing economic forces, local responses and environmental and social change in the urban areas of less developed countries, with a special emphasis on the Caribbean.

Chapter 2

Methodology, Logistics and Reflexivity

Introduction

Over the last two decades, a significant literature has focused on the practical, methodological and ethical issues involved in doing research in the South (Sidaway, 1992; Hoddinot, and Devereux 1992). A special emphasis has been placed on the ethical dilemmas that Western researchers face while conducting fieldwork in developing countries. These include issues of ownership, exploitation and the power imbalance between the researcher and the researched. Thus, the purpose of this chapter is to review such dilemmas and to illustrate the theoretical and practical research methods adopted in this research. The chapter is divided into two main parts. The first provides a concise overview of some potential pitfalls of doing research in the South which have been unearthed in the recent development studies literature. The second part explains the methodology adopted in the present research, with a special emphasis on the questionnaire survey and the logistics and other practical matters involved in two fieldwork periods in Cuba conducted as part of the present work.

Issues and Dilemmas of Doing Research in the South

In recent years there has been a proliferation of publications which have raised concerns over the dangers of conducting unethical and politically-insensitive research in developing countries (Laws *et al.*, 2003; Scheyvens *et al.*, 2003). The primary concern maintains that the traditional model of research now concentrates internationally recognized expertise in a few centres in the North. Further, even within developed nations, knowledge and skills are increasingly being concentrated in fewer research centres. Examples of such centres are Oxford and Cambridge in the United Kingdom and Harvard and Boston in the USA. At the national level, these centres concentrate an unfair share of economic and educational resources to the great disadvantage of less traditionally established research centres.

The unequal distribution of research and expertise at the international level is illustrated by Laws *et al.* (2003:15) who argue that:

> [a] situation has developed where research knowledge and skills belong to an elite. For example, much of the research into the issues of the South is carried out by people who are based in the North. Frequently, research is done by highly paid academics or consultants

who make brief visits to poverty-stricken areas and then return to their base, taking their data with them.

Along with the concentration of knowledge in the North, their critique also underlines the problem of non-reciprocity which permeates much of current development research practice. Indeed, often data never return to the country or place they relate to. This, in turn, generates few opportunities for Southern people or non-academics to learn from the research processes. In other words, individuals and local communities who provide North-based researchers with assistance often do not get anything in return for their time and efforts.

Another area of concern which relates to doing research in developing countries is the power imbalance between the researcher and the researched. Scheyvens *et al.* (2003) argue that power asymmetry exists on two levels. Firstly, real differences associated with access to money, education and other resources, may make participants feel inferior to researchers. Secondly, perceived differences which exist in the mind of participants can reinforce feelings of low self-esteem, which may be common in marginalized or less advantaged groups within society.

Although the validity of these assertions can be criticized, there can be little doubt that much of the current social science research agenda is dominated by Western scholars, researching 'other' people's lives, culture, economy and environment. People from the South are often guinea pigs to be examined in Western research projects, with little interaction occurring in the opposite direction (Scheyvens and Storey, 2003). Often, researchers hold all the control in the research process while participants are not actively engaged with the research and play a merely consultative role. For this reason, the recent debate on development studies has urged researchers to reconsider their role in the investigation process and to assess how their relatively privileged position may influence the research process and its outcomes.

The critical issue of a fair and ethical management of the cross-cultural relationship with the 'host' community has also encouraged an increasing number of scholars to consider how their 'positionality' can have an effect on the topic they study. Indeed, researchers are ever more encouraged to be 'reflexive' and assess how elements such as their social background, age, sex, ethnicity, religion, sexuality, education, work experience and skills might have a bearing on their research findings (Laws *et al.*, 2003). In the research process, it is important that researchers are open about their viewpoint on, and their involvement in, specific issues which include their beliefs, interests and experiences of a given topic.

Methodology of the Research, Practicalities and Reflexivity

The issues of power, positionality and reflexivity introduced in the previous section are linked to different types of research in which scholars can become engaged. Broadly speaking, two main research traditions in the social sciences have been identified in the literature. The first is traditional or 'positivist' research which tends to deny the power dynamics involved in research. According to Laws *et al.* (2003:

27), this tradition claims that the scientist is a disinterested, unbiased observer, who can produce 'objective truths' about reality, a reality which is out there to be observed value-free. Researchers can be committed to certain sets of values but can still be seen as non-partisan in some respects and in some situations.

A second and more recent tradition in social science research challenges the notion that a value-free and truly objective science is possible. Within this tradition, several approaches to research, including social constructionism, critical theory and postmodernism, contend that the observer's point of view affects how reality is studied. Indeed, reality is socially constructed through the researcher's values and beliefs because the observer tends to see what he or she is looking for. This leads to the conclusion that truly unbiased research and an objective truth cannot exist.

The in-depth analysis and the wider theoretical implications of these two traditions are outside the scope of this research. Here, it suffices to highlight that these conflicting strands have conventionally been associated with quantitative research (the traditional-positivist approach) on the one side and qualitative techniques (the alternative strands) on the other. Quantitative techniques have dominated most social science research in the past and are characterized by many of its proponents as objective, 'facts-based', and most importantly, as leading to quantifiable results (Overton and Van Diermen, 2003). Quantitative data can mainly be collected through observations, questionnaires, structured interviews and secondary data, encompassing published government statistics, local or national reports and archival material.

In contrast, qualitative research techniques are often used to investigate myriad subjective and contested 'truths', as opposed to a universal and objective truth. Qualitative methods include a variety of techniques, including oral histories group discussions, semi-structured interviews and writings of ethnography, among many others. Qualitative research can incorporate quantitative data and quantification. But, as Brockington and Sullivan (2003: 79), forthrightly point out:

> [t]hey (qualitative methods) go beyond numbers to consider the meanings of quantitatively derived findings to the people they affect, and to problematise, rather than accept uncritically, the production of such data.

It would be wrong to assume that qualitative and quantitative techniques are mutually exclusive (Murray and Overtone, 2003). There is no reason why methods cannot be mixed and researchers use both, avoiding falling into the trap of being either qualitative or quantitative. Indeed, the spectrum of research methods can be seen as a continuum where observers position themselves according to their research objectives, values and preferences.

In the context of this research, the methodology employed was based on a multi-method approach which made primary use of interview techniques and questionnaire analysis in the context of urban tourism. This approach blends political economy and tourism studies of urban areas with planning theory. Mainstream research on tourism in urban areas has often been conducted according to demand and supply models which will be reviewed in more depth in chapter 3. In simple terms, Pearce (1999: 4) specifies how:

> Demand or origin studies stress the changes in market conditions which affect people's motivation to travel and the factors which influence their ability to do so, for example increase in leisure time and disposable income, improved technology and travel organisation. Supply-side or destination research tends to address the benefits that the development of tourism bring or is perceived to bring, to consider what leads both public and private sectors to foster its growth and how it is best achieved.

Hall (1994) argues that there is a tendency for many tourism researchers to focus on 'practical' or 'applied' studies, such as the economic dimensions of tourism or aspects of marketing, consumer research or visitor flow. Little attention has been paid to the wider philosophical, political and societal implications of such work. In addition, such frameworks often emphasized 'hard' data measurement and thresholds reflecting the quasi-positivistic, 'value free' nature of much tourism research (Hall, 1991). By contrast, he contends that 'tourism is not a continuation of politics but an integral part of the world of political economy' (Hall, 1994: 68).

The approach adopted in this volume focuses on the political economy of urban tourism in Havana which encompasses the study of the allocation of tourism resources, the generation of tourism policy and the politics of tourism development in Cuba. The study will look at these issues through the lenses of urban studies, impact assessment research and participatory planning theory. This allows for the critical study of the interwoven relationships between the dynamics of tourism promotion in Havana and the city's overall development and urban management process.

This approach does not deny the importance of the other components of urban tourism; rather it seeks to explore these areas in greater depth. On the demand side, for example, it is worth mentioning the theory of tourism urbanization put forward by that part of the literature (Page, 1995; Mullins, 1991). According to this theory, the shift from a fordist to a post-fordist mode of production has led to a re-interpretation of the city's essence in the function of consumption rather than production (Page, 1995). As a consequence, cities are developing ever more as places of consumption, relaxation and leisure and therefore as tourist destinations (Mullins, 1991).

Data Gathering and Fieldwork

The research entailed the collection of quantitative data and, to a lesser extent, qualitative data. Most of the data were collected during two periods of fieldwork in Havana. The first two-month fieldwork investigation was conducted between October 2002 and December 2002. The second four-month fieldwork investigation was carried out from May 2003 to September 2003. However, an initial one-month visit to Havana had been conducted in July 2000 by the first named author in order to collect data for a Masters dissertation on the environmental impact of tourism in Havana which was completed at the Institute of Latin American Studies, University of London (Colantonio, 2000). It was during this time that first contact with Havana's academics, planners and officials was established and the potential topic for research identified.

The fieldwork visits presented a number of difficulties which are not uncommon for foreign researchers working in Cuba. The main difficulty was faced during the first fieldwork visit and involved both administrative and research-related components. In fact, the fieldwork was conducted by means of a tourist visa and this had two main implications. Firstly, the maximum stay in Cuba was limited to two consecutive months. Secondly, access to policy documents was strictly prohibited because of the nature of the visa. Nonetheless, the first fieldwork visit represented a useful opportunity to re-establish and expand contacts with academics, policy-makers, planners and key informants in Havana.

The first fieldwork period for this research was carefully prepared for in the UK during the nine months preceding the visit. During the preparation, the literature on urban tourism in Havana was reviewed in order not to duplicate other research and the aims and objectives of the research were defined. It is worth pointing out that the original research design focused on the impact of both FDI and tourism on urban change of Havana. However, after the first few weeks in Cuba, the first author realised the difficulty of gaining access to economic data concerning the external sector as a whole. As a result, it was decided to concentrate the research efforts on the tourism sector alone.

After the completion of the first fieldwork period, the data gathered were examined, the theoretical background of the research was re-worked, the research methodology was refined and the second fieldwork plan and checklists were devised. The second fieldwork trip was carried out by the first author through a student visa which allowed access to policy-documents and texts that had previously been restricted.

During the fieldwork investigations, both primary and secondary data were collected at Havana's main universities and institutions. These included the University of Havana, the José Echéverria Polytechnic Institute, the Ministry of Tourism, Havana's Tourism Board (OTH, *Oficina de Turismo de la Habana*), the Provincial Office of the Institute of National Planning (DPPF, *Dirección Provincial de Planificación Física*), the Ministry of Economy and Planning (*Ministerio de Economía y Planificación*), the Ministry of Science, Technology and Environment (CITMA, *Ministerio de Ciencia, Tecnología y Medioambiente*) and the Group for the Integral Development of the Capital (GDIC, *Grupo para el Desarrollo Integral de la Capital*).

The data sources ranged from academic texts, to departmental policy statements, to policy documents, including Havana's development plans. The main texts consulted also encompassed documents concerning legislation from local and national government bodies and planning authorities. The advantage of using such materials stems mainly from the authenticity and credibility that they offered. However, the main disadvantage associated with these documents was the ideological and rhetorical structures that were intrinsically embedded within them. In fact, the textual and documentary analysis of official writings and institutional publications required an elaborate distilling process aimed to filter data and hidden meanings out of the writings. In this context, it could be argued that an interesting topic for future research could be the study of the relationship between the discourse analysis of texts concerning tourism and urban planning and their actual translation into practice.

The data gathering was a slow process because most State-related data sources, including official statistics and Havana's development plans, have restricted access which requires authorization for consultation. Hence, an essential component of the data collection was to gain the trust of state authorities. In the past, researchers adverse to Castro and the Cuban revolution have conducted research within the island and used their data to criticize Cuba's socialist experiment. Cuban authorities have, therefore, become increasingly suspicious about foreign researchers, especially because as a well known Cuban academic (who cannot be named) put it: 'Cubans are aware of their weaknesses and mistakes. However, it is up to them to criticize themselves as the island has been in a constant and unbalanced struggle with the USA for over forty years'.

During the fieldwork, it was essential to create 'a good impression' and to establish good working relations with Cuban authorities in order to obtain permissions to access confidential data. At the outset, the first author explained clearly the academic purpose of the research to all participants and showed them his awareness of Cuba's current delicate situation. This reassured the majority of contacts that his interest in the research topic was genuine rather than commercial or military. As a matter of fact, in order to reciprocate their participation in the research process and allow data to return back to Cuba, the author agreed to give soft copies of this research to specific institutions, including the Ministry of Tourism and the University of Havana.

Interviews

During the fieldwork a total of 26 in-depth interviews were carried out. These were conducted with 9 officials, 3 academics, 7 practitioners and 7 residents in Havana, as summarized in Table 2.1. The interviews constituted a vital tool to access experts' and local residents' opinions and ideas which have subsequently been used to inform questionnaire design (see the next section). However, on a few occasions interviews with officials were time consuming because the researcher had to call them several times in order to arrange an interview. Moreover, some interviews required a lengthy introductory and ice-breaking discussions on themes such as the weather and food in Cuba, which were not directly related to the research topic. On a few occasions, the questions asked were answered only in the last few minutes of the interview.

However, the main difficulty involved with the interviewing process with officials was to extrapolate hidden meanings from the 'official account of the story'. In fact, the interviewees were clearly bridled by their institutional role while answering the questions. However, this hindrance has been overcome through the use of 'data triangulation'. This technique implies asking opinions and questions on sensitive issues to a range of people working in different state institutions. The various answers were subsequently cross-checked with one other in order to authenticate diverging data and accounts.

The access to 'institutional' interviewees was gained mainly through gatekeepers, intermediaries and snowballing techniques (see Flowerdew and Martin, 1997, for an in-depth description of these techniques and associated terminology). A smaller number of interviews were arranged following an extensive website search carried out before the fieldwork and after the presentation of the research at various faculties of the University of Havana and the Institute of Tropical Geography. Almost all interviews with 'institutional actors' were arranged by telephone, carried out in institutional settings and audio-taped, with two or three exceptions. By contrast, interviews with local residents were carried out in a more casual environment, mostly public places, cafes or bars. Further, these interviews were not taped and were arranged usually by friends and acquaintances of the researcher.

The interviews were either open or semi-structured for two main reasons. Firstly, the varied backgrounds of the participants precluded the use of a standardized interview schedule (Barriball and While, 1994). Secondly, open interviews were carried out first to identify what were the main issues involved in the development of tourism in Havana, and in its planning. Subsequently, these issues constituted the basis for the development of themes to be explored in semi-structured interviews and, to a lesser extent, through the questionnaire survey. The anonymity of the interviewing process was guaranteed to all the 'non institutional' participants.

It is worth pointing out that all interviews began with an introduction of the research and the first author's background in order to stimulate interest in the respondents. The interviews were conducted relatively informally and without using high-tech devices such as digital sound recorders. This helped reduce the power imbalance with the participants who often do not have access to state of the art technology. The interviews were carried out in Spanish, a language in which the first named author is fluent. This also helped in avoiding ambiguities concerning the author's positionality with regard to Cuba's current political situation. Indeed, views on Cuba by Western researchers are often polarized between those in favour and those against the country's communist experiment. In this context, the researcher clearly stated to all interviewees that he arrived in Cuba without any preconceptions on Communism and he was neither in favour or against Fidel Castro's leadership. By doing so, on many occasions the author gained the trust of the participants who consequently enjoyed interviews and answered openly during the interviewing process.

Table 2.1 Interviews undertaken by Andrea Colantonio between May 2003 and September 2003 that have been referenced in the main text of the book

Code	Interviewee	Date	Type of Interview
1	Planner, Institute of Physical Planning, Havana	28/05/03	Informal
2	Policy-maker, Provincial Office of CITMA, Havana	02/06/03	Informal
3	Resident of Cerro municipality, Havana	14/06/03	Informal
4	Member of Staff, Institute of Tropical Geography, Havana	15/06/03	Formal
5	Researcher, Provincial Office of the Institute of Physical Planning, Havana	16/06/03	Formal
6	Member of Staff, Provincial Office of CITMA, Havana	20/06/03	Informal
7	Head of Environmental Commission, Havana's Municipal Assembly, Havana	24/06/03	Formal
8	Maria, resident of Miramar	29/06/03	Informal
9	Resident of Vedado, Havana	30/06/03	Informal
10	Policy-maker, Provincial Office of the Institute of Physical Planning, Havana	04/07/03	Informal
11	Professor, CUJAE and ex-director of GDIC, Havana	10/07/03	Formal
12	Engineer at Plan Maestro, Havana	11/07/03	Formal
13	Member of Staff, Mintur	15/07/03	Informal
14	Director of Investments, Oficina del Historiador, Havana	17/07/03	Formal
15	Director of 'Sibarimar' Programme in East Havana	21/07/03	Formal
16	Professor, University of Havana	24/07/03	Informal
17	Researcher, CICA	26/07/03	Formal
18	Researcher, Provincial Office of the Institute of Physical Planning, Havana	16/08/03	Informal
19	Member of Staff, CITMA	18/08/03	Informal
20	Architect at Plan Maestro, Havana	19/08/03	Formal

21	Hotelier, Hotel Naciónal	21/08/03	Formal
22	Hotelier, Hotel Vedado	21/08/03	Formal
23	Planner, Provincial Office of the Institute of Physical Planning	22/08/03	Formal
24	Resident of Centro Habana	28/08/03	Informal
25	Resident of Old Havana	01/09/03	Informal
26	Engineer, INRH	02/09/03	Informal

This table lists the code number and details of the interviews undertaken between May 2003 and September 2003 in Havana.

Questionnaires

As noted earlier, one specific objective of the research was to survey residents' perceptions concerning urban tourism as part of overall development in the Special Period. Thus, the methodology employed in the research included a questionnaire survey which was carried out in Havana between May 2003 and September 2003. The questionnaire survey and its findings are presented in detail in chapter 9. Here, it suffices to say that the survey sample was randomly chosen in Havana's four newly established 'tourist poles', and consisted of 160 interviewees, 40 in each tourist pole.

The sample size was selected taking into account the time and facilities available. Moreover, the survey could not have been conducted on a larger scale as it was carried out without any formal authorization or approval and, indeed, it would have drawn the unwanted attention of state institutions. The validity and reliability of the survey results obtained have been tested according to statistical significance tests, such as the Chi Square or the Fisher tests whenever possible (see chapter 9).

Survey methodology – The sampling methodologies used in questionnaire surveys are wide and diverse, ranging from probability sampling to purposive or non-random sampling. For the purpose of this study, the sample was randomly chosen within Havana's four newly established tourist poles and consisted of 160 interviewees, 40 in each tourist pole. The identification of the sample was carried out employing a 'multi-stage' probability sampling technique based on a two-stage process. The first stage entailed the stratification of Havana's tourist areas by type of district. The second stage identified the sample areas which showed a high density of tourism facilities and which had undergone noticeable environmental and economic change since the 1990s tourism re-development.

The sample areas are shown in Figure 2.1. More specifically, Area 1 includes the plot delimited by 60th Street and 90th Street in Montebarreto; Area 2 comprises areas surrounding the Meliá Cohiba Hotel and 23rd Street in Vedado; and Area 3 consists of the Cathedral square and Obispo street in Old Havana. The sample choice in East Havana was more complex due to the more scattered spatial distribution of tourist facilities in this district. However, Marina Tarará, and Guanabo in the Eastern municipality were eventually selected to conduct the survey. These areas are characterized by different socio-economic and environmental conditions which will be reviewed in greater depth in Chapters 6 and 8.

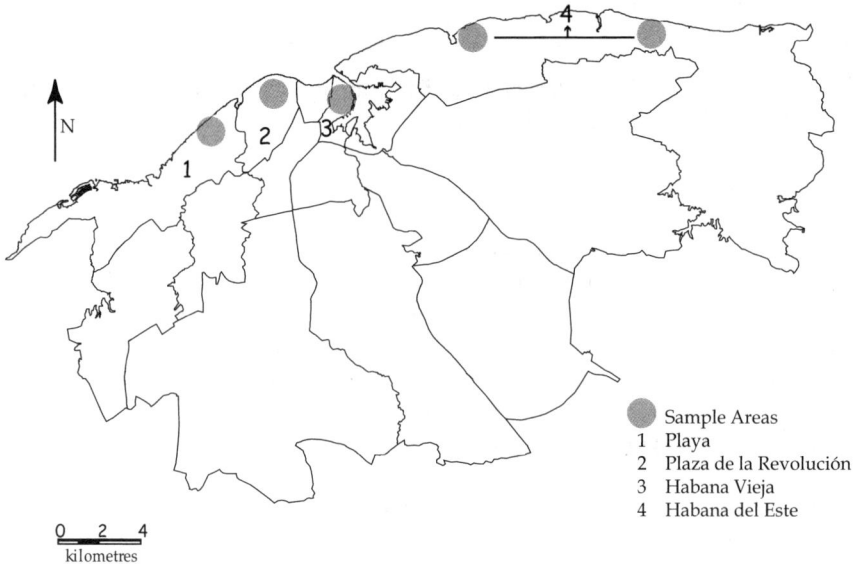

Figure 2.1 The sample areas for the questionnaire survey

The survey was conducted without any formal authorization or approval. This was necessary to minimize the risk of the survey being discovered and blocked by governmental authorities. After several consultations with an Italian scholar who has been researching in Cuba since early 1990s, this choice emerged as the only viable solution to carry out a systematic research survey on tourism in Havana. This task has never been attempted before in Havana. The author had initially thought about asking for the help of the Committees for the Defence of the Revolution (CDRs), a mass organization with wide popular support at the local level. However, he was discouraged by the Italian researcher. Indeed, in the past she had asked them for help but was actively discouraged by the CDRs to complete a similar research project.

In order to carry out the survey 'in the field', it was decided to ask for help from a qualified and practicing sociologist based in Havana, who cannot be named and who the first author had met at a conference in July 2000. This was needed in order to benefit from her local knowledge and experience in conducting surveys in Cuba and because it seemed an adequate practical solution to avoid possible institutional censorship.

The sociologist was remunerated for her time and work. A sum of US$ 1 per questionnaire was agreed. The advantages and disadvantages of payment for external researchers have been amply discussed in the literature (Boyden and Ennew, 1997 and Kirby, 1999). In the context of this particular questionnaire survey, the author decided to remunerate the Cuban sociologist in order to recognize her contribution to this research, to make her feel the work was valued, to increase her motivation and to help ensure she completed the surveying task. At no time, did payment represent a form of control over her actions or work schedule.

After two preparatory meetings, it was commonly agreed to conduct door-to-door interviewing and to hand the questionnaires to the respondents and leave them to complete it at their own pace over one or two days. In the sociologist's view, this technique was in line with surveying techniques employed by governmental authorities in Cuba. Further, as Parfitt (1996) notes, the self-completion questionnaire gives respondents more time to consider their response and minimizes the risk of them being influenced by the presence, personality and intonation of the interviewer. For similar reasons, the sociologist suggested that the author did not take part in the distribution and collection of the questionnaires, as this could have led respondents to provide 'biased' responses. According to her, many Cubans are reluctant to portray governmental policies or actions in a negative light when they are confronted by 'outsiders' in official settings or interviews.

At the operational level, the questionnaires were translated to Spanish by the first author and linguistically enhanced by the Cuban researcher (a copy of the questionnaire can be found in Appendix 1). Once the sample areas were identified, the Cuban researcher distributed the questionnaires to the first few houses of each street included in the sample areas. During the administration of the survey there were a number of standard ethical practices which were observed by the sociologist at the author's request. These practices were essential to protect the basic rights of the research participants. Firstly, no participant was coerced to participate in the survey. Indeed, respondents participated in the questionnaire survey by their own voluntary initiative. Secondly, all participants were informed on the academic aims of the research and were given background information on the project. Lastly, both confidentiality and anonymity were guaranteed. Indeed, participants were assured that identifying information would not be made available to anyone and that they would remain anonymous throughout the study.

It is important to underline that it was agreed that the findings of the questionnaire would be made available to the Cuban sociologist so that she could use them as part of her continuing work. The results of the questionnaire survey are presented in chapter 9.

Conclusions

This chapter has highlighted how researchers from Western countries have been forced to reconsider their role in the research process in the context of the South thanks to concerns raised by the recent development studies literature. These concerns encompass ethical dilemmas, issues of ownership, exploitation and power imbalance between highly qualified and wealthy Western researchers on the one hand and less advantaged individuals and communities in developing countries on the other.

The chapter has illustrated the steps taken in this study to avoid potential problems in the field. The approach adopted in this research has been pragmatic and empirical but has endeavoured to be fully ethical within the Cuban social and political situation. It was necessary to fully take into account the administrative and political difficulties of doing academic research in contemporary Cuba. Lastly, the present chapter has provided an overview of the philosophical debate surrounding qualitative and quantitative research and has explained the mix of data which will be used throughout the remainder of the book.

Chapter 3

Tourism and Development:
The Cuban Context

Introduction

Tourism is widely regarded as the world's third largest industry, after oil and vehicle production, contributing directly to over 4 per cent and indirectly to over 11 per cent of global Gross Domestic Product (GDP). Global tourist arrivals jumped from 25.3 million in 1950 to 703 million in 2003, while total expenditure climbed from US$ 2.1 billion to US$ 474 billion over the same time period (UNCSD, 2001; WTO, 2003).

Employment generated by the tourism industry is also significant. WTO (World Tourism Organization, 1993) figures indicate that tourism-related activities, including travel, accommodation, catering, retail establishments, leisure, entertainment, recreation and sport, provide over 200 millions jobs worldwide. Furthermore, the geographical distribution of tourism has increasingly spread worldwide after World War II. In 1950 the top 15 tourist destinations, all in Western Europe and North America, attracted 97 per cent of the world's total arrivals. By 1999 this figure had fallen to 62 per cent, with market shares increasing for developing countries and economies in transition.

It is thus comprehensible why international tourism was declared a priority sector after the onset of the Special Period in Cuba and has played a key role in the country's reinsertion into the world economy. Indeed, the tourism industry has become a sector based on a new foreign-investment regime that has led to new forms of direct and mixed investment and new management contracts in Cuba. Further, priority efforts have been made to link tourism with the rest of the economy and increase the domestic content of the sector's inputs in both goods and services. To this end, new institutions, new laws and new concepts of work have been created (ECLAC, 2000).

The main purpose of this chapter is to look at the political economy of tourism promotion in Cuba during the Special Period. The chapter examines the rationale that underpins the 1990s economic and institutional reforms and assesses how these have shaped Cuba's new development strategy. Indeed, it is argued that this strategy has been grounded on the implementation of an Import-Substitution policy cantered on tourism, aiming to reduce the country's leakages and economic dependency from external markets.

The chapter is divided into four sections. The first part provides an account of the position of tourism in both Western (capitalist) and socialist countries. It outlines the political and economic dimension underpinning governments' intervention in this sector, and casts light on the politics of tourism in an international context. This is of particular salience in examining Cuba in the context of this book. The second section examines the viability of tourism as a tool for the national development of transitional economies and developing countries, and discusses the main issues involved in tourism promotion strategies for such countries. The third section assesses the role and the significance of tourism in Cuba's new development strategy. In this section, the analysis will focus on the study of the nature and the impacts of the 1990s reforms in Cuba, with a special emphasis on the promotion of FDI and the setting up of the State Tourism Corporation. Lastly, some conclusions will be drawn in the final section of the chapter.

Tourism in Western (Capitalist) and Socialist Countries

Tourism in Western (Capitalist) States

Over the last fifty years, the tourism literature has attempted to position the growing importance of leisure and tourism within western capitalist societies in order to understand the political economy of tourism development and to explore the reasons for the public sector's involvement in tourism. For example, Hall (1994) argues that tourism is a product of capitalist society and cannot be understood without reference to it. In his view, the dominant ideology of tourism in Western societies portrays leisure and tourism as essentially a private and individual choice. According to this account, individuals are ever freer to decide the allocation of their time between work and leisure because of the changing politics of space and time of mature capitalism. Along similar lines, other sociological interpretations contend that tourism, as with all leisure phenomena, is part of the struggle for the control of space and time in which social groups are continually engaged (Wilson, 1988).

The study of leisure activities has also impinged on theories concerning the current dynamics of modernization (see Harrison, 1992) and the globalization of tourism. Urry (1990: 40) observes that 'the internationalisation of tourism means that we cannot explain tourist patterns in any particular society without analyzing development taking place in other countries'. From an economic standpoint, he goes on to highlight that the result of such internationalization has been that different countries and regions have come to specialize in providing particular kinds of tourism. Most specifically, countries, localities and tourist sites have specialized within an emerging international division of tourism in the last decade. Britain, for example, has come to specialize in its tourism on history and heritage whilst Spain has promoted 'sea, sun and sand' tourism.

Within the globalization process of tourism, capitalist States have the task of defining their tourism policy in the light of national objectives. States have to create suitable frameworks for the promotion of specific forms of tourism which are in line with priority development goals. For example, after the economic decline of the manufacturing sector in the late 1970s, tourism has been increasingly used by governments as a tool in the economic restructuring of national and local economies (Page, 1995). To this end, States have had a direct and indirect involvement in the tourism industry through government business enterprises, operating in the commercial spheres of the economy and the establishment of regional tourism development agencies.

In other instances, ideology has played a crucial role for the intervention of the state in tourism through the selection of particular development objectives linked to a set of overt and covert values (Hall, 1994). From a political perspective, international tourism has allowed host governments the possibilities of offering a positive image of itself to the outside world and of reiterating a strong nationalistic message to its citizens. For instance, large-scale tourism events, especially sports events such as the Olympic Games and the football World Cup, have been used by regimes as a means of enhancing image and ideology. Examples of these are the 1936 Olympic Games in Nazi Germany and the 1978 football World Cup in Argentina.

In fact, the nature of governments' involvement in tourism varies according to the conditions and circumstances peculiar to each country. These depend upon factors such as the politico-economic-constitutional system, the level of socio-economic development, and the degree of tourism development. For example, in Western nations there has been an almost universal tendency to privatize and often commercialize functions in the tourism sector that were once performed by the State. On the other hand, in socialist states, governments' intervention in tourism has always had a strong ideological component. States have played a central role in shaping tourism policy at the collective and individual levels. This is because tourism was not conceptualized as an individual choice, as will be explored in the next section.

Tourism in Socialist States

The theoretical approach to tourism in socialist states is not an easy one and the conceptualization of a socialist model of tourism has been attempted only on a few occasions (Hall, 1984, 1990; Böröcz, 1990). It can be argued that in socialist states the understanding of the role played by tourism is complicated by the theoretical lacuna that exists in the Marxist tenets on this issue. As Hall (1984) forthrightly points out, tourism posed something of a philosophical problem during the State-socialist period. Indeed, neither Marx nor Lenin provided guidelines for a distinctive socialist approach to tourism development or to development itself (Potter *et al.*, 2004a).

In socialist states, the service industry, including tourism, was considered to be of relatively minor importance. Tourism was classified as 'unproductive', that is, as an inefficient activity with a low priority in the national development strategy. The requirements of the tourism industry, which entailed the availability of a flexible, entrepreneurial and self-financing sector responsive to changing demands and fashions, were the antithesis of the centralized socialist economy based upon heavy industry. Broadly speaking, the main role of tourism was to regenerate the labour force and to satisfy the workers' demand for recreation.

The nature of recreation was supposed to be based on the 'socialist way of life'. Holidays, for example, had to be spent with other members of the worker collective. For this purpose, a tourist industry was established to serve these needs (Williams and Baláž, 2000) while recreational spaces were constructed through a high concentration of publicly organized amenities. In this context, Scarpaci (2000a) notes that public spaces shaped under socialist regimes were designed for mass organization and demonstrations, as opposed to smaller more intimate encounters found at cafes or small shops in market economies.

Despite these philosophical hindrances, D. Hall (1991b: 83-84) suggests that there are a number of ways in which socialist development strategies can subordinate international tourism to Stalinist economic priorities. These are:

i. It should provide assistance in the implementation of policy seeking the equal distribution of goods, services and opportunities across the state area.

ii. It should be used as a catalyst to improve economic performance and stimulate rapid economic development.

iii. Infrastructural improvements and elaborations should follow in its wake to benefit the indigenous population as well as, if not to a greater degree than, foreign tourists.

iv. The natural environment should not be adversely affected, and whenever possible, should be positively enhanced by the process of tourism development.

v. The much needed hard currency brought by foreign tourists should be employed for the purchase of essential imports to improve the country's qualitative and quantitative performance.

vi. A preclusion, within the tourism process, of alien influences, should be secured – whether of an ideological, cultural or economic nature likely to affect those coming into contact with foreign visitors or likely to cause significant economic 'leakages' from the country (these will be explained in the next section of the chapter).

vii. International peace and understanding, as defined by the state socialist society itself, should be promoted.

viii. Visitors' ideological appreciation should be enhanced by imbuing them with a sense of the superiority of the socialist system in general, and of the host country's own interpretation of socialist development in particular.

ix. Tourism should thereby be employed to project a deliberately constructed, self-conscious image of the host country to the outside world.

Hall's (1991b) analysis thus suggests that in socialist countries, ideology has played a significant role in tourism policy-making in two main ways. At the domestic level, tourism development policy was highly centralized because tourism activities were a substantial concern of the State. Tourism policy was intended to serve primarily state ideological interests and to ensure that mass leisure was in line with broader State goals. Consequently, State enterprises were responsible for the provision of many collective and individual items of welfare, including leisure and recreation, housing and medical care (Harloe, 1996). At the international level, the countries belonging to the Soviet block imposed restrictions on travel both within the country and to Western nations 'for fear of ideological contamination' (Hall, 1994: 61). In fact, international tourists' visits were mainly geared to convince visitors of the superiority of socialism.

With the downfall of socialism and the establishment of a new geo-political global order, the approach of former and continuing socialist countries to tourism has changed radically. Tourism represented an effective route for the development of economic and political linkages with other trading blocks. As Hall D. (1991a) notes, tourism has been central in the social and economic transition of former Eastern Europe socialist states in many fashions:

- Tourism activities have acted as a catalyst for social change by permitting greater interaction between host populations and visitors from the outside world.
- Tourism has represented a symbol of new found freedoms by permitting the region's citizens to travel freely within and outside their country.
- The tourist industry has played an integral part in economic restructuring through privatization and the encouragement of a shift toward a service economy.
- Tourism flows have been a component to commercial development through a growth of business and conference tourism reflecting the region's re-entry into the world economic system.

Tourism and Development: Issues for Transitional and Developing Countries

In recent years, transitional States have not been the only countries to deploy tourism as a tool for national development. Many governments of developing countries such as Costa Rica and Mexico, have adopted tourism as an important vehicle to promote economic growth and to spread the benefits of modernization. Indeed, as Hall (1994) and Pearce (1999) note, international tourism has been seen as:

- bringing foreign exchange into the country
- improving the level of foreign debt
- attracting Foreign Direct Investment
- creating employment
- increasing state corporate profits
- boosting tax revenue

- diversifying the economy
- aiding regional development.

Furthermore, according to a recent UNCTAD (1998) document, tourism has been chosen as a major driving force for national and local development for three additional reasons. Firstly, the multiplier and spillover effects of tourism on the rest of the economy are felt sooner than those engendered by other sectors. Secondly, tourism is a large generator of jobs. Thirdly, in some countries, especially island micro-states, tourism is the only development alternative available.

Despite general optimism expressed by many governments in the South concerning the benefits of tourism promotion, several authors have highlighted a variety of issues and potentially negative outcomes that can stem from tourism-oriented development strategies embarked upon by vulnerable and unstable economies (see Brohman, 1996; Harrison 1992; Momsen, 1998; Potter 2000 for a review). Amongst the most important of these issues is that tourism has been deemed responsible for the generation of dependent development because of the existence of several elements characterizing the nature and the functioning of the global tourism sector. These include the political and economic role played by FDI, the existence of 'leakages' and the quality of jobs generated by the tourism sector. These aspects will be reviewed in the next section.

The Role of Foreign Direct Investment in Productive Capacity Building

Globalization and neo-liberal policies, including liberalization and privatization, have generated a significant growth of FDI in recent years. FDI is considered an important source of private capital and foreign currency which is capable of spurring economic growth in developing countries (De Welde and Morrisey, 2002). FDI in developing countries has increased from US$ 24 billion (24 per cent of total foreign investment) in 1990 to US$ 178 billion (61 per cent of total foreign investment) in 2000 (World Bank, 2001). The economic literature displays burgeoning examples of theory-led and empirical research approaches aimed to identify the determinants of FDI and to assess its economic impact.

De Welde and Morrisey (2002) investigate claims that FDI is a central policy tool in achieving three main development goals. These are: poverty reduction, the equal redistribution of the benefits of growth and the generation of employment. On the one hand, their study acknowledges that foreign-owned firms tend to pay higher wages in developing countries. On the other hand, it highlights a systematic lack of evidence concerning the effects of FDI on income distribution and poverty in developing countries. Moreover, from an employment standpoint, they conclude that the benefits of growth are not equally redistributed among workers because highly-skilled jobs are usually better remunerated than low-skilled positions.

Another study by Li and Yue-Man (1998) examined the effects of FDI and Trans-National Corporations (TNCs) on China's regional inequalities. They establish a comparison between changing patterns of socio-economic indicators such as GDP growth per capita, employment level and the location of FDI in Chinese regions. They conclude that foreign investors helped to reduce China's regional imbalance in the 1980s, the first decade of their involvement with China. However, after this initial positive impact, large TNCs contributed to the increase of regional disparities throughout the 1990s.

FDI has often been associated with the formation of productive clusters that facilitate the transfer of technology and human capital, as well as helping domestic producers to develop (UNCTAD 2001). States from the South have encouraged cluster-driven development strategies to enhance domestic capacity building and, to a lesser extent, to defend domestic markets. Gallup *et al.* (2002) point out that clusters lay the groundwork for accelerating the formation, expansion, and attraction of industries. As shown in Figure 3.1, they provide a model of clusters for tourism highlighting the complexity of structures and inter-linkages which exist among a variety of societal and economic elements that are involved in tourism.

Figure 3.1 Tourism Cluster

(*Source*: Gallup *et al.*, 2002)

It can be seen in Figure 3.1 that cluster-based economic development aims to achieve high-performing regions through building the value-chain, which encompasses key foundation elements, supplier industries and final export, within each cluster of a given region. Cluster studies focussing on the successful expansion of tourism in developing countries have highlighted the fundamental importance of heavy investment in tourism infrastructures, which range from transport systems to accommodation. Seldom do governments from the South have access to public funding from international agencies to finance such infrastructural upgrading without a significant string of economic structural adjustments being attached to the lending. Therefore, the governments of developing countries have increasingly sought FDI as a source of private funds for investment, especially in the accommodation sector where large capital is required to develop major projects.

FDI can take a variety of forms and shapes when establishing linkages with national economies. These are summarized in Table 3.1 in relation to the accommodation sector. Table 3.1 provides a review of the main costs and benefits associated with the variety of FDI agreements, ranging from total private ownership of the project by the foreign investor to total public ownership by the host government. The table shows how the encouragement of specific types of FDI can be functional to the achievement of state national development goals and closely linked to the ideological and political beliefs of national governments. For example, full national ownership will be pursued by governments which aim to retain control in tourism decision-making. By contrast, governments which are not willing to take the financial risk of tourism development strategies encourage full private ownership.

The political dimension of FDI in tourism and the economic globalization process as a whole has been debated extensively in the literature. It has been suggested that tourism TNCs may have been politically useful to Western government in terms of influencing the foreign policy of host or recipient countries (Francisco, 1983). Similarly, Matthews (1978) argues that the covert interrelations between the foreign policies of Western governments and their own corporations lead to suspicions within developing countries that corporate tourism has hidden motives. Indeed, while profit is the apparent goal of these corporations, they may serve parent governments as a tool to exercise political influences that eventually result in economic and political domination. The validity of this argument would seem confirmed if examined in the context of contemporary party politics in many governments of the North, especially USA and Canada, where the intermingling of politics and corporate power manifest itself covertly and overtly during political campaigns, as well as through party funding mechanisms.

Investigations of the political implications of FDI in tourism and corporate hidden agendas have also been conducted within the broader framework of dependency theory and its component concept of 'core' and 'periphery'. The dependency theory school emerged from influential and seminal works by Prebish (1950), Frank (1969) and Cardoso and Faletto (1970). Hall (1994), reviewing the salient tenets of dependency theory, notes that dependency can be conceptualized as a historical process which alters the internal functioning of economic and social sub-systems within a developing country. This conditioning causes the simultaneous disintegration of an indigenous economy and its reorientation to serve the needs of exogenous markets. This internal transformation determines the specific role of articulation of various modes of production within a developing country, and thereby creates specialized commodity export enclaves, such as tourism or primary agricultural production (cocoa, copra, sugar) and structural inequality between social groups (Britton, 1982).

Table 3.1 FDI in the accommodation sector

Types of investment	Benefits	Costs
Total ownership 100 per cent ownership of equity by a foreign subsidiary for an unlimited time	• No financial risk to the host country	• Large outflow of income from tourism ('leakage') • Difficult to reflect government policy on tourism development
Joint venture Partial ownership of equity by foreign capital for an unlimited time	• Access to extra capital • Access to international marketing networks • Lower social/political cost of FDI Reduced income leakage	• Requirement for a certain base capital • Risk-sharing • Possibly unfavourable contracts due to limited bargaining power
Franchising The right to do business in a prescribed manner under an existing brand name is sold to a local firm	• Transfer of managerial and marketing skills • Assured standard of quality • Brand image	• Management risk is with the host country's firms
Management contracts The business is controlled and managed by a foreign firm, without the ownership	• Possible transfer of knowledge, skills and technology (e.g. GDS) through a cooperation agreement	• No control over the finance, management and planning
Hotel consortia Independent hotels pool resources together in order to compete with integrated and franchised chains	• Joint national and international publicity campaign	• Small-size hotels may not be considered attractive to a consortium • Initial lack of brand reputation
Full national ownership Domestic investment without foreign links	• Reduced international leakage • Independence in adoption of corporate strategies	• Lack of international reputation • Higher marketing costs

(*Source*: UNCTAD, 1998)

The significance of the dependency approach as an overarching structural element capable of explaining much of the underdevelopment in the South has been tested by authors at a variety of geographical scales. For example, Potter (2000: 54) assesses the impacts of tourism promotion in the dependent development of Caribbean islands and concludes that:

[D]espite efforts to engineer economic change by enclave industrialisation and the promotion of tourism, the economies of Caribbean territories have remained characterised by highly constrained and limited production possibilities. Indeed, in so far as development in the tourist and manufacturing sectors have strong connotations of dependency and emulation through the demonstration effect, it can be argued that they have in all probability served to increase the import of commodities for consumption.

The notion of dependency is also closely tied to the concepts 'neo-colonialism' or 'neo-imperialism'. These concepts highlight how the development of core-periphery relationships between developing nations and their former colonial powers are reflective of former colonial relationships. In these relationships the range of foreign economic and tourist interests in developing countries is greater than that which existed during the colonial period (Hall, 1994: 124). Crick (1989) goes further and argues that the manner in which the tourism industry is planned and shaped will recreate the fabric of the colonial situation because tourism is a form of leisure imperialism which represents the hedonistic face of neo-colonialism.

Other authors have researched the social implications of neo-colonial relationships and contend that they reinforce class stratification in host countries along racial and socio-economic divisions. Conway (1998: 53), for example, highlights how:

[P]ower relations institutionalised during the colonial era are not easily expunged, and the racial and ethnic divisions that were part of the colonial models of authority and dominance are societal legacies with persistence, especially when rearticulated by political rhetoric, class allegiances, and other contemporary forces that see political economic benefits in such societal divisiveness.

In recent years, the dependency theory and neo-colonialism theoretical frameworks have stagnated. It has been argued that the traditional division between core and periphery does not exist any longer because of globalization and its implications for the dissolution of national cultures, national economies and national borders. Scholars have called for new research capable of overcoming 'tired old conceptual dichotomies (e.g., modernization-dependency, internal external) [which] seem no longer to afford needed explanatory power' (Brohman, 1997: 25).

However, Klak (1998) maintains that core-periphery relations remain highly relevant to understanding specific regions such as the Caribbean. In his study of the impacts of globalization and neoliberalism in the Caribbean, Klak acknowledges that the narrow distinction between 'core' and 'periphery' has changed because of spatial changes in commodity chains and more geographically dispersed production across nation-states. However, he contends that the deeper meanings of such terms refer to power relations, authority and the accumulation of wealth. Future research therefore should not abandon the notion of dependent development. Instead, it should incorporate the analysis of these issues within the changing nature of core and periphery.

Leakages and Employment in Tourism

Tourism leakages stem from foreign domination of the tourism industry and are considered to be a major obstacle to the positive contribution of tourism to development (Brohman, 1996). UNCTAD (1998) defines leakage as the process whereby part of the foreign exchange earnings generated by tourism, rather than being retained by tourist-receiving countries, is either retained by tourist-generating countries or is remitted back to them. It takes the form of profits, income and royalty remittances; costs for the import of equipment, materials, capital and consumer goods to cater for the needs of international tourists; the payment of foreign loans; several mechanisms for tax evasion, and overseas promotional expenditures (UNCTAD, 1998: 4).

Leakages can be categorized into external, internal and invisible. Gollub *et al.* (2002) provide examples of these three types of leakages in the tourist sector. External leakages originate outside of the tourism destination and its domestic industries. These leakages consist mostly of repatriated profits and the amortization of external debt often required financing the construction of tourism infrastructures and the provision of services. Another example of external leakages consists of financial flows to external intermediaries for booking tour operators, foreign airlines and cruise-ships.

Internal leakages primarily arise from imports that are paid and accounted for domestically. The importing of catering-related products such as wine or organic products and leisure services is often needed to meet international tourists' demands. Lastly, invisible leakages mostly coincide with tax avoidance, informal currency exchange transactions and off-shore saving and investments. These leakages are difficult to document. Furthermore, they may take the form of depreciation of a destination's value in environmental, cultural and historic terms. An increase in tourist arrivals is often said to impinge on a destination's natural and anthropogenic resources, causing the deterioration of local residents' quality of life.

Very often, leakages also occur because the international tourist industry presents the characteristics of an oligopoly with anticompetitive practices. Souty (2002) reports a study by the United Nations which describes the 'Greek squeeze case'. According to this study two large British tour operators, Air Tours and Thompson, abused their market share position and squeezed the prices paid to their suppliers in Greece to push up profit margins during the 1980s. As a result, despite international arrivals in Greece increasing from 5.5 million in 1981 to 8 million in 1989, the real value of revenues of the Greek tourist sector shrank by 20 per cent because of anticompetitive practices.

Along with leakages, employment generation in tourism has been addressed in the literature as another potentially negative outcome of tourism development. Tourism is a heterogeneous sector encompassing a wide array of labour-intensive industries, activities and services ranging from the 'old' and, to a lesser extent, the 'new' economy. According to UNCTAD (1998) for each job created in the tourism industry, some five to nine jobs are generated in other areas. Nevertheless, tourism has often been deemed responsible for generating mainly low skilled jobs and, only marginally, a few highly skilled jobs in a limited number of specialized international activities. It can be argued that while this job creation promotes employability among the unskilled or semiskilled workforce, it may trap such workforce member in low paid, flexible and seasonal jobs.

The study *Employment and Tourism: Guidelines for Action* by the European Commission (1997) describes three main qualitative elements of employment in the tourism sector. Firstly, a big share of employment is provided by Small and Medium Enterprises (SMEs), which account for 95 per cent of the sector in Europe. They are often very small businesses with low levels of productivity, especially in the catering industry. Secondly, there is a high rate of turnover of staff which restricts professionalism in the industry. This turnover provides a springboard for less skilled individuals or young people to enter the labour market, but limits tourism workers' ability to increase their skills at the same time. Lastly, jobs in tourism are unattractive as tourism is often perceived as a sector linked to 'servility' rather than 'service' (EU, 1997).

The main findings of the study by the European Commission (EU, 1997) are important because they can be used to highlight some differences that exist in tourism's employment generation between the Global North and the South. In developing countries, jobs in the tourism industry are often better remunerated than jobs in other economic sectors. These jobs provide a stable source of food from the workplace and the possibility of receiving tips. Furthermore, unlike in developed countries, the tourist industry represents one of the few formal opportunities to enter the job market rather than a first access to remunerated work. In the context of transitional economies, tourism has often been linked to the loss of human capital since highly skilled and specialized personnel including doctors, teachers or civil servants have been forced to re-train and take up less skilled jobs in the tourist sector.

Another potential problem for economies in transition is the absence of tourism SMEs. At the theoretical level, these enterprises are deemed essential to the 'trickle down' of the economic and employment benefits of tourism to other sectors of the economy. The development of small and family businesses is a pre-condition, a *sine qua non*, necessary to spread the economic benefits of tourism at the household level. However, in transitional economies the vacuum left by large state-run enterprise has only been filled with difficulty by SMEs in the provision of services. Small entrepreneurs have often lacked access to financial capital to start an economic business because priority has been given to the privatization of large State enterprises. Until this hindrance is eliminated, for example, by the setting up of special *ad hoc* lending programs by international financial institutions or donors, the development of household business will be replaced by service provision offered by large foreign corporations. These themes are highly pertinent to the case of Cuba, as it will be shown throughout this book.

Tourism in Cuba's New Development Model

Cuba is one of the countries which have recently undertaken a new development strategy centered on the promotion of tourism and the external sector. However, unlike many other countries, Cuba's new development model has been inward-looking and based on an Import-Substitution policy aimed at guaranteeing economic and political independency for the country. There are three milestones of the new development policy: the institutional re-organization of the tourism sector; the establishment of joint ventures with foreign capital; and efforts to link tourism with other sectors of the economy. The remainder of this section will therefore provide basic figures on the economic performance of tourism in the 1990s and examine these three measures in turn and in light of the theoretical tools provided above.

The Economic Importance of Tourism in the Special Period

The economic importance of tourism within the Cuban economy has grown steadily throughout the Special Period. Thus, international tourist arrivals increased at 17 per cent per annum, leaping from 340,300 in 1990 to 1,774,000 in 2000 as shown in Table 3.2. In the same period, the gross income of the tourism sector rose at an annual rate of 21 per cent from US$ 243 million to US$ 1,952 million as shown in Table 3.2. Between 1990 and 2000, international tourism accounted for one fourth of total investments (Gutierrez Castillo and Gancedo Gaspar, 2001) and increased its contribution to the balance of payment from 4 per cent in 1990 to 43 per cent in 1999 (ONE, 2002). Hence, since 1997, tourism has become the main contributor to the balance of payments, eroding the supremacy of the sugar industry as the main export. This indicates that in the Special Period, Cuba has entered a tourism-dominated era for the first time in its history, as displayed in Figure 3.2.

The growth of the tourism sector has also been significant in term of the contribution to Gross Domestic Product (GDP) and the new employment created. Indeed, Table 3.2 shows how tourism's contribution to Cuba's GDP increased nearly six fold from 1.2 per cent in 1990 to 7 per cent in 1999. Similarly, employment in tourism doubled between 1990 and 2000, growing at 6.4 per cent per annum from 52,000 to 100,000 workers respectively (Mintur, 2001a). At the national level, the Cuban Chamber of Commerce (2002) contends that in the 1990s, 200,000 new jobs were created directly or indirectly, as a result of the development of tourism. Other sources exaggerate these figures by arguing that 300,000 new jobs were created in the same period (Figueras, 2003).

In this context, it has been argued that the employment multiplier effect of tourism has been high. Recent estimates maintain that for each job directly generated in tourism, another 2.7 or 3 are indirectly generated in other sectors (Pérez Mók and Garcia, 2000; ECLAC, 2000). However, other estimates contend that the employment multiplier has been just 1.4 (Figueras, 2003). More specifically, for every 100 jobs created in tourism, another 53 jobs are created in the manufacturing industry, 36 in construction, 14 in agriculture and forestry, 29 in transportation, 3 in urban services and 3 in communication.

Table 3.2 Gross income of and employment in the tourist sector in Cuba, 1990–2000

Year	Tourist arrivals to Cuba (thousands)	Gross income from tourism (US$ millions)	GDP (CP millions*)	Gross income from tourism/ GDP (percentage)	Employment in tourism
1990	340.3	243	20,879	1.2	52,000
1991	424.0	402	17,554	2.3	n/a
1992	460.6	550	16,382	3.3	n/a
1993	546.0	720	16,617	4.3	n/a
1994	619.2	850	20,375	4.3	n/a
1995	745.5	1,100	23,025	4.8	n/a
1996	1,004	1,333	24,481	5.4	64,000
1997	1,170	1,515	24,675	6.1	70,900
1998	1,416	1,759	25,863	6.8	81,000
1999	1,603	1,901	26,146	7.3	n/a
2000	1,774	1,952	28,206	7	100,000

* CP = Cuban Peso (current). See Mesa Lago, 1998, for a re-assessment of the Cuban GDP in both current and constant (1981 value) Pesos

(*Source*: Calculated from Mintur, 2001a; ONE, 2002; ECLAC, 2000; Pérez Mók and Garcia, 2000)

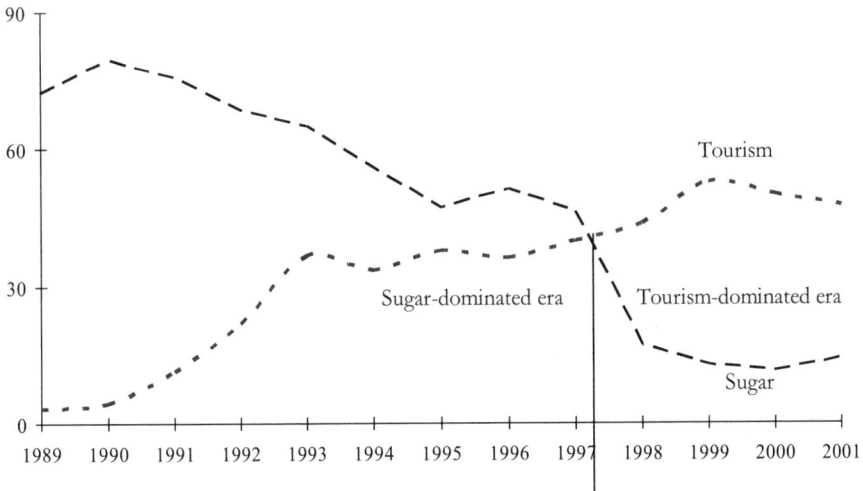

Figure 3.2 Structure of exports of sugar and tourism (%) showing Cuba's transition to the tourism-dominated era in the Special Period

(*Source*: Calculated from ECLAC, 2000 and ONE, 2002)

The Institutional Re-organization of Tourism

The tourism promotion strategy of the 1990s has entailed the design of new institutional structures specific to tourism, along with the instruments for the general adjustment of the economy (see Appendix 2 for a summary of the main economic and administrative reforms). In 1994, two tourism circuits were established in order to maximize tourist revenues: one for domestic tourism and another one for international tourism. The former, operating in pesos and involving decaying facilities, soon became a low priority sector for Cuban policy-makers. The latter, operated exclusively in US dollars[1] and involved better quality lodging and catering facilities in order to meet the more demanding standard of international tourists.

The distinction between national and international tourism has been part of a larger re-organization of the tourism sector. In 1994 the Ministry of Tourism (*Mintur*) was set up for the first time, replacing INTUR. The main aims of the new Ministry were to design, implement and control the policies and development strategies of

---

1   In November 2004, the government halted the circulation of the US dollar in Cuba. As a result, formerly US dollar-operated facilities and businesses currently operate in Convertible Pesos, a new currency introduced in 1994 (see appendix 2). Until 2005, one US dollar was exchanged to one Convertible Cuban peso and both currencies corresponded to roughly 25 regular Cuban pesos. Thus, throughout this book the terms US dollar and Convertible peso will be used interchangeably to indicate a currency which has a bigger purchasing power than the regular Cuban peso.

tourist areas and to supervise the modalities in which foreign investors might enter the sector (ECLAC, 2000). *Mintur* consisted of decentralized structures which encompassed territorial delegates of the Minister of Tourism, specialized policy units and newly established State Tourism Corporations.

The new State Tourism Corporations or Holdings are the most innovative component of the modernization and decentralization process of the tourism sector in the Special Period. They operate with foreign currency, enjoy some autonomy in decision making and have to pay dividends to the State through a tourist industry-finance fund. These resources are subsequently re-allocated in the sector itself or in other branches of the country's economy. The nature of these new firms blends together elements of centralized decision-making with capitalist entrepreneurialism. Indeed, as Jones (2000) puts it:

> [State Holdings] operate as free from the Government control and oversight as any private sector firm in any country in the world. They borrow on the international financial markets for their own account, they are audited by leading Western accounting firms, and they are as flexible to undertake any business deal they want. But they have only one shareholder, the Government of Cuba. If they make their profit targets and operate with acceptable margins, they keep going. If they do not, people are fired, new management is inserted, and changes are made (Jones, 2000: 3).

Despite this partial decentralization process, other authors have pointed out that in 2003, state companies were relieved of their limited independence, their ability to compete commercially against each other, and the privilege of obtaining credit (McIntosh and Nülle, 2004). In addition, after 2003, hard currency transactions require central bank approval; imports and exports decisions are taken by the Foreign Trade Ministry, while prices for internally traded goods in Cuba are determined once again by the state agencies.

Each of the new State Holdings works in specific tourism segments ranging from accommodation to transport, as shown in Figure 3.3. If taken together, it could be argued that the corporations' overarching aim is to provide full coverage of the economic and organizational activities involved in tourism in Cuba. Figure 3.3 also illustrates how after the 1994 re-organization, the number of institutions and agencies involved in the tourism sector has increased dramatically. Thus, while in 1991, there were only four institutions responsible for developing and administering the tourist sector – INTUR (1976), *Corporación* CUBANACÁN (1987), *Grupo Gaviota* (1988) and *Campismo Popular* (1981) – these had increased to nearly fifty in 2002.

As previously noted, the overall restructuring of the tourism sector has paid little or no attention to the domestic sector, being skewed toward international tourism. This is noteworthy, emphasizing that only *Izlasul* Corporation and *Campismo Popular* with its five agencies are responsible for domestic tourism while all the remaining holdings are oriented toward international tourism. This clearly reflects governmental authorities' unbalanced allocation of resources and efforts between the two distinct tourism circuits.

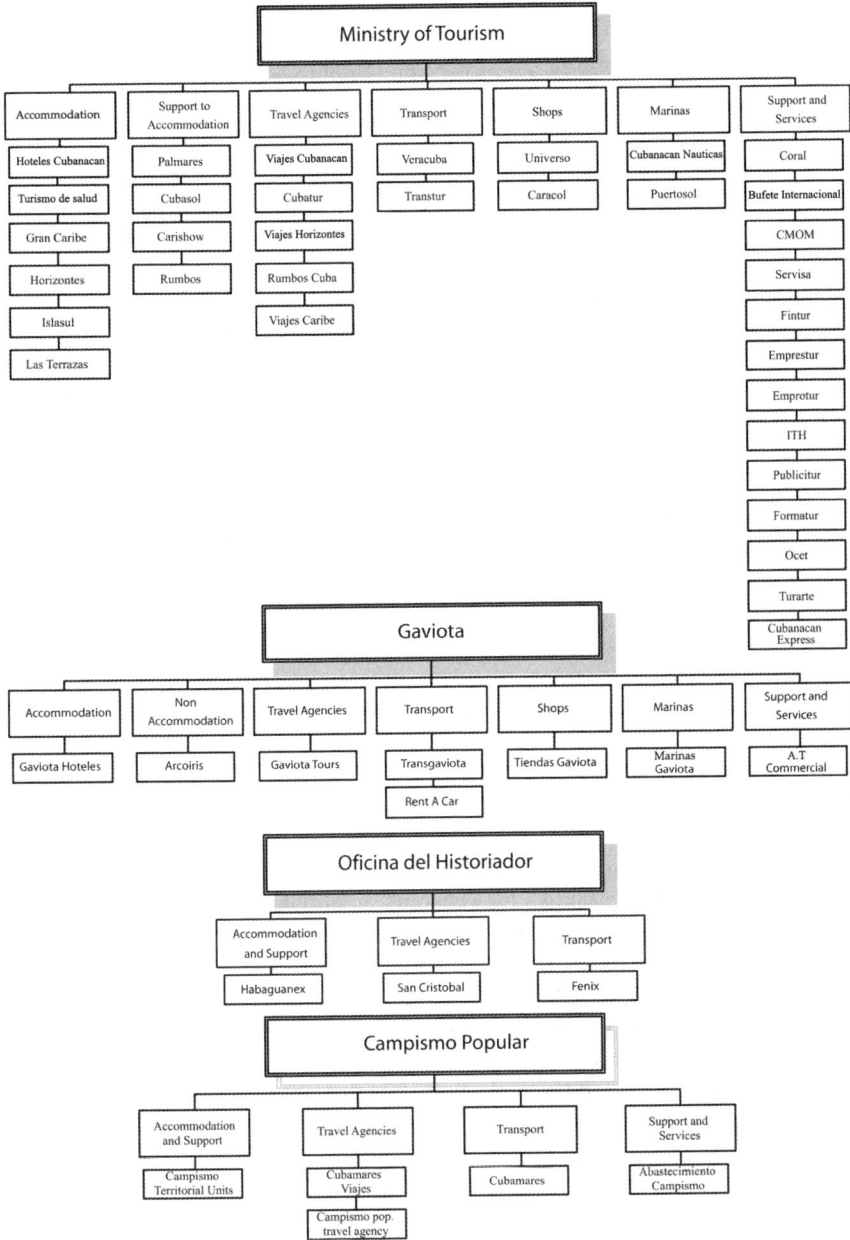

Figure 3.3 The institutional re-organization of the Cuban tourist sector after 1994

(*Source*: Mintur, 2001a)

Foreign Direct Investment and Tourism in the Special Period

As noted in Chapter 1, an essential measure within Cuba's international tourism promotion strategy has been the promotion of FDI. The country's effort to attract FDI can be traced back to the 1980s when the government first passed *Decree Law 50* in 1982 which legalized the establishment of joint ventures between Cuban-State-run and foreign firms. There is, however, general agreement that this initiative generated little interest among Western investors. The main reason was because it set the limit to 49 per cent for the foreign share of joint ventures and provided a low level of investment protection for foreign firms (Spadoni, 2002).

It was only in 1992 that Cuba endorsed an aggressive campaign to attract FDI when the National Assembly passed several amendments to the 1976 Constitution clarifying the concept of private property and providing the legal basis for transferring state property to joint ventures (Pérez-López, 1998). This campaign culminated in the enactment of *Law 77* of 1995, *the Foreign Investments Law* which has generated contrasting views among scholars. Pérez-López (1998) contends that the new Law codified the *de facto* rules under which joint ventures had already been operating and introduced some minor innovation to the legal framework for foreign investors such as the theoretically possible elevation to 100 per cent for the foreign share within the joint venture.

By contrast, other authors argue that the changes introduced by Law 77 have been substantial because, for example, the new initiative offers specific guarantees for foreign firms against expropriation (Spadoni, 2002). Furthermore, the Law created an *ad hoc* agency, the Ministry of Foreign Investment and Economic Cooperation (MINVEC) to speed up the approval process of projects involving foreign capital (Travieso-Diaz and Trumbull, 2002). This new ministry is responsible for the receipt, screening, processing and the distribution of foreign investment applications among other government agencies.

It proves difficult to establish the economic importance of FDI in today's Cuba due to restricted access to official data. Publicly available figures of foreign capital are limited to the number of International Economic Associations (*Asociación Económica con Capital Extranjero*, AECEs) by year, by sector and by country. These include both joint ventures and International Economic Association Contracts, where the contracting parties do not set up a separate legal entity. Figure 3.4 demonstrates how these associations increased threefold from 129 in 1993 to 400 in 2001, recording a 23 per cent average annual growth rate. Although this data precludes an in-depth analysis of the strategic nature of AECEs, it provides hints as to the magnitude of the penetration of foreign capital in today's Cuba. In this context, Spadoni (2002) quotes figures by the Cuban Central Bank according to which, between 1993 and 2001, FDI in Cuba has been tantamount to US$ 1,964 million.

International Economic Associations are not the only type of foreign investments currently allowed in Cuba as two more legal and economic agreements are permitted between Cuban and foreign firms. These are management contracts and production contracts. Management contracts are reached when a Cuban firm contracts a foreign entity to manage their infrastructure or business for a stipulated period of time and with a remuneration based on the results of the activity agreed upon. Production contracts are agreements according to which the foreign party supplies finances, material resources and technology to their Cuban counterpart in exchange for the production of goods by the Cuban firm at a set price for the domestic or international markets.

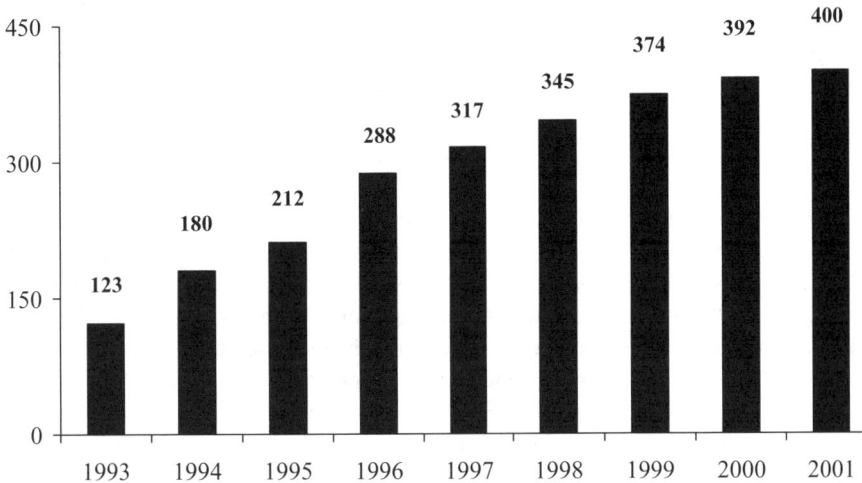

Figure 3.4 Active International Economic Associations from 1993 to 2001

(*Source*: BNC, 2002)

Most of these new forms of direct and mixed investments and new management contracts can be found in the tourism sector. Official statistics report that at the end of 2000, there existed 29 joint ventures in tourism, with a total capital of US$ 1,089 million, 26 of which were hotel chains managing 15,600 rooms. Of these, 3,700 rooms (about 10 per cent of the total) were already operating while the remainder were in the design or construction phase (Mintur, 2001a). In the same year, 17 international hotel chains were reported to have management and marketing contracts with Cuban counterparts, for a total of 54 hotels and about 16,120 rooms under management. These contracts had a validity of five to seven years but could be prolonged if the partners agreed.

A large share of the joint ventures and management contracts in the accommodation sector are with Spanish (Sol Meliá, Grupo Riu, Iberostar), French (Accor and Club Med), German (LTI), Italian (Ventatur), British (Qualton), Canadian (Life Hotel) and Dutch (Golden Tulip) companies. It is estimated that joint ventures will account for 20 per cent of total room capacity by 2005 (Figueras, 2003). The advantages stemming from an affiliation with large hotel chains are multiple as described earlier. ECLAC (2000) highlights that in the Cuban case the chain's advantages are of two kinds.

Firstly, large hotel chains, such as Sol Meliá, can facilitate a series of easy accesses, encompassing: (i) access to financing; (ii) access to the advertising and marketing programs and to the distribution and reservation networks of the foreign chain; (iii) access to suppliers and purchaser groups; (iv) access to the transfer of a wide range of technologies and the use of an internationally recognized brand image. Secondly, foreign partners normally appoint the Managing Director, the auditor and a limited number of personnel in each establishment. These, in turn, divulge the mother branch's operating manuals and facilitate the transfer of know-how especially concerning principles of market management.

The Linkages Between Tourism and Other Economic Sectors

The linking of the tourism industry to other productive sectors has been of vital importance in Cuba's new development strategy. The backward linkages spur the development of the production of goods and services and import substitution (ECLAC, 2000). In this light, it is argued that tourism in Cuba has contributed to national development in two main ways. Firstly, the increased demand for goods and services, such as food, furniture and transport generated by the growth of tourism has been met by local industries. Secondly, tourism revenues have been used to finance development projects in other economic sectors and to establish productive clusters.

Thus, in 1992, *Finatur*, a financing agency working as a development bank, was set up to finance tourism sector supplies. This agency offered credits under favourable conditions for capital investment and projects in the manufacturing industry and the agricultural sector. From 1992 until the end of 1998, *Finatur* provided US$ 437.2 million in financing and had 246 ministries and enterprises of different sizes as its clients (ECLAC, 2000). Examples of projects financed by *Finatur* include the construction of 500 greenhouses all over the island to make it an all year-round producer of vegetables (Brundenius, 2002), and the establishment of *Gambinas*, a fresh pasta factory which currently supplies 118 hotels and 16 restaurants in Cuba.

As a result of such efforts, officials and researchers in Cuba insist that the new Import-Substitution strategy has been a success (Rodriguez, 2000). They maintain that the benefits of tourism development have spread to other economic sectors through the creation of linkages with local suppliers (Ferradaz, 2002). These linkages have coupled with the transfer of skills, capital and technology from foreign partners contributing to the upgrade of the domestic productive capacity. This has led to the diminishing import of goods required by the tourist sectors and helped the development of productive clusters which, in turn, have reduced tourism leakages.

The effectiveness of the Import-Substitution policy has been supported and proved by detailed official statistics. Indeed, recent reports state that sales by local suppliers in the dollar economy have steadily grown since the legalization of hard currency holding,[2] increasing from 25 per cent in 1996 to 61 per cent in 2000 (Rodriguez, 2000). Further, it is argued that the domestic share of deliveries to the tourism industry increased from 10 per cent in 1990 to 65 per cent in 2001, as shown in Figure 3.5 (Marquetti Nodarse, 2001). That is a high figure compared to other destinations in the Caribbean (Brundenius, 2002).

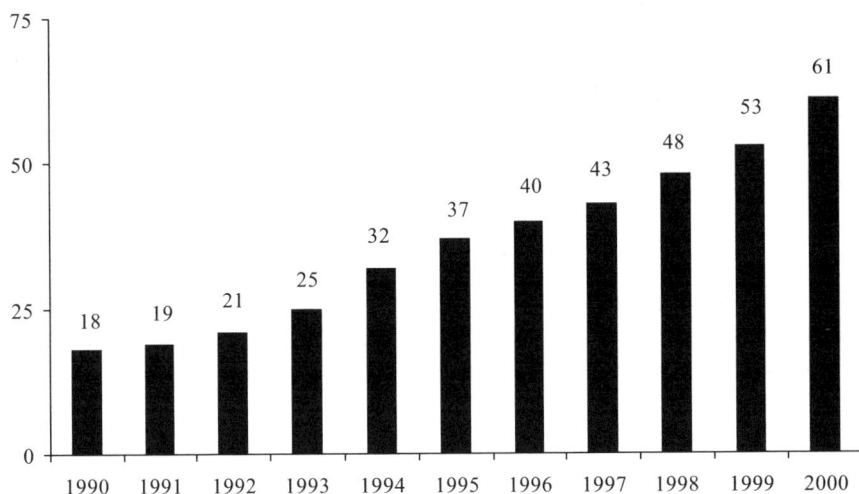

Figure 3.5 Domestic share of deliveries to the tourism industry (%), 1990–2000

(*Source*: Marquetti Nodarse, 2001; Figueras, 2003)

Moreover, beginning in 1994 production was channelled to the dollar-denominated shops (TRDs), which can be considered as yet another effect of tourism on the economy. TRDs constitute the local dollar market where Cubans and foreigners buy goods in US dollars. Indeed, it has been noted that the national participation in the sales of TRDs increased from 29 per cent in 1996 to 51 per cent in 2000 (Brundenius, 2002). Further, ECLAC (2000) estimates that 60 per cent of total domestic production is placed in TRDs, while 30 per cent goes to tourism.

Despite these notable data, other authors have expressed sceptical views concerning the real success of Cuba's new development model and have questioned the reliability of official figures. Brundenius (2002) notes that data concerning import substitution may be inflated since official reports normally do not explain the

---

2   After November 2004, the US dollar is still a legal currency but cannot be used to pay in dollar-denominated shops and other tourism facilities which currently operate in Convertible Cuban Peso. A 10 per cent fee has also been introduced for converting dollars into the local currency.

methodology deployed in calculations. For instance, in the context of the domestic share of deliveries to the tourist industry, it is not clear whether imports of raw material to the local industries are deducted from total figures or not. Along similar lines, Dolores Espino (2001) quotes a recent interview with Ibrahim Ferradaz, previous Minister of Tourism in Cuba, in which he maintains that in 1999 the cost of generating one dollar in the tourist industries was about 78 per cent. In her view, that gives a clearer indication of the real tourist import component than data published by Cuban researchers. Lastly, Brundenius (2002) points out that the extent to which official figures are the outcome of successful productive capacity upgrading, rather than the result of tariff and non-tariff barriers, is unclear.

Conclusions

This chapter has highlighted some of the main advantages and pitfalls of tourism-oriented development strategies for transitional and developing countries and applied them to the Cuban context. After the beginning of the Special Period, Cuba implemented institutional and economic reforms that have *de facto* transported the island into a tourism-dominated era and determined the country's transition toward a mixed economy. Nonetheless, despite this driving role played by tourism within Cuba's long-term development strategy, there is general disagreement on the rationale underpinning the new model of development, its economic results and the policy-making tools deployed in the strategy.

For example, the use of FDI in the new model has generated a debate among scholars. On the one hand, some scholars argue that FDI in Cuba merely represents an instrument of economic survival that the Cuban leadership had to adopt in order to maintain political control (Werlau, 2001). However, other authors maintain that FDI has played a key role in contributing to the transfer of capital, know-how, technology and organizational skills from Western economies towards Cuban State holdings and that this, in turn, contributed to the upgrading and modernization of Cuban local industries (Pérez Villanueva, 2002; Spadoni, 2002).

After this overview of the new model of economic growth embarked upon by Cuba, the next chapter will investigate how Havana, with its tourist attractions and infrastructures, has played a key role within the national development strategy.

Chapter 4

Urban Tourism in Havana:
An Overview of the Special Period

Introduction

The promotion of Cuba as a tourist destination has been undertaken mostly in the 'Sun and Beaches' segment of the global tourism market. Promotional campaigns in this regard have been prepared mainly in Europe and Canada because of the USA embargo. Nonetheless, urban tourism has been an important component of Cuba's tourism development strategy in the 1990s. As the principal city and national capital, Havana dominated much of this tourist segment despite efforts made to promote tourism in four main other Cuban cities, namely Santiago de Cuba, Trinidad, Cienfuegos and Santa Clara (see Figure 4.1).

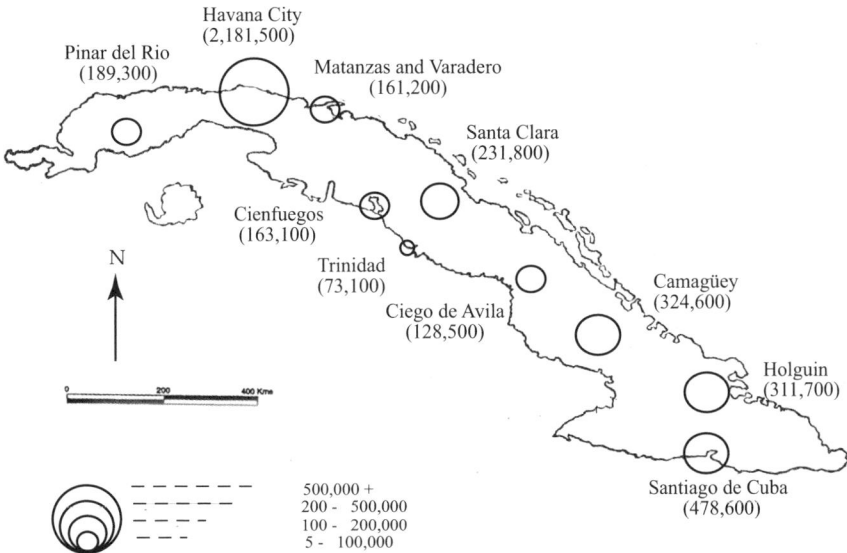

Figure 4.1 Main urban tourism destinations in Cuba (inhabitants)

(*Source*: ONE, 2002)

At the beginning of the Special Period, Havana was designated by Cuban governmental authorities as one of the country's most important tourist destinations because of its colonial heritage, extensive beaches and pre-existing tourist facilities. Furthermore, the city was equipped with good transport infrastructure. These included the José Martí International Airport, an active commercial harbour and the Carretera Central, the backbone of the nation's highway system. These infrastructural elements, connecting Havana with the country's other major population centres and tourist areas, proved of vital importance in receiving international tourists and in allowing them to travel across the island.

The main aims of this chapter are twofold. The first is to provide an overview of Havana's tourism re-development in the 1990s and its importance within the national development strategy. This preliminary study will be complemented by the findings of chapter 6 where an in-depth analysis of the historical role played by tourism in Havana within Cuba's national development will be provided. The second aim is to provide a theoretical framework for the study of urban tourism in order to allow the reader to understand concepts and terms that will be used throughout this volume. Thus, the chapter is divided into three main parts. The first part reviews approaches to urban tourism developed in the literature while the second outlines the main key features of tourism development in Havana during the Special Period. The chapter concludes with an outline of the role played by urban tourism in Havana within Cuba's tourism development strategy.

Urban Tourism

Urban tourism was one of the earliest forms of tourism by the mid-eighteenth century, when European aristocrats and nobility started to 'tour' European cities with their courtesans. With the development of transport facilities in the fordist era and the advent of mass tourism during late-1960s, there was a major shift from this kind of tourism towards coastal, rural or mountain destinations. Over the last decade, however, urban tourism has re-emerged as a mainstream form of tourism and is increasingly being incorporated into urban policies as a tool for the regeneration of post-industrial cities (Law, 1993) and strategic-sector activities capable of promoting local, regional and national development (EU, 2001).

Academic research into tourism developed during the 1960s and 1970s as a sub-discipline of other social sciences rather than as an area of study in its own right. This prevented the development of an independent body of literature on the study of urban tourism until the 1980s. Researchers were unable to separate tourism from recreation, hence, they studied cities under the moral assumption that they were for work, while rural areas were for recreation (Ashworth, 2003).

This separation denied two main arguments which were to be developed by the urban tourism literature throughout the 1990s. First, cities are multifunctional entities in which tourism is one of the city's functions. Tourism and urban functions are interdependent with tourist and residents sharing and sometimes competing for many services, spaces and amenities (Pearce, 2001). Second, there exist several forms of tourism within urban areas. For example, cultural and heritage tourism depends on the existence of cultural facilities or old historic centres in cities; business and conference tourism is linked to the economic and cultural vitality of cities as well as to their image and the availability of facilities.

Approaches to Urban Tourism

Various approaches have been devised by researchers to provide a theoretical framework for the study of urban tourism through the lenses of geographical research. The most influential approaches so far have been conceptualized by Ashworth (1988, 2003), Page (1995) and Pearce (2001). These authors endeavour to understand why tourists seek cities as places to visit. In addition, they investigate the implications for policy making and urban development that stem from such tourism.

Ashworth (2003) identifies six approaches to urban tourism which have been adopted through the years. These include:

- *The facilities approach* deployed by early researchers, during the 1970s and 1980s, who began producing a taxonomic classification of tourism facilities in an attempt to isolate the object of study, that is, urban tourism.
- *The ecological approach*, which seeks to re-integrate tourism into regions within the city and contends that urban tourism can be found in specific tourist areas within the city, often referred to as the 'Central Tourism District' or the 'Tourism Business District' (as explained in chapter 5).
- *The user approach* based on behavioral and sociological studies which defines urban tourism according to what visitors actually do in cities and why.
- *The policy approach* which highlights the role of planning authorities.
- *The economic approach*, adopted especially during the formative period of the discipline, which attempts to measure the economic impacts of tourism.
- *The city marketing approach* developed alongside business studies in an attempt to market cities as a product or brand.

Other authors have impinged on the more traditional 'systems' approach used in tourism literature based on the supply-demand components. For example, Page (1995) developed a systems approach where the complexity of urban tourism is reduced to a number of constructs, each of which highlights the nature and the role of different elements affecting the system. Drawing on Laws' work (1991), Page argues that the urban tourism system consists of three key features: (i) the inputs that include the supply of tourism products and tourism demand; (ii) the outputs provided by the tourist experience, and (iii) external factors conditioning the system, for example, the business environment, consumer preferences and political factors. These features allow a conceptualization of urban tourism based on a high degree of customer services; a simultaneous supply component; an inconsistent demand which varies according to seasonality, and an intangible product which is often consumed.

Within the tradition of the systems approach, Jensen-Verbeke (1986) offers the most comprehensive and, so far the best-established description of the elements of urban tourism supply. In her analysis, Jansen-Verbeke, identifies three types of elements:

- The primary elements include a combination of cultural, sport and amusement facilities and leisure settings consisting of physical characteristics (harbours, historical street patterns, interesting buildings and parks) in addition to socio-cultural features: friendliness, local customs and folklore. These elements may be considered the city's attractions.
- The secondary elements consist of the supporting facilities and services that tourists consume during their visit: hotel and catering facilities, and shopping facilities.
- Additional elements consist of the tourism infrastructures related to transportation and tourism information and other tourism-specific services.

Other authors go further and note how urban tourism supply is embedded in other broader functions of urban areas. Thus, Burtenshaw *et al.* (1991) argue that tourists are only one set of city visitors as urban environments provide the setting for the matching between a variety of demands by users and several existing resources. As a result, the 'tourist city' stems from the overlapping of 'other cities' that include: the 'historic city', the 'cultural city', the 'night-life city' and the 'shopping city', as shown in Figure 4.2. The functional boundaries between these sub-cities are often blurred and inter-changeable, making the study of urban tourism a complex task to carry out.

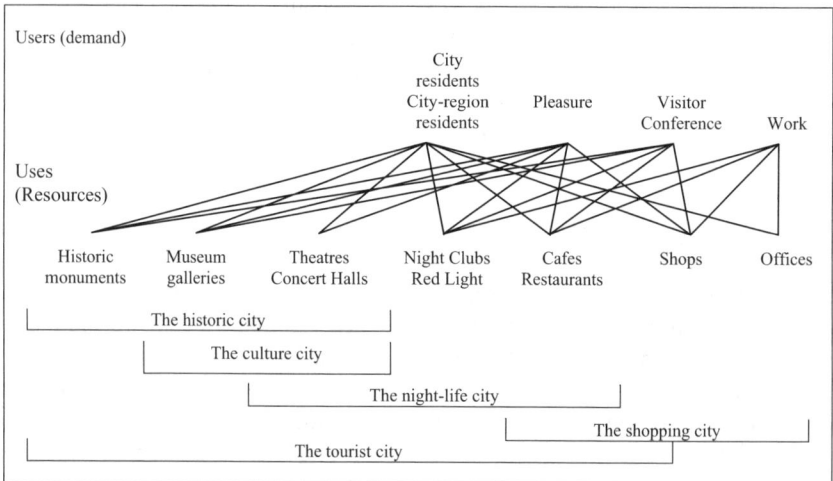

Figure 4.2 The tourist city

(*Source*: After Burtenshaw *et al.*, 1991)

In a similar vein, Pearce (2001) pinpoints that the difficulty of disentangling urban tourism from other urban functions has determined that the tourism and urban studies literature scarcely overlap. This has resulted in an incoherent corpus of literature fragmented along the lines of various disciplines and spatial scales. Furthermore, this difficulty has hindered the pursuit of common goals and comparisons between studies. Pearce (2001), therefore, provides an analytical framework based on a matrix (see Figure 4.3) which integrates different tourism research themes horizontally to various spatial scales vertically. In his account, the linkages between each cell, for example, between the marketing and supply of a site or a city, might be seen in terms of approaches to research or management.

		Themes								
	linkages / *linkages*	Demand	Supply	Development	Marketing	Planning	Organization	Operations	Impact-Assessment
Scale	Regional/ National/ International								
	City-wide								
	District								
	Site								

Figure 4.3 An integrative framework for urban tourism research

(*Source*: Pearce, 2001)

Tourism in Havana During the Special Period

Urban tourism in Cuba's main cities has been an important component of the island's tourism development strategy in the 1990s. One way to discern the magnitude of the urban tourism phenomenon in Cuba is to look at the tourist sector's structure based on existing rooms. This is displayed in Table 4.1 which reveals that the importance of urban tourism has doubled between 1990 and 1998. Indeed, while in 1990 only 10 per cent of total rooms were to be found in urban areas, this figure rose to 27 per cent in 1998. In the same period, rooms in beach resorts decreased from 86 per cent to 65 per cent, while rooms in other tourism segments, such as nautical and health tourism, doubled from four per cent to eight per cent.

Table 4.1 Number of rooms by broad geographical areas, 1990–2000

Tourism Segment	Rooms*		Percentage of total rooms	
	1990	2000	1990	2000
Sun and Beaches	11,094	22,945	86	65
Urban	1,290	9,531	10	27
Other	516	2,824	4	8
Total	12,900	35,300	100	100

* International tourism only

(*Source*: Elaborated from Mena, 2001; ECLAC, 2000)

As noted earlier, most of the new rooms were built or refurbished in Havana because the city played a significant intermediate role in receiving international tourists. For example, Table 4.2 shows how in 2001, the total number of rooms to be found in Havana was six times greater than the number of rooms in Santiago de Cuba, the second biggest Cuban city. Havana's intermediate role as a tourism destination can be deduced from the Trip Index. This indicator consists of the number of days spent in a given city as a percentage of total days spent on the whole trip. Thus, if we take into account that in 1998:

- over 54 per cent of tourists arriving in Cuba visited Havana first (Castro, 2001)
- the average length of the visit to Havana was 4 days against the national total of 11.5 days

the Trip Index calculated for Havana in 1998 is tantamount to 0.16 (see Appendix 3). This indicates that on average, almost one fifth of total national holiday days were spent in Havana immediately after tourists' arrival in Cuba.

Table 4.2 Tourist accommodation (rooms) in two major Cuban urban tourism destinations,* 1990–2001

Urban area	Rooms**		Percentage of total rooms	
	1990	**2001**	**1990**	**2001**
Havana City	3,122	12,002	24.2	28.8
Santiago de Cuba	276	2,164	2.1	5.2
Total	12,900	41,659	26.3	34

* Data for other urban areas are not available

* * International and domestic tourism

(*Source*: Elaborated from Espino, 2000 and Mintur, 2001a)

The economic significance of urban tourism in Havana has also been noticeable at the local and national level. International tourist arrivals tripled between 1995 and 2002, jumping from 332,600 to 912,700, as shown in Table 4.3. The gross income of the tourist sector in Havana grew from US$ 260.6 million in 1995 to US$ 510.3 million in 2002, as indicated in Table 4.4. The gross income fell in 2002 after the 11th September 2001 terrorist attack in New York that slowed down world tourism flows. Further, between 1995 and 1998, the cumulated gross income of Havana's tourism sector was US$ 1410.2 million, which represented on average 48 per cent of the national total (OTE, 1997). Lastly, in 1998, 11 joint-ventures between Cuban and foreign firms were operating in Havana, mostly in the accommodation sector. In 1999, 25 out of 29 investment project proposals for the provision of tourism facilities and services stemmed from joint venture projects (OTH, 2000).

It is worth pointing out that the distribution of tourists' expenditures has also changed over time. According to a report by Havana's Territorial Office of Statistics (OTE, 1997), in 1995 over 65 per cent of the total income of Havana-based state holdings came from the accommodation sector. By 2002, this percentage had halved to 30 per cent (OTE, 2002) while the total revenues continued to grow. The shift in the composition revenues indicates that the newly established State tourist corporations have diversified and increased the supply of tourist infrastructures outside the accommodation sector. This in turn suggests that, following the 1994 re-organization of the tourist sector, the corporations have made some initial efforts to develop other city's functions including 'night life' and 'shopping' functions outside the accommodation sector. These efforts, however, have been inconsistent, prompting urban planning problems as will be explained in chapter 10.

Table 4.3 International tourist arrivals in Havana, 1995–2002

Year	Tourist arrivals (thousands)
1995	332.6
1996	506
1997	648.9
1998	780.7
1999	866.8
2000	951.3
2001	979.7
2002	912.7

(*Source*: Mintur, 2001b and OTH, 2003a)

Table 4.4 Gross income of the tourist sector in Havana, 1995–2002

Year	Gross income from tourism (US$ millions)
1995	260.6
1996	323.6
1997	371.3
1998	421.2
1999	523.4
2000	531.9
2001	542.8
2002	510.3

(*Source*: Mintur, 2001b and OTE, 2003)

On the demand side, the main flow of tourism to Havana, and Cuba as a whole, came from the Western Hemisphere, as shown in Figure 4.4. The main countries of origin of the travellers are Italy, Canada, Spain, France, Germany and Mexico. In 2001, Canada ranked in first place with a total of 350,400 visitors, followed by Germany and Italy with 171,800 and 159,400 visitors, respectively. Furthermore, figures provided by the Cuban National Statistics Office (ONE, 2002) show that the historical trend of visitors to Cuba by country of arrival has not changed significantly during the second half of the 1990s.

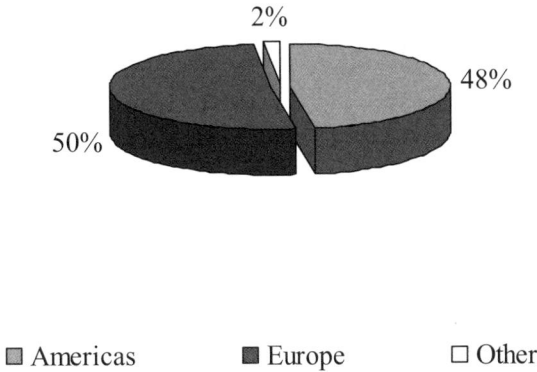

2%

48%

50%

▨ Americas   ▩ Europe   ☐ Other

Figure 4.4 International tourist arrivals to Havana by generating areas

(*Source*: OTH, 2003b)

In terms of the purpose of travelling to Havana, a recent survey conducted by Havana's Tourism Board (OTH, 2002a) indicates that in 2002 over 82 per cent of passenger arrivals in Havana were for the purpose of recreational tourism. Business tourists made up four per cent of the total while tourism for conventions and events of all types corresponded to 11 per cent. The remaning three per cent included health tourism and other smaller niche markets. The survey also highlighted that almost half of the interviewees were first time visitors to Havana.

Tourism Poles in Havana

As part of the national tourism development strategy, between 1990 and 1995, the *National Plan for the Development of International Tourism* was devised by the National Institute of Physical Planning, identifying 67 'tourist poles' to be developed throughout Cuba. This plan and its political economy implications will be examined in detail in chapter 6. Here it suffices to highlight that five of these tourist poles are currently to be found in Havana, as listed in Table 4.5 (see also Figure 4.5). Four different types of tourist areas can be recognized (Ponce de Leon, 1997). The first represented areas of established historic and cultural value that already represented significant tourist attractions. Secondly, areas suitable for the construction of new tourism infrastructures and facilities were identified. A third type comprised areas that were connected with existing tourist zones within the city. Finally, areas that are not suitable to be urbanized but which are suitable for the development of tourist-oriented services were delimited.

Table 4.5 Tourist Poles in Havana as designed in 1995

Area	Pole	Type of Tourism
West Coast	1. Marina Hemingway	Nautical
	2. Montebarreto	Business, Conventions and recreation for elderly
Central	3. Vedado- Centro Havana	Cultural and health
	4. Old Havana	Cultural and business
East Coast	5. Eastern Beaches and Cojimar - Sub-poles: - Villa Pan Cojimar - Bacuranao - Tararà - Santa Maria del Mar - Boca Ciega - Guanabo - Veneciana-Brisas	Sport events conventions Sun and beach Nautical and health Sun and beach Sun and beach Sun and beach Nautical and Ecological

(*Source*: DPPF-CH, 1999)

Since the tourism poles were identified, the total number of rooms available for tourists in Havana has increased rapidly throughout the 1990s growing from 4,682[1] rooms in 1988 to 12,002 rooms in 2002. However, the growth of tourist rooms in Havana has been spatially uneven among the poles, as shown in Figure 4.5 and Table 4.6. East Havana has experienced the largest increase in rooms in relative terms. While tourist accommodation was very limited in this part of Havana in 1988, in 2002 there were 3,878 rooms available for both national and domestic tourism. This increase stems mostly from the conversion of existing housing units from domestic tourism to tourism accommodation for international tourist or foreign workers in Havana.

1   This figure does not coincide with data provided in Table 3.2 because for several years after 1988 many hotels in Havana were closed for refurbishment. As a consequence, rooms available in 1990 were lesser than in 1988.

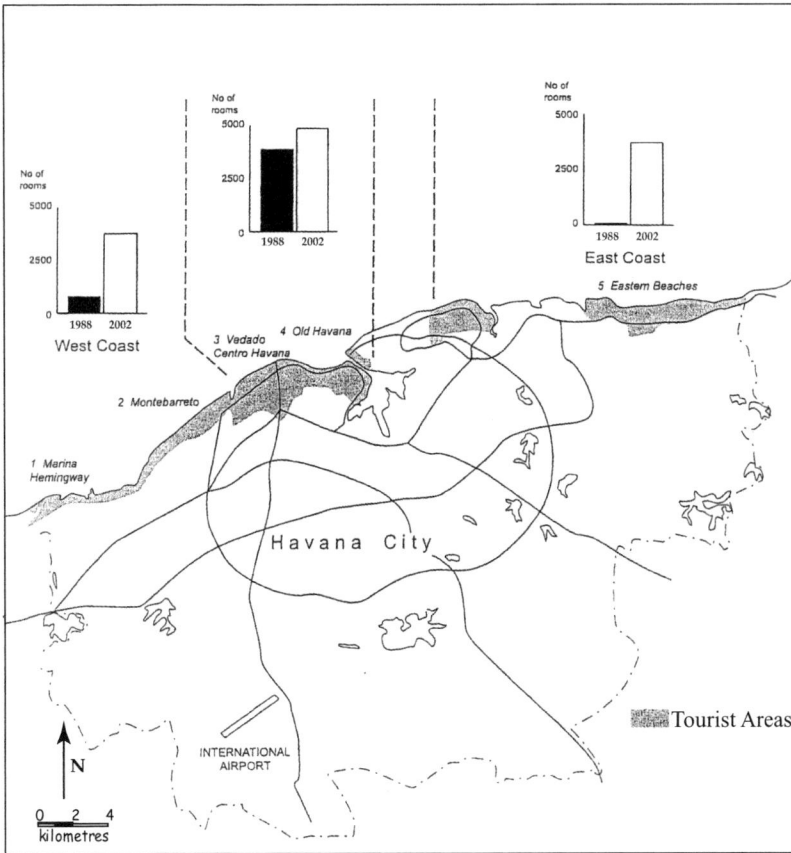

Figure 4.5 Tourism poles in Havana

(*Source*: After DPPF-CH, 1999; Intur, 1988)

In West Havana, the supply of tourist accommodation has also increased significantly, growing from 867 rooms in 1988 to 3878 in 2002. These new rooms were distributed among 21 new or modernized hotels. The array of new tourist accommodation and associated rooms can be discerned from the listing for the years 1988 and 2002 which is provided in Table 4.6. Central Havana's tourist poles, especially Old Havana which was declared a World Heritage by UNESCO in 1982 (see chapter 9), have been characterized by the application of a different development strategy grounded on the rescue of architectural heritage and the consolidation of existing tourist infrastructures. As a result, four hotels were refurbished and re-opened in Havana's historic district, El Telégrafo, Hotel Florida, Parque Central, Plaza. At the aggregate level the accommodation supply of the area grew from 3,783 rooms in 1988 to 4,246 in 2002.

Table 4.6 Hotels and rooms available in Havana in 1988 and 2002

Area	Pole	Hotel	Total hotel rooms available in	
			1988	2002
West	1. Marina Hemingway	Acuario		314
	2. Montebarreto	Bello Caribe		120
		Bosque		62
		Club Arenal		166
		Comodoro	124	460
		Complejo		
		Neptuno - Tritón	272	532
		Copacabana*	138	168
		Chateau Miramar		50
		El Viejo y el Mar and		
		Marina Hemingway	140	272
		Kohly		140
		La Pradera		154
		Mariposa		48
		Melía Habana		413
		Hotel Novotel Miramar		428
		Neurovilla		52
		Palco		182
		Panorama		317
		Paraiso	73	
		Royal Palm*	120	
Sub-total			**867**	**3878**
Central	3. Vedado- Centro Havana	Ambos Mundos		52
	4. Old Havana	Beltrán de Sta Cruz		11
		Bristol*	124	
		Bruzon	51	42
		Capri	216	215
		Caribbean	36	38
		Colina	80	80
		Comendador		14
		Deauville	150	144
		El Telégrafo		63
		Gran Hotel*	82	
		Habana Libre	534	572
		H.Conde de Villanueva		9
		Hotel Florida		25
		Inglaterra*	84	83
		Isla de Cuba	67	
		Lido	72	65
		Lincoln	139	131
		Los Frailes		22
		Melía Cohiba		462
		Meson de la Flota		5
		Naciónal	463	439

Area	Pole	Hotel	Total hotel rooms available in	
			1988	**2002**
Central	3. Vedado- Centro Havana	Nueva Isla*	110	
	4. Old Havana	New York	94	88
		Packard*	86	
		Park view*	55	55
		Parque Central		284
		Plaza*	195	188
		Portales de Paseo		18
		Presidente	144	158
		Regis*	70	
		Riviera	330	352
		Tejadillo		32
		San Miguel		10
		Santa Isabel*	30	27
		Santander		39
		Sevilla	192	190
		Saratoga*	52	
		St´John´s	97	88
		Valencia		11
		Vedado	198	203
		Victoria	32	31
Sub-total			**3783**	**4246**
East	5. Eastern Beaches and Cojimar	Aparthotel Atlántico		96
		Aparthotel Costazul		400
	- Sub-poles:	Atlántico		82
	- Villa Pan Cojimar	Bacuranao		52
	- Bacuranao	Casas del Este		1751
	- Tararà	Hotel Gran Via		10
	- Santa Maria del Mar	Las Terrazas		154
	- Boca Ciega	Marina Tarara		216
	- Guanabo	Mégano		83
	- Veneciana-Brisas	Mi Hacienda		6
		Mirador del Mar		115
		Motel Las Vistas		9
		Miramar	32	24
		Playa Hermosa		28
		Río Cristal		12
		Tropicoco		188
		Villa Panamericana		481
		Villa Loma		39
		Villa Tarara		132
Sub- total			32	**3878**
Total			4682	12002 **

* Hotels closed as in 1988; ** Includes rooms for international and domestic tourism

(*Source*: Elaborated from Intur, 1988; OTH, 2000 and various tourist directories)

Conclusions

Urban tourism is an important tourism product which has re-emerged as a mainstream form of tourism, attracting the attention of policy-makers and researchers alike in recent years. This chapter has looked at the main used to study urban tourism, and its key characteristics and components, illustrating the critical contribution of tourism in Havana toward local and national development in Cuba. Indeed, as the capital of Cuba, Havana has played a pivotal role within the national tourism promotion strategy, at least in its initial stages. The city's utilities, recreational facilities and natural resources have proved an essential asset upon which governmental authorities have capitalized to promote tourism in Cuba. Nonetheless, most of the emphasis has been placed on the development of the accommodation sector, despite some initial efforts which have also been made to promote the city's other functions.

The promotion of tourism in Havana, however, has had an impact on the city's urban fabric in several ways. The next chapter, therefore, will focus on the examination of the potential economic, environmental and social impacts of tourism on urban areas and the planning implications stemming from them. This exercise is indispensable to (i) provide a theoretical context for the study of the effects of tourism in Havana which follows, (ii) to help understand the criteria underpinning the selection of the main variables deployed in the presentation of the findings of the research, and (iii) to identify planning issues at the local and national levels which need to be taken into account for the future development of tourism in Havana and Cuba as a whole.

Chapter 5

The Impacts and Planning of Urban Tourism

Introduction

The previous chapter has outlined how researchers have approached and analyzed the city as a context for tourism activity. This is because the expansion of tourism in cities has important implications for the process of urban development and planning. Tourism activities imply a resource use and generate several impacts as their development and operations are interrelated with the environment, economic activities and the population of tourist destinations. Thus, in recent years tourism planning at all levels of government has had to adapt its program to include new objectives such as environmental considerations and concerns over the social impact of tourism.

This chapter investigates the impacts of tourism in urban areas, studies the difficulties of incorporating tourism and its impacts within a given city's management process and suggests methodologies and approaches to overcome these difficulties. The chapter endeavours to address three main questions: (i) are the impacts of urban tourism the same in cities in the developed and developing world? (ii) what are the possible approaches to tourism planning within the broader framework of urban management? (iii) why is participatory planning important for the sound management of the impacts of tourism in urban areas?

The chapter is divided into four main parts. It begins with the investigation of the impacts of tourism in urban areas, highlighting similarities and differences in these impacts between cities in the North and the South. Next, it turns to the review of recent developments in planning theory, such as the move towards 'collaborative planning'. These developments are often employed to indicate a 'third way' in planning between market forces and centralized forms of governance. A special emphasis will be placed on the linkages between state and civil society and the role played by intermediary agents, such as NGOs, in enhancing public participation in planning in developing countries. The fourth section defines several approaches and tools for the planning of urban tourism which will provide a useful methodological and theoretical framework for the study of Havana throughout this book. The chapter concludes with an outline of the main methodological and theoretical key features reviewed in the chapter.

The Impacts of Tourism

As all human activities, tourism generates direct and indirect, single and multiple impacts. However, the tourist industry is structured in such a way that the consumer is brought to the product, rather than the product being delivered to the consumer (ICLEI, 1999). As Urry (1990: 67) expresses it: 'Tourist services develop in very particular places and cannot be shifted everywhere; they have a particular "spatial fix"'. In other words, tourism products and services comprise elements which are not produced by the tourism industry but, for example, by geography, history and culture (Vourc'h, 2001:40). This has implications for the material and immaterial resource assets of tourist destinations which are not always straightforward.

The literature has identified two main problems that hinder the impact assessment of tourism development. Firstly, as mentioned earlier, there is no 'one' tourism industry (Pearce, 1989; Forsyth, 1997; EU, 2000; Gunn, 2002) but instead a combination of many activities whose economic, environmental and social outcomes are often not easily measurable. In this light, Pearce (1995) notes that certain types of impacts are more readily measured than others. For instance, from an environmental standpoint, atmospheric particulate levels can be established more easily than levels of visual pollution. Secondly, some impact assessments of tourist development pose theoretical quandaries that hamper practical measurements which have been extensively debated in the literature.

The main theoretical difficulties that hinder practical measures of impact assessment can be articulated in three broad analytical categories. These include:

- *The nature of the impacts*: there are conflicting impacts, for example, gains in the transport system may be associated with environmental deterioration. Moreover, there could be difficulties in distinguishing tourism impacts from changes that may be generated by local processes (natural and anthropogenic causes).
- *Cumulative and derived impacts*: the overall impact of a tourist development plan differs from the sum of the single development projects contained in the plan.
- *Lack of longitudinal studies*: there could be difficulties in establishing the pre-development conditions of a given area or the significance of the change is not assessable due to lack of longitudinal data.

Despite these theoretical and methodological quandaries, scholars have endeavoured to identify tourism's main economic, environmental and social impacts. It is these that will be discussed in the next three sections of this chapter.

The Economic Impact of Tourism in Urban Areas

Tourism has been used by governments as a tool of economic policy capable of generating income and employment, of diversifying the economy, and of promoting regional development through multiplier effects and the building of local productive capacity. Nonetheless, some authors express sceptical views concerning our understanding of the economic impact of tourism and its underpinning mechanisms. As Hall (1994: 118) points out:

> Tourism is clearly of significance to many governments as a mechanism to promote national and regional development. However, the analysis of the economic impacts of tourism indicates that our understanding of its effects is incomplete, not only in terms of macro and micro economic impacts but also in terms of its social consequences. Policies do not always lead to desired outcomes. There is no clear consensus as to tourism's role in economic development. The picture is clouded not only by the different assessments of economic development, but also by its socio-cultural and environmental implications.

As noted in chapter 3, the economic impact of tourism is mediated by the existence of leakages, the level of local productive capacity building and the structure of the international tourism industry. Furthermore, much of the economic effects of tourism will depend on the scale and the form of tourism being promoted. Cultural and business tourism, for example, is normally characterized by high levels of expenditure (Shaw and Williams, 1994). On the contrary, more traditional forms of tourism such as 'sand, sun and sea' generate lower volumes of tourist expenditures. This is particularly true for large-scale tourism enclaves which, as Butler (1999: 66) notes:

> while having certain advantages in terms of potential environmental and quality control operations, such developments have been criticised for minimising tourist expenditures in local communities and high levels of economic leakage. The fact that many of the larger developments are externally owned and often import much of their food or other items aggravates this situation.

Throughout the 1980s, a considerable literature has highlighted the significant role that tourism has played in the economic and socio-environmental regeneration of inner city areas, especially in the USA and the UK. In these experiences municipal authorities have replaced old local industries with tourism which has generated tangible economic, environmental and social outcomes. Law (1992) argues that investments for tourism involve the development of facilities, physical environments and infrastructures which have many benefits for local communities. This development may lead to the creation of new jobs and have a visible effect on the physical regeneration of inner city areas, either in the form of specific buildings such as museums, concert halls, convention centres or stadia, or in the promotion of specialized districts. The physical regeneration of the area and the arrival of visitors in turn increase civic pride in local communities. This identifies local residents with their environment and encourages them to take greater care of it (Law, 1992:61).

Despite numerous examples of inner-city regeneration, the interpretation of tourism as a catalyst for socio-economic and environmental regeneration has been questioned by scholars. Shaw and Williams (1994) express three major concerns within this context. Firstly, they question the social distribution of the benefits generated by tourist developments. In their view private-sector investments have often aimed to develop national and international conference facilities, business centres and international hotels with little regard for the leisure needs of local people.

Secondly, they dispute the ability of the environmental benefits of these developments to spread out equally within the urban area. They agree that tourism development schemes produce rapid changes in the physical environment. However, they argue that there is little evidence that this environmental upgrading has been able to spread out to other parts of the inner city. Lastly, one presumption underpinning the argument that tourism can spur regeneration is that tourism developments are multifunctional, incorporating new hotels, tourist attractions and conference facilities, together with retail and leisure components.

With globalization, the economic benefits of tourism have also increasingly been associated with FDI inflows towards urban areas. Ever more cities compete to attract FDI in tourist infrastructures, especially in large-scale convention and exhibition facilities since meetings and conference tourism have grown significantly in recent years. Hence, the municipal authorities of several post-industrial cities have vigorously pursued this market niche for two main reasons. Firstly, meetings and conference tourists are high spending. In turn, this can generate more levels of inward investment (Law 1993; Shaw and Williams, 1994) as companies perceive this market to be lucrative. Secondly, the potential for direct and indirect job creation is high (Bradley *et al.*, 2002).

The growing competition amongst cities to attract FDI has generated an increasing body of literature which has explored the role of promoting a new image for certain cities and place marketing to attract investments in tourism. Bradley *et al.* (2002) examine the impacts of place promotion and urban image enhancement on the locational decision-making processes of convention, exhibition and meeting organizers in the UK. They conclude that externally perceived images are a key determinant for investment locations and cannot be ignored by local authorities engaged in the promotion of their localities.

The competition between cities also occurs because cities attempt to develop themselves as strategic regional 'hubs' or gateways. It can be argued that cities with developed communications systems and transport infrastructures, including international airports, ports and railway stations, often assume a networking functional role among cities, surrounding regions and other areas. In this context, Ashworth and Turnbridge (1990) argue that visits to cities are often incidental rather than intentional. In their views, cities are largely recipients of transit tourism by people who stop off before moving on to visit a foreign country or a region as well as destinations for tourists on holiday in the surrounding towns and cities. As a result, urban tourism areas are increasingly being considered as nodes with high connectivity capable of providing information as well as linkages with other destination regions.

The Environmental Impact of Tourism in Urban Areas

Several studies have been conducted concerning the environmental effects of tourism on rural destinations and coastal resorts (see France, 1997 for a detailed review). During the 1980s, the promotion of mass tourism in fragile environments was yielding a clear negative impact in terms of loss of bio-diversity and diffuse environmental pollution. This stimulated political interest and academic research which has given considerable attention to the notion of carrying capacity in the recreation and tourism literature. Hall (1994) maintains that the notion of capacity is of significant interest to tourism planners because of the increased concern over negative aspects of tourism and the long-term viability of tourist destinations. Ultimately, this concept is inter-linked with the needs of tourist destinations to be able to cope with increased visitor numbers and markets. The result is a need for changes in the provision of physical and social infrastructures.

Tourist carrying capacity from an ecological standpoint may be defined as 'the maximum level of recreation use in terms of visitor numbers and activities that can be accommodated before a decline in ecological value sets in' (Coccossis and Parpairis 1992: 26). Despite the theoretical usefulness of this definition, several authors have stressed the difficulties of making the concept operational. For instance, Briassoulis (1992) highlights four operational limitations linked to the assessment of tourist carrying capacity. These are:

i.   carrying capacity is multidimensional.
ii. it is difficult to identify the 'critical' limiting resource to be used as a basis for estimating the carrying capacity of a region.
iii. the number of individuals a region can accept without undergoing significant environmental deterioration depends on the type and intensity of tourist activity.
iv. there are usually more than one set of competing explanations for environmental degradation, one of which may be tourism impacts.
v.   the management practice itself may be a cause of environmental degradation rather than the actual development (Farrel and Runyan, 1991).

Much of the literature on the environmental impact of tourism has been focused on the context of developed nations while there has been virtually no attempt to investigate these impacts in continuing socialist countries. One exception is provided by Hall's (2000) work. He argues that under state socialism, tourism and transport tended to be developed by targeting economies of scale, often with little consideration for their environmental impact. In his views, such impacts included visual amenity loss from poorly designed and located buildings and installations, soil and water contamination from untreated sewage and poor litter disposal, the excessive use of water resources, traffic congestion and pollution from exhaust emissions. Transport infrastructures related to tourism also exerted a negative impact on the environment. Thus, the destruction of natural environment can result from infrastructure development and other pollution problems associated with airport development, the direct and indirect consequences of road construction and other tourism transport forms, encouraging the degradation of previously less accessible areas (Hall, 2000: 418).

Significant attention to the analysis of the environmental impacts of tourism in urban settings has also been neglected for a long time. Hinch (1996) notes that the self-destruction of tourism in a wilderness setting is much more dramatic than its demise in urban areas. Nonetheless, he points out that 'not only does the city's complexity make the problem difficult to diagnose but it makes the cure difficult to prescribe and to administer' (Hinch, 1996: 107). The incremental deterioration prompted by urban tourism is less evident other than in instances such as the Mediterranean coast of Spain where the economic needs of the tourist industry to concentrate its activity has prompted urbanization with a clear negative environmental impact.

A recent UNEP (2000) publication has summarized the main environmental issues associated with urban areas. These include resource consumption, land use, water use, energy use, solid waste, wastewater collection and treatment of water pollution, air pollution and global warming, brownfields and natural and industrial disasters. The remainder of this section will directly or indirectly establish a relationship between these issues (except natural and industrial disasters which are outside the realm of tourism) and the environmental impact of tourism in urban areas.

Resource consumption – It is widely recognized that city dwellers consume a greater amount of natural resources than the immediate region can provide. Cities transfer environmental cost associated, for example, with the production of city imports to distant destinations where these goods are produced. This is expressed by the concept of the 'ecological footprint' (Rees and Wackernagel, 1996) of a region or a city. For example, Rees and Wackernal (1996) calculated that London's ecological footprint or the land area required to supply its environmental needs is 120 times its size. Similarly, tourist destinations, including urban areas, produce environmental footprints. Gössling *et al.* (2002) apply this methodology to calculate resource consumption of the ecological footprint of the roughly 117,690 international tourists who visited the Seychelles in 2000. They divided resource and area use into four categories 'transport', 'accommodation', 'activities', and 'food and fibre consumption'. According to their estimates an average 10.4 day holiday in Seychelles requires almost the same area available globally per human being (2 ha).

Land use – As cities expand their tourist functions, an increased amount of land is often lost to the development of tourist facilities and attractions such as new accommodation or theme parks. Island cities with a waterfront, especially in developing countries, often experience urban and tourism development along their coastlines (Pearce 1995; Weaver, 1993; Potter and Dann, 2000). For example, Page (1995), points to the extreme case study of the resorts of Buggiba and Quawra on the island of Malta, which have now merged to form a continuous urban tourist development. This process can prompt the loss of agricultural land as well as exacerbate environmental problems due to the construction of new tourist facilities and the loss of coastal ecosystems.

Water use, wastewater collection and treatment and water pollution – Availability of water and its treatment are two major issues for many urban areas of developing countries which have poor water distribution and collection systems. These infrastructural networks can lose large amounts of water to leaks or illegal connections or they may have inadequate treatment capacity. Urban tourism can contribute to increase the seasonal demand on these systems, especially in tropical and hot cities, during the summer. In this context, Stonich (1998) carried out a study of the political ecology of tourism development in Bay Island, Honduras and showed how tourists consume substantially greater water levels than local residents. Her study does not compare quantitatively water use between tourists and residents. However, it reports that tourists bathe an average of 3.1 times a day by showering while residents bathe only 1.2 times a day by taking sponge baths. This exemplifies how tourists consume larger amounts of water than residents which, in turn, exerts an extra pressure on water systems that are already running at their full capacity.

Energy use – Tourist attractions and facilities consume a considerable amount of energy. This can exert stress on deficient energy production sources and may determine a rationalization of energy or long power shortcuts for local residents at various stages. Becken and Simmons (2002) carried out research on the energy consumption patterns of tourist attractions and activities in New Zealand. Their study analyzed the total energy use of tourist industry businesses and energy use per tourist visiting attractions and activities. These ranged from art galleries, museums and shopping to air activities and nature recreation. They conclude that tourism infrastructures such as museums, theatres and historic buildings require a moderate energy use per tourist. These tourism activities could be found predominantly in urban environments with clear implications for the overall urban energy demand as well as the emission of greenhouse gases derived from fossil fuels that may affect global climate.

Solid waste – Solid waste disposal and collection creates environmental concern in two ways. First, in cities of the developing world only 30 to 50 per cent of waste is collected, the rest is dumped in illegal landfills or left in the street (UNEP 2001). Second, the waste collected may not be adequately treated because, for example, urban areas are running out of suitable landfills sites. Although there are no direct studies of urban tourism's impact on solid waste, it could be said that often tourists' consumption patterns can generate problems for waste disposal and collection systems which are already underperforming. ICLEI (1999) argue that tourism related consumption has a negative impact on destinations because, upon their arrival, tourists often maintain their high levels of consumption, despite the fact that the destination area may not have adequate infrastructural facilities to manage such consumption patterns. Furthermore, other studies contend that the composition of waste changes as income rises with a lower proportion of biodegradable organic wastes and more plastics and other synthetic material (UNEP 2001: 8).

Air pollution and global warming – International tourism is ever more related to the increase in flight numbers. Airports are often located near cities, despite the fact that air transport is amongst the most polluting of industries (EEA, 1997). At the international level, this contributes to the greenhouse effect. At the local level, it poses environmental threats for residents who live near the airport in terms of high carbon dioxide emission levels. Furthermore, cars associated with tourism are deemed responsible for increasing levels of air pollution. Indeed, urban tourism in transitional economies has generated more demand for private car rentals and taxis, all of which contribute to the increase of atmospheric pollution, congestion and noise as urban areas lack adequate road systems.

Brownfields – Brownfields are environmentally ruined sites, usually abandoned, vacant or underused former industrial facilities. The redevelopment of such sites is complicated by the environmental liabilities of potential developers and by the fact that they require a delicate process of participatory planning which will involve a vast array of actors often with diverging interests. Contrary to the previous examples which pointed to ways in which tourists can exert negative impacts on the urban environment, there are instances in which brownfields have been redeveloped with a tourist function. For example, Bilbao Metropoli-30, a public private partnership set up in Bilbao, Spain, devised a strategic revitalization plan for the city which entailed the strategic location of the new Guggenheim museum on a brownfield along the highly polluted river La Ria (Andersen Consulting, 1990). The museum is now a well establish tourist attraction in Europe which attracts thousands of visitors per year.

Previous sections have pointed to theoretical ways in which tourism can impact on urban environments in both negative and positive terms. The potentially negative impacts of tourism in urban areas, however, are summarized in a more systematic way in Table 5.1. These impacts have been enumerated in six main categories ranging from land use to social and cultural patterns. It is important to highlight that these categories do not apply to cities in developed and developing nations alike. For example, the impacts of tourism on the urban infrastructures are more significant to cities in the South than to urban agglomerates in the North, as will be examined in greater depth in chapter 9. Furthermore, Table 5.1 displays some impacts that stem from the introduction of new social and cultural patterns associated with tourism. These exogenous patterns are generally more noticeable in the cities of the South and play a crucial role in the social construction of the urban space through resource sharing and interactions between tourists and residents. This particular aspect will be discussed in the next section of this chapter.

Table 5.1 The negative impact of tourism on the urban environment

1. **Land use**
   - Land lost through the development which may have been used for agriculture
   - Conversion of land which has valuable ecological functions (e.g. mangrove swamps or wetlands)
   - Change to the hydrological system

2. **Visual impact**
   - Expansion of the built area
   - Standardisation of the architectural style
   - Excessive seasonal population growth

3. **Infrastructure**
   - Overloading the urban infrastructure with the following utilities and developments:
     - roads
     - railways
     - car parking
     - the electricity grid
     - solid waste disposal
     - liquid waste disposal
     - water supply
   - Municipal authorities' investments in infrastructures and services may be bias to serving tourist areas

4. **Urban form**
   - Changes to the land use as residential areas see hotels/boarding houses develop
   - Alterations to the urban-fabric from pedestrianisation and traffic management schemes to accommodate tourists
   - Changes to the built environment lead to contrasts in the quality of the urban areas used by tourists and residential areas

5. **Natural features**
   - Surface and underground water pollution
   - Air pollution
   - Change of green areas use for tourist facilities development (e.g. golf course)

6. **Cultural and social pattern**
   - Introduction of drugs, crime and prostitution
   - 'Irritation' of city dwellers caused by tourist
   - Shrinking of household available space to leave rooms free to provide Bed & Breakfast accommodation
   - Displacement of local activities

(*Source*: Adapted from Page, 1995)

The Social Impact of Tourism in Urban Areas

The social impact of tourism has been debated extensively in the literature (see Shaw and Williams, 1997 and France, 1997, for reviews). In recent years, the tourism-community relationship issue has become central to arguments about sustainable tourism which seek the well-being of host communities. This has been reflected in a significant increase in case studies concerning tourist-resident relationships. The most comprehensive literature review of such studies has been provided by Pearce and Moscardo (1999). They reviewed 262 studies of tourism- community relationships and pointed out how the methodological tradition has followed two main approaches to such studies. The first approach consists of the ethnographic case studies which have been mostly carried out in developing countries taking a cautionary perspective that emphasizes the negative impact of tourism. The second approach draws upon social survey research and typically attempts to detail and examine host community attitudes towards tourism and its impacts.

Research efforts have converged on both the study of the factors underpinning the social impacts of tourism and methodological issues concerning the assessment of the modalities through which these impacts occur. Thus, Urry (1990: 57-59) argues that the social impacts of tourism depend on the intersection of a wide range of factors. These include:

- the number of visitors in relationship to the size of the host population.
- the predominant object of the tourist activity, where this could include a landscape, a townscape, an ethnic group, a life-style, historical artefacts, bases for recreation (e.g. a golf course) or 'sand, sun and sea'.
- the character of the tourist experience, ranging from a quick visit to deeper immersion.
- the organization of the industry (e.g. private- or publicly-owned).
- effects of tourism on pre-existing agricultural and industrial activities.
- the economic and social differences between visitors and the majority of the host society.
- the particular standards of accommodation required.
- the degree to which the state actively seeks to promote tourism.
- the extent to which tourist can be identified and blamed for negative impacts.

Other authors have shown a more methodological concern for the impact assessment. They have highlighted how tourism has been identified as a factor of change that may affect traditional family values and cause cultural commercialization, leading to a loss of authenticity. Furthermore, tourism has been linked to increases in crime, prostitution and gambling among host communities (Mathieson and Wall, 1982; Pearce, 1989; Ryan, 1991). In addition, tourism development may create social conflicts at the destination due to socio-cultural differences, economic welfare and a purchasing-power gap between local residents and tourists (Tosun, 2002). Similar to the environmental impact assessment of tourism, the evaluation of social impact has heavily relied on the notion of carrying capacity. From a social standpoint, this may be defined as 'that point in growth of tourism where local residents perceive on balance an unacceptable level of social disbenefits from tourism development' (D'Amore, 1982: 144).

Several models based on stages or life-cycle techniques form the major theoretical framework for investigating local communities' response to the increase in tourist flows and to assess destinations' carrying capacity. Two well-established models have been proposed by Butler (1980) and Doxey (1975). The first one maintains that visitor numbers will decline as soon as the infrastructural and social carrying capacity of a given destination is exceeded. The second consists of a four stage model including Euphoria, Apathy, Annoyance and Antagonism which leads to the postulation of an 'irridex', an *ad hoc* index to measure the changing attitude of communities to tourism development. Indeed, Doxey (1975) argues that an initial phase of tourism development (stage I) is followed first by indifference toward tourism (stage II), then by increasing uneasiness by residents toward tourist activities (stage III) and eventually by irritation (stage IV).

Recent studies have noted that these stage models are over-simplistic and unidirectional. They do not take into account that different individuals or groups within the host community may respond to tourism in different ways according to their economic dependence from the tourist sector and the personal benefit that can be gained from it (Gilbert and Clark, 1997; Tosun, 2002). Moreover, as highlighted earlier, there are several hindrances to the 'measurement' and implementation of tourist carrying capacity. These mainly stem from the fact that individuals and collective responses to tourism are not unidirectional in nature and move from positive to negative according to the personal economic benefits that individuals receive from tourism.

Notwithstanding these difficulties, tourist carrying capacity may indicate the limit to the development of tourism. This indicator is often used in life cycle models and relies on the assumption that there exists a resource access and use conflict over the same urban facilities between local residents and visitors. However, local city dwellers may not be the only group to be disadvantaged from the struggle for control of urban infrastructures. Indeed, D'Amore (1982) applies Doxey's model to a life cycle model for urban destination and concludes that irritation can be felt alike by both tourists and residents. When this happens, negative interactions between residents and tourist develop and tourism visitation begins to decline.

Tourism Planning

Planning for Tourism

As noted earlier, tourism may have an impact, either positive or negative, with evident implications for local resources. Planning is therefore a vital tool to maximize the positive impacts of tourism and mitigate or eliminate altogether the negative impacts.

For this reason, planning for tourism tends to be an amalgam of economic, social and environmental considerations which reflect the diversity of factors that influence tourism (Heeley, 1981: 61). Nonetheless, planning is rarely exclusively devoted to tourism *per se*. For example, Butler (1999) notes that as tourism becomes tied ever more firmly to global processes and agents, its planning is becoming increasingly involved with many activities and processes unrelated directly to leisure. This has resulted in planning for aspects of tourism rather than tourism planning as a separate activity in its own right.

In the former socialist countries of Eastern Europe, tourism planning encompassed social, ideological and political goals as well as economic objectives and was completely subservient to the interests of the State (Hall D., 1991b). Instead, in Western nations, planning for tourism has traditionally been associated with 'zoning' or development planning at the local government level (Gunn, 2002). Hall (1994) points out how planning concerns have typically been focused on site development, accommodation and building regulation, the density of tourism development, the presentation of cultural, historical and natural tourist features, and the provision of infrastructure, including roads and sewerage. In addition, planning has often focused on land-use issues within a political arena of stakeholders' interests.

The variety of actors, often referred as 'stakeholders' involved in tourism planning, and the plethora of forces (cultural, economic and social) influencing them, has traditionally been articulated into four main interest groups: public and private sectors, Non Governmental Organizations (NGOs) and local communities. Authors have debated the role played by these stakeholders in the planning arena. Thus, De Lacy *et al.* (2002) explain how the role of national governments is to set the broad policy agenda and provide the framework in which tourism development takes place. National governments intervene therefore in four main areas: the establishment of legal and regulatory frameworks, the provision of infrastructure, investments in marketing and the promotion of tourism destinations and in the provision of training. Local governments, on the other hand, provide 'on-the-ground' interface for national policies and help the capacity of localities to host tourism. The private sector's role mainly entails the provision of capital to develop tourism projects and organizational skills necessary to a profitable management of tourist infrastructures. Lastly, NGOs play a key role in representing and acting for the community. Their action is often crucial to advocate bottom-up approaches to tourism planning and promoting consultation planning.

Along similar lines, Page (1995) illustrates the distinction between the role of the private and public sectors in the supply of the tourism product. He contends that the main reason for the private sector's involvement in tourism is economic profit, whereas the public sector's involvement can include economic, social, cultural, environmental and political reasons. The economic reasons are related to fostering economic development while the socio-cultural ones often involve the achievement of specific objectives such as the well-being and health of individuals, and/or the promotion of the cultural awareness of citizens.

Recent works have highlighted the importance of citizen and community involvement in planning, not only through the incorporation of their views and perceptions on tourism within the development plan, but also though an active participation in the decision-making process. The desirability of public involvement in planning practices and interactive governance has been emphasized since the mid-1980s (see Potter, 1985). Public participation in planning also received widespread attention in the literature during the 1990s. As Rydin and Pennington (2000: 153) note:

> the emphasis on the inherent desirability of public involvement is part of a tradition which seeks to 'open up' planning processes to democratic scrutiny and to expand the scope of public involvement as an integral part of improvements in policy delivery.

The next section will review developments in planning theory, such as the concepts of participatory and collaborative planning, in the light of the importance they have acquired among academics and practitioners alike. This discussion is essential in order to understand the main rationale underpinning planning practice in Western and socialist nations and will prove useful in assessing the main shift that has occurred in planning practices in Havana and Cuba during the Special Period.

Participatory and Collaborative Planning

Public participation in planning can be rationalized following two different approaches. The first approach focuses on the democratic right to be involved in the public policy process. The second argument is associated with the greater effectiveness of policy delivery if it is 'more in tune with society's values and preferences' and could thereby result in 'better' policy delivery (Rydin and Pennington, 2000: 155). This efficiency argument is based on the assumption that a more democratic participation in planning can raise awareness of the cultural and social qualities of localities at the policy-making stage and avoid conflicts that may emerge in policy implementation later.

Whichever approach is chosen to justify public participation, they both assume a renewed validity in the context of both development planning practices and highly centralized socialist planning systems. Thus, after the Second World War, development planning has been grounded on the implementation of technocratic and blueprint projects that considered space and communities as organically undifferentiated wholes to be filled with social and cultural content. Similarly, communist countries have been characterized by a democratic gap deemed instrumental by communist parties to achieve the prescription of the communist paradigm.

Meurs (1992) argues that the incompatibility between participation and planning in communist systems of governance is often explained in terms of two arguments. Firstly, central planning removes most real decisions from the level of enterprises, depriving 'workers' democracy' of its content. Secondly, major tensions between local interests and national goals may force the central authority to choose between abandoning planning or repressing participation.

Orthodox Marxist theories hold that one goal of socialism is to allow people to regain control over the products of their labour and avoid alienation. A second goal of socialism is to prevent recurrent economic crises and to achieve steadier and equally redistributed economic growth (Meurs, 1992). Central planning is therefore crucial to avoid the booms and busts of the economy. It permits the best resource allocation by co-ordinating information concerning economic and social variables at the level of the state, which would not otherwise be available to individuals or societal groups.

Planning theories have recently become interlinked with communication theories. Healey (1999), drawing from Habermas' communication theory, argues that societies are built of social networks that overlap and intersect in complex ways. Many people operate in several networks at once which link multiple social worlds. In Healey's view 'communicative planning' is the interactive process through which problems of governance are defined, interests constituted, policy agendas identified, and governance programs followed through. This is a desirable form of planning both in terms of greater effectiveness for planning systems and in terms of moving towards a more communicative democracy (Colantonio and Potter, 2002).

The academic planning community has often referred to the outcome of planning activities as the development of dynamic and inter-subjective interactions between state and groups within civil society. Broadly speaking, the state is often seen as a set of institutions for the protection and maintenance of society. Thus, the government, the judiciary and the armed forces secure the reproduction of social relations through the enforcement of law, the supply of public good and varying extents of intervention in the economy. Civil society, on the other hand, is regarded as the segments of society that lie outside the realms of the state and the market-place (Potter *et al.*, 2004a). It forms a 'third sector' where individualism and societal self-organization guarantee the reproduction of society in co-operation with the state. Within this context, it is possible to distinguish two approaches to planning: traditional institutionalism and new institutionalism.

Traditional institutionalism envisages institutions in the orthodox way of the formal set of structures and procedures as in the traditional view of public administration. Within this approach state and civil society groups are often seen as negotiating agents in the policy making-implementing-monitoring process. Planning results from the position and power of the agents of governance (Phelps and Tewdwr-Jones, 2000). Factors such as 'partnership' and 'empowerment' become central in the analysis.

Rydin and Pennington (2000: 156) argue, however, that these accounts often assume 'that non-participation reflects either a lack of interest in the policies under discussion or barriers to frustrated participation put in place by political and professional structures'. This 'uncollaborative' practice is based on the often misconceived assumption that policy-makers obstruct public participation.

Professionals therefore can change this by altering their values, institutional norms and working practices.

In the theory of New Institutionalism, an institution is not understood as an organization as such but as an established way of addressing certain issues (Healey, 1999). Here the power redistribution exercise between institutions and civil society, planners and individuals becomes blurred into collaborative action and social communication. Governance does not stem from the struggle for power, since institutions are already the expression of societal values, beliefs and norms. This allows policies to be locally-informed and place-based.

Recent developments in planning theory reviewed so far have highlighted the importance of communicative action and public participation to broaden participatory and democratic governance. Phelps and Tewdwr-Jones (2000: 112) note that these developments 'have each found favour as possible formulations of a "third way" between market-based and centrally planned forms of economic and political governance'. The application of these developments to tourism planning studies has been limited, both in number and in scope, especially in urban contexts. Hence, the next and final section of this chapter proposes a set of approaches and tools to assess how tourism can be included within the broader framework of the urban management process.

Urban Tourism Planning: Indicators, Approaches and Tools

Approaches and Tools to the Management of Urban Tourism

Because of the impacts that tourism can have, several authors hold that tourism planning should be included in the broader process of urban management (Page, 1995) and highlight the need of the environmental, economic and social management of tourism activities (ICLEI, 1999; Forsyth, 1997; Goodall, 1996). The sound management of tourism activities has also been urged by urban planners, because the effects of tourism in cities are more acute in particular areas where tourism facilities and amenities are spatially concentrated (Pearce, 1995). These functional areas often form what urban geographers have termed 'Tourism Districts' or 'Tourism Business Districts' (TBD) (Getz, 1995).

Getz (1993: 583) elucidates how 'the term Tourism Business District can be used to describe concentrations of visitor-oriented attractions and services located in conjunction with the urban Central Business District (CBD) functions'. The TDB results, therefore, in a combination of tourist attractions and CBD functions, including offices, retail, government, meetings and essential services, such as transport catering, accommodation and information. In some centres, tourism is viewed as a major catalyst for desired changes. Thus, many municipalities have planned the development of a TBD often in conjunction with economic development, urban renewal or redevelopment schemes.

Getz (1993: 587) goes on to identify four major issues related to the TBD planning process:

i. Developing tourism: to create attractions, infrastructures and services; to promote urban tourism; to co-ordinate public and private activities; and to provide appropriate land use/development incentives and control.

ii. Using tourism as a catalyst: to attract other development/investments; to generate a positive image of the area; and to facilitate conservation and amenity provision through tourism.

iii. Balancing tourism with other urban functions: to determine the role and priority of tourism along with resident-oriented services and businesses or industrial development; and to evaluate opportunity costs.

iv. Dealing with negative impacts: to account for such negative effects as the reduction of affordable housing, inflated land costs, traffic, prostitution, crime, and the loss of leisure opportunities for residents.

Notwithstanding that theoretical constructs such as the TBD are important concepts developed in the literature, research into the conceptualization of tourism's contribution to overall urban management may be considered to be at a very early stage. This is especially true if such research is compared to the volume of environmental and social studies undertaken in urban areas. Thus, Table 5.2 outlines a set of methodologies that suggest distinct ways to conceptualize the integration of tourism activities to urban management. As shown in Table 5.2, these approaches are reflected in a broad spectrum of methodologies relying upon a wide set of criteria. These range from deterministic attempts based on environmental criteria, such as the measurement of the ecological carrying capacity of a given place, to approaches which have a more social and political connotation, encompassing sustainability and public participation in planning.

Many of the concepts contained in the last column of Table 5.2 (Urban tourism) are only intuitive applications of the general theories expressed in the first three columns of the table. Although these applications can be criticized for not fitting the implications stemming from the theories themselves, they represent a stimulus to further research in this direction. Furthermore, the table provides a theoretical framework to answer important questions related to tourism planning in urban areas such as (i) who is involved in planning? (ii) what are the roles, responsibilities and interest of agents responsible for planning? (iii) who wins and loses according to the approach implemented? (iv) what are the best indicators to be used to achieve specific urban management goals?

Thus, the table demonstrates how at one end of the spectrum, environmental planning (groups A and B) places a greater emphasis on deterministic concepts such as environmental carrying capacity. According to these approaches, it is the task of municipal authorities to define critical threshold values for this indicator and impose limitations to the growth of tourism accordingly. Middle range approaches (groups C, D and E), emphasize a greater role for private sector initiative and for public-private partnerships in defining objectives and policies, promoting economic sustainability and implementing management systems and action planning. At the other end of the spectrum (group F), are to be found approaches based on public participation and decision-making sharing with local residents. These approaches underline the guidance role that urban communities can play to inform policy according to their perception of how urban tourism affects its environment.

Another issue underlined by the table concerns the difficulty in selecting indicators and variables to be used as instruments to inform tourism planning and development policies. Hughes (2002), for example, argues that there are two main issues linked to the use of environmental indicators applied to tourism. Firstly, the extent to which tourism is the agent responsible is not clear since it may prove difficult to isolate the impact of tourist- from non-tourist industries. Secondly, it is difficult to establish what criteria need to be used to define the minimal base level indicator. In other words, considering that the local natural condition of destinations could absorb unequal levels of different forms of tourism, who should set critical threshold values for the indicators? And how should these thresholds be set? Further, as other authors have pointed out, at present, environmental criteria are often more developed than social criteria in the development of indicators (Font and Bendell, 2002).

Despite these methodological quandaries, examples of tourism indicators have been developed at the international and national levels under initiatives encouraged by the WTO (1993) and the English Tourism Council (2002). However, these indicators mostly apply to rural areas and have not been tested in urban areas because of the measurement problems reviewed above. In the context of this research, the authors have elaborated a list of multidimensional variables which can be used in the impact assessment process and the identification process of policy issues related to the urban management of tourism. These variables are reported in Table 5.3 and will be used throughout this research in the context of Havana.

The variables described in Table 5.3 are derived from urban monitoring indexes deployed by international organizations and indicators developed in tourism studies. These encompass four main dimensions (or themes) of urban tourism: social, economic, environmental and institutional. For each of these dimensions a set of variables has been selected, although some of them, such as jobs created in tourism can be more easily measured than others, for example, tourist industry discharges into water bodies. Lastly, it can be seen how emphasis has been placed on the effects of tourism on urban infrastructure and social phenomena, such as the informal economy, which are significant in the context of cities in the developing world. This choice is directly related to the difference of the impacts of tourism in cities in the North and the South. These types of indicators informed the original research carried out in Cuba as part of this book.

Table 5.2 Tools for, approaches to, urban and tourism management

Group/Purpose	Name	Details	Urban Tourism
(A) Establish environmental carrying capacity and human impacts on them	Environmental footprint	Estimates the land area required by any human activity, both directly – the land occupied by buildings or infrastructures – and indirectly – including the land needed to grow crops and assimilate pollutants. For example the 'land equivalent' of fossil energy is the area needed to grow the equivalent of biofuel or to sequester the carbon released. 'Footprint' may offer a meaningful single measure of all global ecological impacts of human activities, at household, municipal national or global level. The degree to which the 'footprint' of human activities exceeds the total productive area is a measure of unsustainability	Resource consumption and waste assimilation requirement by tourist population in terms of corresponding productive land area
	Environmental space	Estimate maximum sustainable rates of human use of key resources (energy, selected non-renewable resources, land wood) and then divides these evenly among the world's population to give each individual's entitlement. The extent to which any country (or household) exceeds this is a measure of unsustainability	Calculation as to whether tourists' are exceeding their 'fair share' of resource consumption and waste generation in comparison to the local population
	State of environment reporting (SoER)	Collection, interpretation and publication of information about the state of local information	Processing the information about the state of tourist development areas
(B) Use of environmental information to guide policy	Environmental budgeting	Local carrying capacities are used to set 'budgets' for the maximum amount of environmental impact permissible in the municipal are. For example the water extraction budget would be based on replenishment rates. The municipality works with all environmental 'consumers' to keep impacts within the budget. For example more consumption of water by households would have to be offset by less consumption by industry, or by more recovery/treatment of water	'Budgets' to be divided between tourists and local residents. Possible limitation of visitor numbers
	Sustainability indicators (Technical approach)	Indicators are chosen and designed as an integrated set linking measures of the *state* (= condition) of the environment itself with measure of the pressures (=actions) taken to reduce those pressures. This clarifies the connection between inputs, output and outcomes (management term related to (response, pressure, state) and helps to design policies and actions to tackle environmental problems and measures their effectiveness in doing so	Planning on capacity standards to be used as indicators as well as optimum capacity levels. For instance: set of densities for hotels and other tourist-oriented infrastructures which depends on image, land availability, cost parameters, building heights and allowable density

	Sustainability reporting	SoER broadened to include quality of life as well as aspects of sustainability, and focused on information needed to guide decision and action	SoER broadened to include quality of life of local residents
(C) Assess environmental effects of policies/actions	Environmental impact assessment	Structured, explicit and systematic assessment of the environmental effects of activities or project. It may be done to identify priorities for improvement in existing activities, or to guide choice between future options	Assessment of environmental effects of tourist development activities or projects
	Strategic environmental assessment	Environmental impact assessment of programmes, plans and/or policies	Environmental impact assessment of programmes, plans and/or policies of tourist development
	Sustainability appraisal	Assessment (of activities, programmes, plans and/or policies) which applies social and economic sustainability criteria as well as environmental ones, and consider the integration and reconciliation of different criteria	Assessment of tourism activities, programmes, plans and/or policies which apply social, economic and environmental criteria
(D) Manage actions towards environmental/ sustainability objectives		Setting of environmental objective, implementation of environmental improvement actions and monitoring and reporting of their effectiveness, i.e. application of familiar 'management by objectives' processes to a municipality's environmental effects	Environmental action planning and Management, Eco-management and Audit (EMAS), Sustainability management and audit applied to the tourist industry (compliance with environmental legislation, minimisation of waste and reduction of over-consumption etc....)
	Eco-management and Audit (EMAS)	A formal management systems standard for environmental 'management by objectives'	
	Sustainability management and audit	Proposed updating of EMAS to include social and economic aspects of sustainability and strengthen involvement of stakeholders in setting criteria and assessing performance, according to social audit principles	
(E) Communicate sustainability problems and solution	Good practice case studies	Diffusion of database of good practice case studies	Database of good practice case studies of tourist development
	Databases, Internet sites	The Internet offers new means of presenting information for varied uses and users	Use of the internet for information exchange/ collection

		Urban Tourism
(F) Build community and political support for sustainability	Sustainability indicators (community approach)	Indicators are chosen by (or with) local communities to express and articulate sustainability problems and aspirations in ways that are meaningful and 'resonant' to ordinary people, and ideally capable of being collected by them	Development of 'irritation index' that indicates when local residents perceive on balance an unacceptable level of social disbenefits from tourist development
	Deliberative consultation methods	Processes such as future research, visioning, focus groups, planning for real community appraisal/mapping which aim to build consensus on public policy goals	Involvement of local communities in decision making/planning for tourism development
	Local Agenda 21 process	Participative process, usually (but not necessarily) initiated and managed by municipality, seeking to build the broadest possible consensus in local community on sustainable development aims and actions to be taken by all sectors. Often using deliberative consultation methods	Application of LA 21's principles (participation, and transparency, partnerships, accountability, systemic approach, etc...) to tourist development projects

(*Source*: Drawn from Levett, 1997, except the column 'Urban Tourism', added by the first named author)

Table 5.3 Selected variables for the measurement of the impacts of tourism and the identification of planning issues in Havana

Theme	Sub-theme	Indicator
Social	Effects on the socio-cultural landscape	• Change in urban population (migration, building workers, etc) • Displacement of residents' activities • Change in life style and quality of life • Social problems (crime and prostitution) • Community stress and conflict because of tourism
	Community participation	• Audit of community perceptions of tourism
Economic	Employment	• Job created in the tourism sector • Wage difference between tourism and other economic sector
	Informal economy	• Workers in the informal sector
Environmental	Tourism and urbanization plans	• Description of the development proposed, comprising information about the design and size or scale of the tourist development • Review of urbanization plans and current land use
	Urban infrastructure and natural resources	• Residues and emissions generated by tourist infrastructures by type, quantity and composition including : (i) discharges to water (ii) emissions to air (iii) noise (iv) deposits/residues to land and soil • Effects of tourism development on local infrastructures: (i) roads (ii) railways (iii) car parking (iv) the electricity grid (v) solid waste disposal (vi) liquid waste disposal (vii) water supply • Effects on aesthetic landscape • Effects on flora, fauna and geology

Continued...

Table 5.3 continued

Theme	Sub-theme	Indicator
Environmental	Urban infrastructure and natural resources	• Effects on land (i) Change of local topography, etc. (ii) Land use/resource effects (iii) Quality and quantity of agricultural land taken by the development (iv) Effects on surrounding land uses including agriculture (v) Waste disposal • Effects on water (i) Effects of the development on drainage patterns in the area (ii) Change to hydrographical characteristics e.g. ground water, water courses flow, flows of underground water (iii) Effects on coastal or estuarine hydrology (iv) Effects of pollutants, waste etc on water quality
	Other indirect and secondary effects	• Effects from traffic (road, rail, air, water) related to the development (e.g. increase of number of taxis and hired cars per residents (impact of tourism on transport) transport. • Effects of other development associated with the project, e.g. new roads, sewers, housing, power lines, pipelines, telecommunication etc. • Secondary effects resulting from the interaction of separate direct effects
Institutional	Institutional capacity	• Percentage of local authorities with Tourism Action Plans
	Environmental assessment of policies	• Policies, programs and plans for which a Strategic Environmental Assessment has been undertaken at the planning stage

(*Source*: Adapted from EEA, 1999; ETC, 2002; UNEP, 2000, 2001; EU Urban Audit, 2002)

Conclusions

This chapter has demonstrated how tourism is a powerful force capable of generating multidimensional impacts in urban areas. These impacts can be different between cities in the developed and developing world and need to be taken into account by municipal authorities within the overall urban management process. Thus, the chapter has reviewed several methodological approaches through which urban tourism can be incorporated in the urban management and planning process. These range from centralized models of planning, which have been adopted in socialist states, to more inclusive forms of tourism planning in common usage in Western democratic societies. Indeed, there are several stakeholders (public, private and community) at different spatial scales (local, national and international) involved in tourism whose contribution to planning is a fundamental prerequisite for a successful urban management process.

The conceptual tools and the variables discussed in this chapter will be employed in Part II of the book to assess the economic, social and environmental impacts of tourism in Havana. In the meantime, the next chapter provides an overview of the interrelationships between tourism and urban development in Havana. This is essential in order to understand how the current impacts of tourism are inevitably entwined with the main characteristics of Havana's urban form and its past urban growth.

PART II
Tourism and Development in Havana

Chapter 6

Tourism and Urban Development in Havana: From the 'Pseudo-republic' to the Special Period

Introduction

As outlined in chapter 1, Havana's fortunes have been closely entwined with the political and economic vicissitudes of Cuba. These encompassed colonial dependency on Spain until 1898; significant political domination from the USA from 1902 to 1959; the Socialist Revolution led by Fidel Castro in 1959 and the beginning of the Special Period after 1989. Throughout Cuba's colonial history, Havana has been the most important city of the island in economic and political terms, concentrating most of Cuba's trade and political power.

After gaining independence from Spain, Havana effectively became a back-door playground for American tourism, capital and organized crime. In 1959, the Socialist Revolution turned its back on this imperialistic history, making every effort to halt gambling, prostitution and organised crime in Havana. Since 1989, the need to look outward to other economies of the developed world has meant that Cuba has specifically targeted tourism as a mechanism for economic growth and development. As a result, over the last decade, Cuba's tourist flows have risen drastically as demonstrated in chapter 3. Throughout the 1990s, Havana has been pivotal in Cuba's new tourism-oriented development model, experiencing a significant increase in tourism projects and tourist flows.

The aims of this chapter are twofold. Firstly, to describe how tourism has historically been a powerful force in shaping Havana's urban expansion, with the exception of the revolutionary period from 1959 to 1990. Secondly, to outline how tourism and specific urban policies have contributed to the uneven spatial development of Havana. The chapter is divided into four main sections, together with a final concluding section. The first section introduces Havana's main physical features and summarizes the city's urban development in the colonial period. The second section provides an overview of the increasing importance of tourism in Havana's urban development in the first half of the twentieth century. The third examines the anti-urban policy embraced by the revolutionary government after 1959 to curb Havana's growth and its development of tourism. Lastly, the fourth section looks at the re-establishment and redevelopment of tourism in Havana since the introduction of the Special Period.

Havana's Main Physical Features and Colonial Development

Havana's Physical Features

Havana is located on the northern coast of Cuba and with 2,200,000 inhabitants it constitutes an administrative province which is composed of fifteen municipalities (see Figure 6.1). The city's main physical feature is the Bay, which represents the centre of its territorial development. The city's territorial extension is 727 square kilometres, which consist of 77 per cent urbanized land and 23 per cent non-urbanised land. This extension represents 0.6 per cent of Cuba's national territory and comprises nearly 42 kilometres of coast, including 15 kilometres of beaches on the Eastern coast (Metropolis-EU, 1995).

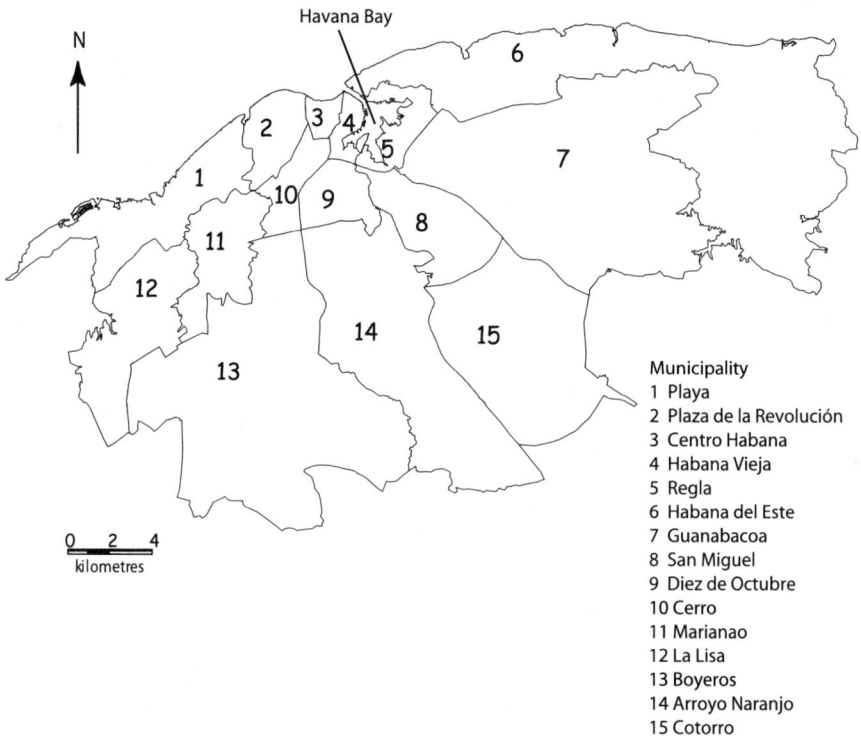

Municipality
1 Playa
2 Plaza de la Revolución
3 Centro Habana
4 Habana Vieja
5 Regla
6 Habana del Este
7 Guanabacoa
8 San Miguel
9 Diez de Octubre
10 Cerro
11 Marianao
12 La Lisa
13 Boyeros
14 Arroyo Naranjo
15 Cotorro

Figure 6.1 Havana's fifteen municipalities

Havana shares with the rest of Cuba a classic wet-dry sub-tropical type of climate. Average temperatures range from 27°C (81°F) in the wet season (May–October) to 22°C (71°F) in the dry season (November–April). The city is cooled by a north-easterly breeze throughout the year and its foundation is composed mostly of Cretaceous limestone. It exhibits marine terraces that expand radio-centrically from the Bay up to a height of 100 metres. These terraces have influenced the layout of Havana, along with a series of capes and escarpments (Scarpaci *et al.*, 2002).

The city is endowed with a good water supply that includes ten rivers and fresh water reservoirs as well as a large underground aquifer located in the southern areas, which until recently has been contaminated by southwards urban expansion. The city's main natural resources and vegetation are concentrated in the eastern municipalities of Guanabacoa and Habana del Este, which are currently less urbanised. These eastern areas account for over 80 per cent of Havana's natural resources (Interview 15), including mangroves and autochthonous vegetation. Almost 95 per cent of the vegetation has an 'anthropogenic' nature consisting mainly of sugar canes and other vegetable and fruit cultivation. The remaining 5 per cent is mostly located in the extreme south eastern city area where isolated patches of wild vegetation thrive (Pérez, 1995).

The City's Colonial Urban and Tourism Development

San Cristóbal de la Habana was founded around 1514 on the southern coast of Cuba. In 1519, the settlement of Havana was relocated to its present site where it immediately became a key transhipment point of commerce between the Old World and the New. As the city began to acquire an independent importance as a trade centre, Spain authorized the building of a coastal defence system based on the construction of three main fortresses to guard the entrance of the bay. These fortresses were La Fuerza (1558–1577), Tres Reyes del Morro (1589–1610) and San Salvador de la Punta (1589–1600), and represent the main contemporary heritage tourism attractions (Scarpaci *et al.*, 2002).

Throughout the next two centuries, Havana continued to be ringed by major fortifications, most of which have survived to this day. According to Diaz-Briquets (1994), the decisive reason for the complete fortification of the city was the English occupation of Havana in 1762 during the Seven Years War (1756-1763). As a result, twelve years later, the fortresses of La Cabaña, Atarés and Principe began to be built on a hill dominating the colonial city. These fortifications determined the city's physical limits along with a defensive wall surrounding the old colonial shell, or *intramuros*, which was built between 1674 and 1797. The walled area, known today as Old Havana (see Figure 6.2), covered an area of 2.9 square kilometres, of which streets and parks occupied 1.3 square kilometres (Diaz-Briquets, 1994).

The growing commercial and communication roles that Havana was acquiring soon clashed with its physical delimitation and at the end of the eighteenth century, the city began to expand outside the walls. The population doubled from nearly 50,000 in 1750 to around 100,000, distributed over 4.43 square kilometres in 1830. The city underwent major administrative restructuring in 1763 and 1807 after this expansion. De Leuchsernring (ca 1952) points out that the *intramuros* population was divided into sixteen neighbourhoods (called *cuarteles*) and the *extramuros* (outside the wall) into six *cuarteles*.

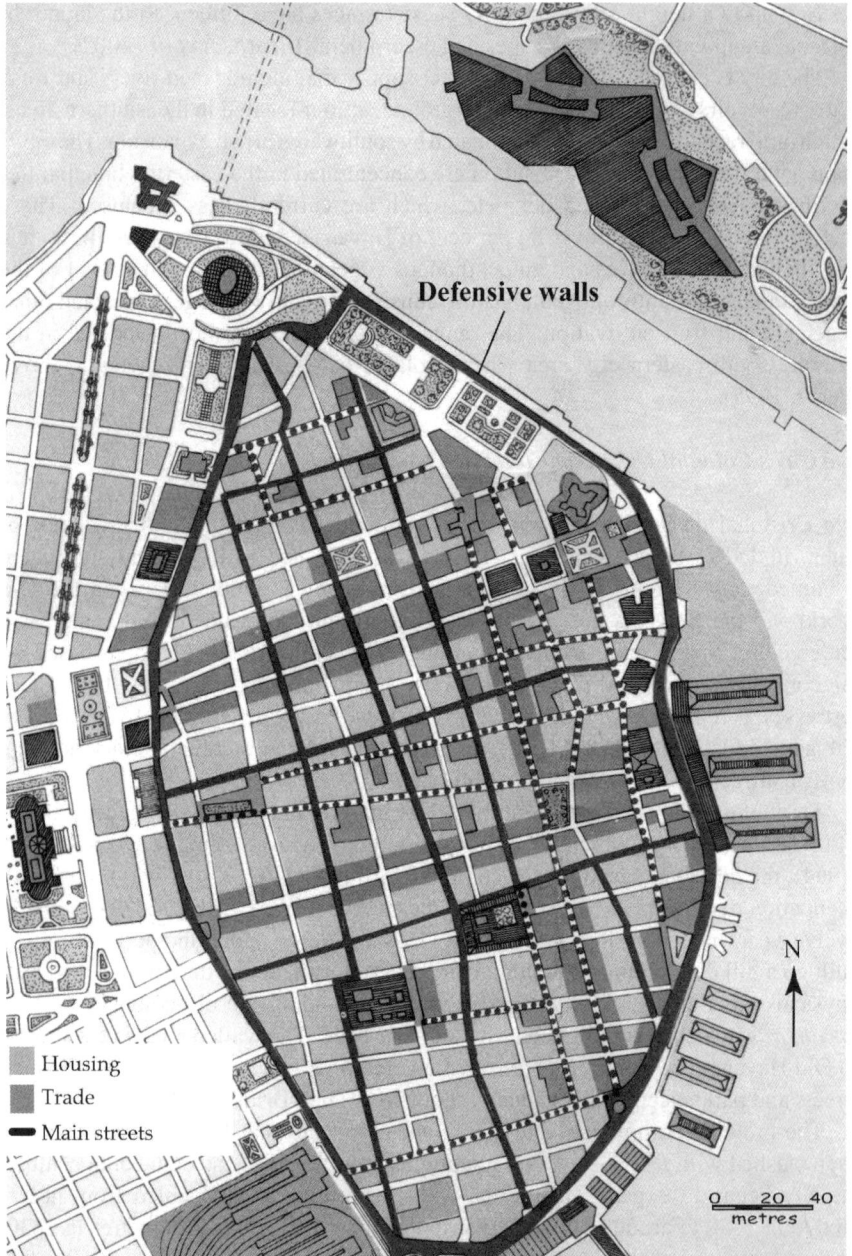

Figure 6.2 Old Havana or *Habana Vieja*

(*Source*: Adapted from DPPF-CH, 1984)

In the nineteenth century, Havana experienced an increase in the importance of its role as a service provider and tourism began to develop. Before 1830, no hotels existed in Havana. Visitors to the city lodged at 'traveller houses' (De Las Cuevas, 1997) or 'interior private rooms' which were reported to number 1,157 in 1830 (Fernandez, 1987). It is argued that the first hotel to be built in Havana, and probably in Cuba, was the Telegrafo Hotel around 1835 (De La Cuevas, 2001). This was the first of a string of hotel developments that started from the 1850s onwards in Havana. Newly built hotels, such as the Inglaterra Hotel (1856), Saratoga Hotel (1879) and Brooklyn Hotel (1899), were mostly located outside the walls while a smaller number of hotels were opened in the fortified district, including Del Comercio Hotel (ca 1841) and Santa Isabel Hotel (ca 1860).

Throughout the second half of the nineteenth century, Havana continued its urban expansion southwards and westwards while the eastern part remained underdeveloped. This was mainly due to the lack of connecting routes that allowed access across the Bay without having to circumvent it. In fact, the development of the road system and other urban utilities played a major role in shaping Havana's urbanization pattern. For example, since the seventeenth century, small factories had been localizing in the Cerro *merced*[1] (today Cerro municipality) to exploit the water flow of the aqueduct built in this area between 1550 and 1592.

Tourism in the 'Pseudo Republic' (1902–1959)

After its independence from Spain in 1898, Cuba became a protectorate of the USA until 1902. This year coincides with the beginning of the republican period that ended with the revolution in 1959. The period between 1902 and 1959 is often referred to as the 'pseudo-republican era', in light of the strong cultural, social and economic influence that the USA exerted on Cuba (Schwartz, 1997). It is to these years that the origin of modern tourism in Cuba can be traced. Thus, Montiel (2001) and Salinas Chavez (1998) argue that the establishment of the *National Commission for Tourism Promotion* (*Comisión Nacional para el Fomento del Turismo*) in 1919 was a turning point in the history of Cuban tourism.

The setting up of the Commission represented the first step toward the institutionalization of the tourism sector in Cuba. These efforts indicated that tourism was beginning to be perceived by government authorities as a valid tool for national and local development. Indeed, the establishment of the commission was included within a much broader *Tourist Law*, formerly known as the 'Monte Carlo Bill', which was passed the same year legalising games of chance and almost every types of amusements at seaside resorts (Swartz, 1997).

The tourism promotion efforts by the Cuban government were also encouraged by external events such as the enforcement of the *Volstead Law* or *Prohibition Act* in the USA, which contributed to triggering a rapid expansion of tourism in Cuba. This

---

1   Land-distribution system established by Spanish authorities where a central point was used to delineate a radius delimiting the circular border of the property.

Law was enforced from 1920 to 1935 and prohibited the production, import, sale and consumption of alcohol in the USA. Many US citizens were encouraged *de facto* to travel for excursions or holidays to nearby countries, in order to have unrestricted access to alcohol.

As a result, tourist arrivals to Cuba grew steadily throughout the 1920s and 1930s until they came to a halt due to two main events: the 1929 world economic recession and the abolition of the Volstead Law in 1935. Table 6.1 shows that tourist arrivals doubled between 1924 and 1928, from 31,566 in the 1924–1925 season to 62,547 in 1927–1928, and then dropped to 29,113 in 1935. They began to increase again for the next five years but plummeted from nearly 80,000 in 1941 to less than 20,000 in 1942, because of the effects of the Second World War. It was not until the end of the war that arrivals rocketed again, reaching over 140,000 in 1948.

Table 6.1 Tourist arrivals in Cuba, 1924/1925–1948

Year	Tourist arrivals
1924–1925*	31,566
1925–1926*	44,395
1926–1927*	48,170
1927–1928*	62,547
1934	20,677
1935	29,113
1936	48,444
1937	62,344
1938	60,667
1939	62,990
1940	77,814
1941	79,895
1942	17,039
1943	17,758
1944	12,365
1945	31,605
1946	114,885
1947	144,566
1948	140,403

* Calculated from December to March, as summer tourism did not exist

(*Source*: Ayala, 2001; Santamarina, 1944; Villalba, 1993)

In the 1930s, interest in tourism continued to mount within Cuba as this economic sector had become the third largest source of foreign currency after sugar and cigar (Figueras, 2003). Thus, in 1934 the *National Tourism Corporation* (*Corporación Nacional de Turismo*, CNT) was set up with the aim of coordinating the plethora of industries operating in the tourism arena. In 1952, the CNT was joined by the *Cuban Institute for Tourism*, a new governmental body with more regulatory powers. The establishment of both agencies epitomises government's efforts towards the further institutional coordination of tourism in Cuba. Nonetheless, it is argued that the CNT was not particularly effective in its first years of activity, because it lacked financial resources and had to rely on voluntary initiatives by industries involved in the tourism sector (Maribona, 1959).

Despite poor economic and political coordination between national and local politicians on the one side and the tourism industries on the other, tourism in Cuba continued to increase until 1959, the year of the Revolution. Room numbers rose from 5,809 (69 per cent of which were in Havana) in 1949 to 7,728 in 1958 at an annual average increase of nearly four per cent. Similarly, tourist arrivals rose steadily throughout the 1950s as shown in Table 6.2. Indeed, while in 1950 tourist arrivals to Cuba were 168,024, in 1958 they increased to 211,807. At a regional level, however, Cuba's share of total tourist arrivals in the Caribbean nearly halved between 1952 and 1958, plummeting from 30 per cent to 16 per cent. This decrease is associated with the development of other Caribbean tourist destinations that absorbed the US market in the 1950s, such as the Bahamas, Puerto Rico and Barbados.

Table 6.2 Tourist arrivals in Cuba, 1949–1958

Year	Tourist arrivals	Cuba/Caribbean (percentage)
1949	150,048	-
1950	168,024	-
1951	188,519	26.4
1952	188,547	30
1953	191,875	21.6
1954	199,315	21
1955	214,126	20.3
1956	223,031	19.2
1957	272,266	21.4
1958	211,807	16.1

(*Source*: Calculated by the authors from data reported in CES, 1981 and Villalba, 1993)

Tourist flows to Cuba throughout the 1950s, however, were closely associated with gambling and other illicit activities such as prostitution and drug trafficking. The importance of gambling was such that data from a Cuban National Bank report, shown in Table 6.3, illustrate how from 1956 to 1958 net revenues from tourism were positive simply because of income linked to gambling. In this context, several anecdotal stories recall that much of these gambling and illicit activities were orchestrated by the Italo-American mafia, which had established directional centres in Havana's best hotels since the 1920s (Ayala, 2001; Figueras, 2003; Villalba, 1993).

Table 6.3 Tourism balance result, 1949–1958

Year	Revenues from tourism (US$ Million)	Revenues from tourism excluding gambling (US$ Million)	Cuban tourists' expenditures abroad (US$ Million)	Tourism balance result (US$ Million)	Tourism balance net result excluding gambling (US$ Million)
	(1)	(2)	(3)	(4=1-3)	(5=2-3)
1949	15.5	-	27.3	-11.8	-
1950	17.1	-	31.6	-14.5	-
1951	19.2	-	29.4	-10.2	-
1952	19.2	-	32.2	-13.0	-
1953	19.6	-	30.8	-11.2	-
1954	24.0	-	31.6	-7.6	-
1955	27.8	-	30.8	-3.0	-
1956	38.1	22.1	33.8	+4.3	-11.7
1957	62.1	28.1	38.5	+23.6	-10.4
1958	56.9	20.9	37.5	+19.4	-16.6

(*Source*: Calculated by the authors from data reported in CES, 1981 and Villalba, 1993)

Urban and Tourism Development in Havana During the 'Pseudo-republic'

There can be little doubt that Havana was the favourite destination of visitors to Cuba throughout the first half of the twentieth century. Villalba (1993) notes that, after the 1919 economic depression, many visitors from the USA to Cuba travelled to Havana with the goal of setting up businesses and investigating investment opportunities. Thus, Havana developed tourist infrastructures and attractions to receive this mix of tourists, businessmen and investment-seekers (De La Cueva, 2001).

Several hotels were built in Havana between 1900 and 1940, many of which became significant city landmarks and key elements of its landscape. The majority of such hotels, including Gran Hotel Habana (1906), Plaza Hotel (1906) and Sevilla Hotel (1908), were built just outside the districts of Old Havana. Others, such as Presidente Hotel (1928) and Hotel Naciónal (1928), were built further westward in the emerging residential area of Vedado, in today's Plaza Municipality, and Miramar in today's Playa Municipality. Indeed, the gradual construction of the Malecón (Havana's waterfront; see Figure 6.3) in 1901 by General Wood encouraged the westward expansion of new elite neighbourhoods along the coast. The development of such neighbourhoods was linked to sugar production wealth, which stemmed from Cuba's insertion in the world economy as a producer of tropical goods in the second half of the nineteenth century.

Figure 6.3 Havana's Malecón

(*Source*: Photo by Andrea Colantonio)

Hotels and recreational facilities in these residential areas were normally built in two main fashions. In some instances Cuban construction companies would build and then sell the property to a Cuban or foreign tourist company (for example the Hotel Sevilla). In others, foreign tourist chains agreed the construction of facilities directly with government authorities. This second business practice is epitomized by the construction of the National Hotel (Figure 6.4) which was agreed in 1925 between the Machado government and the National Hotel of Cuba Corporation. The latter was part of the North American hotel chain 'Intercontinental', which, in turn, was the property of Pan American Airways, an airline company belonging to the Chase Manhattan Bank. It has been noted that such agreements, not uncommon in Havana, cast light on the extent of the collusion between the Cuban government and United States firms and the vertical integration of the Cuban tourist industry of the 'pseudo-republic' (De La Cueva, 2001).

Figure 6.4 Hotel Naciónal in Havana

(*Source*: Photo by Andrea Colantonio)

The involvement of United States firms in the tourist industry was not limited to the accommodation sector. Villalba (1993) notes that in 1915 a United States entrepreneur, H.T. Brown, built the Oriental Park Hippodrome in Marianao, located in the western part of Havana. In 1925, the Hippodrome became indirectly managed by the firm Biltmore, which was already managing the Hotel Sevilla as well as the Biltmore Club. The latter was part of the 'Big Five' clubs (Scarpaci *et al.*, 2002: 111), which included The Yacht (or the Habana Yacht Club), Vedado Tennis, Biltmore and Miramar. These were later joined by Profesionales to make the 'Big Six', which were among Havana's main exclusive clubs holding sporting events.

The development of these exclusive clubs and recreational facilities in wealthy coastal areas of Havana generated a number of problems which encompassed foreign dependency, socio-economic and spatial polarisation and the loss of social identity amongst Havana's dwellers. These socio-economic, cultural and environmental problems are accurately described by Roberts (1953) who argues that the Havana of 1900 was divided into three distinct parts: 'Old' Havana (the older quarters behind the walls), 'New' Havana (parts of Centro Havana, Vedado and Cerro), and 'Suburban' Havana (new developments in west and south districts).

According to Roberts' (1953) description, 'Old' Havana was characterized by less desirable qualities mainly linked to environmental health concerns. These ranged from flooding and industrial pollution to the stench of the Bay. By contrast, 'New' and 'Suburban' Havana were served by better urban utilities and services and displayed healthier socio-environmental conditions. 'New' Havana showed a regular layout and wider streets than the historic city centre. It was mainly populated by affluent white Spaniards working in trade or agricultural production. Lastly, 'Suburban' Havana would spread farther westward of Vedado, welcoming exclusively wealthy Americans.

Although tourism played a significant role in crystallizing differences among Havana's areas, it would be naively over-simplistic to ascribe the city's polarized and fragmented growth exclusively to the development of tourism. Indeed, between 1900 and 1935, Havana witnessed a vigorous phase of urban expansion because of two main factors. Firstly, the Cuban capital returned to the island after being temporarily deposited in the United States for safekeeping during the war of independence (Scarpaci *et al.*, 2002). Secondly, for a few years after the enactment of the 1902 republican constitution no legal framework was devised to regulate municipal discipline and establish clear mechanisms of municipal governance (Roig De Leuchsenring, ca 1952). This in turn hindered urban planning and land use management by municipal authorities, which had little power to halt illegal fragmentation and inappropriate use of Havana's land by foreign real estate developers (Segre, 1995).

Between 1900 and 1924, the population of Havana more than doubled growing from 250,000 to 600,000. Between the same years, urbanized land increased nearly fourfold from 8 to 30 square kilometres (DPPF-CH, 1984). Central government authorities set out to build a hierarchy of classical monuments and landmarks that symbolized middle-class power. Such efforts resulted in the construction of several national icons and urban landmarks. These include the Lonja de Comercio (1906–1909) the Cuban stock market building, and the National Capitol (*Capitolio Nacional*, 1925–1930). The latter was financed with almost 20 million dollars lent by the Chase Manhattan Bank (Segre, 1995), its shape recalling the White House.

In the first years of the republic, the urban planning of Havana remained confined in the theoretical realm of debates between a small cadre of urbanists and did not translate into tangible results. Nonetheless, two development plans for Havana were devised in 1925 and 1926 by Martinez Inclan (Figure 6.5) and Forestier (Figure 6.6) respectively. The *1925 Master Plan* envisaged the formation of a Big Civic Centre as an expansion of the existing one in the area immediately contingent to Old Havana. Furthermore, it proposed the creation of a road system composed of streets that resemble Parisian boulevards and a system of green areas that form today's Metropolitan Park along the Almendares River.

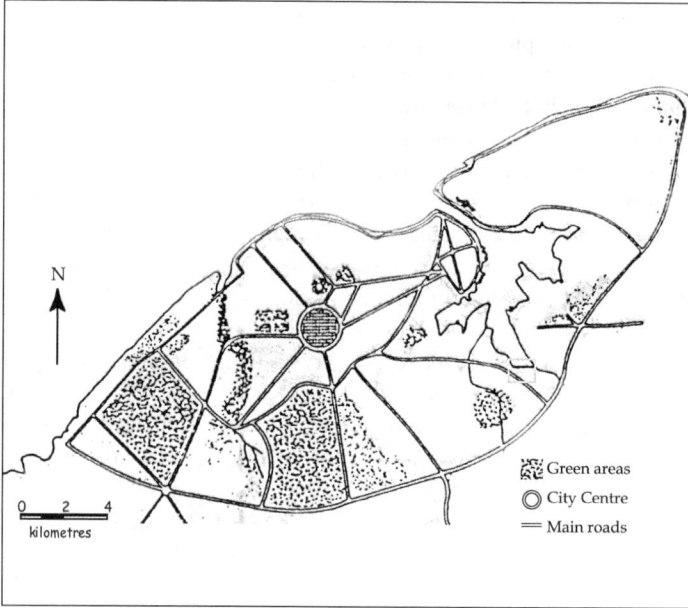

Figure 6.5 The 1925 Master Plan for Havana by Martinez Inclán
(*Source*: Gonzalez, 1995)

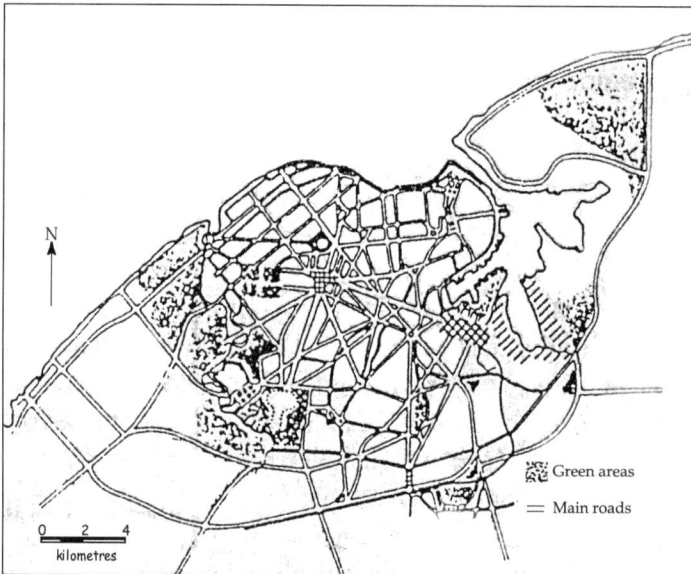

Figure 6.6 The 1926 Master Plan for Havana by Forestier
(*Source*: Gonzalez, 1995)

The *1926 Master Plan* was devised by Jean-Claude Nicolas Forestier, the chief of parks and streets of Paris, and underlined two key aspects of Havana: the political and administrative role played by the Cuban capital, and the city's increasingly important tourist function (Gonzalez, 1995). This plan forecast a majestic development of Havana which was cut short by the depression of 1929, the popular uprising of 1933, which toppled Machado, and the subsequent coup d'état led by Batista in 1935.

The development of Havana's urban area slowed down in the 1940s due to the Second World War, until the following decade when the city underwent the most significant changes of its urban structure since the start of its neo-colonial era (Fernandez, 1987). Thus, in the 1950s, Havana consolidated its traditional centre as the city's main commercial district and began its expansion eastward of the Bay along a West–East coastal urban development axis (see Figure 6.7). New infrastructural roadworks, including two tunnels under the Almendares River, which connected Vedado to Miramar, enabled car access to this exclusive suburb and triggered the full urban development of this area. In 1956 a tunnel under the Bay was opened allowing easy transit from the Malecón to East Havana (Segre, 1995). It is no secret that Batista, who first came to power in 1940 and then again in 1952 through a coup d'état, bought vast amount of land in East Havana with the aim of urbanizing the area (Interview 11, 23).

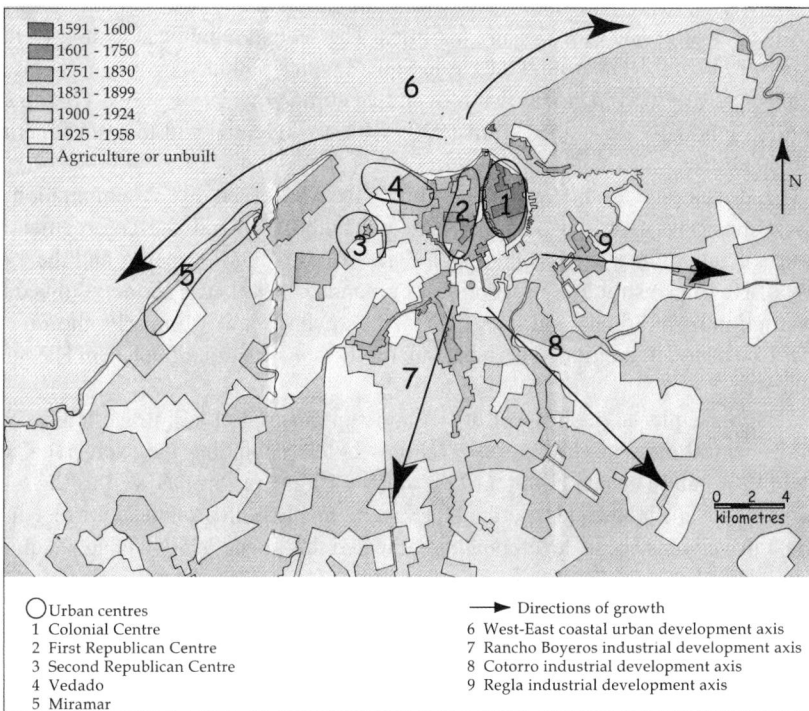

Figure 6.7 Havana's development axes, 1900–1958

In the same years, the worldwide post-war industrial boom and transferable technology spurred the industrial development of Havana along three main axes (see Figure 6.7) emanating from the Bay: (i) Casablanca and Regla where heavy and polluting industries such as a petrol refinery developed; (ii) San Francisco de Paula and Cotorro and (iii) Rancho Boyeros towards Santiago de las Vegas (Arquitectura Cuba, 1974). New industries, especially in the textile, food and building materials sector were located in Havana because:

- the Cuban capital had become an important centre of consumption
- cheap labour was widely available
- there was an active port that allowed the easy supply of imports of raw material
- the city offered a good infrastructural network encompassing roads, electricity and water.

At the end of the 1950s, Havana exhibited a mix of old and new centralities. Figure 6.7 shows how at least four nodes or centres can be identified in Havana of 1958. The old colonial node retained political, residential and trade functions. Further, it was the site of many worship venues. The first republican centre, developed between 1902 and the 1930s, hosted the main landmark administrative and government buildings as well as theatres and other leisure facilities. The second republican centre, formed between 1930 and 1958 around the Civic Square which included mainly government buildings, is still working today. Moreover, two complementary centres, Vedado and Miramar, gradually developed from 1920s with a residential and tourism function, as noted earlier.

The development of Havana in the 1950s was eased by a combination of laissez-faire policy on the part of municipal authorities and the enforcement of pro-urbanization laws such as the 1952 'Law of Horizontal Property' and the 1953 'Law of Hotel Construction Exemption' (Fernandez, 1987). The former allowed the construction of buildings and flats in the city's central area. Similarly, the *Law of Hotel Construction* facilitated permissions for the construction of hotels in Havana's urban area.

As a consequence, a string of hotels and supporting tourist infrastructures was built in central parts of Havana. Several new hotels, including the exclusive Capri Hotel (1956) and Havana Hilton (1958, today's Habana Libre) as well as the more affordable Colina Hotel and St. John Hotel were mostly built around 23rd Street or La Rampa in Vedado. These developments indicated that in the 1950s Vedado acquired a new central role in Havana's urban structure. La Rampa, in particular, boasted a mixture of functions and land use that included cinemas, theatres, art galleries, restaurants, cafeterias, offices, bars and parks.

The liberalization of the tourism sector in the 1950s resulted in mushrooming construction activities in Havana. This, in turn, meant that the room stock of the Cuban capital increased from 4,098 in 1949 to 4,892 in 1958, as shown in Table 6.4. In these years Havana consolidated its primacy as Cuba's major tourist site, followed by Matanzas (where Varadero is located) and Camagüey provinces, with 702 and 445 rooms respectively. The spatial localization of these provinces can be discerned from Figure 6.8. The development of accommodation was coupled with the construction of tourist-oriented infrastructures. These mainly consisted of cabarets, such as 'Tropicana' in Marianao and 'Sans-Souci' and 'Montmartre' in Havana's central areas, and marinas such as Marina Barlovento (today's Marina Hemingway) in the western suburbs.

Table 6.4 Tourist accommodation (rooms) in Cuban provinces, 1951–1958

Province	1951	1958
Pinar del Rio	172	237
Havana City	4,118	5,119
Matanzas (Varadero)	1,000	999
Las Villas	462	536
Camagüey	418	458
Oriente	382	379
Total	6,552	7,728

(*Source*: Banco Nacional de Cuba, 1952; Instituto Cubano del Turismo, 1958 in Villalba 1993)

The economic expansion of Havana attracted migration from less developed areas of the interior as well as other Caribbean islands (Segre, 1981). According to various censuses the population of Havana increased from 823,558 (20 per cent of Cuba) in 1931 to 1,361,600 (24 per cent of Cuba) in 1958 (DPPF, 1984). Similarly, Havana's urban extension grew nearly 70 per cent from 30 square kilometres in 1924 to 50 square kilometres in 1958. Thus, during his dictatorship Batista commissioned a new plan for Havana. This new scheme should have served him as a guide to buy land that would have acquired value for future urbanization (Gonzalez, 1995).

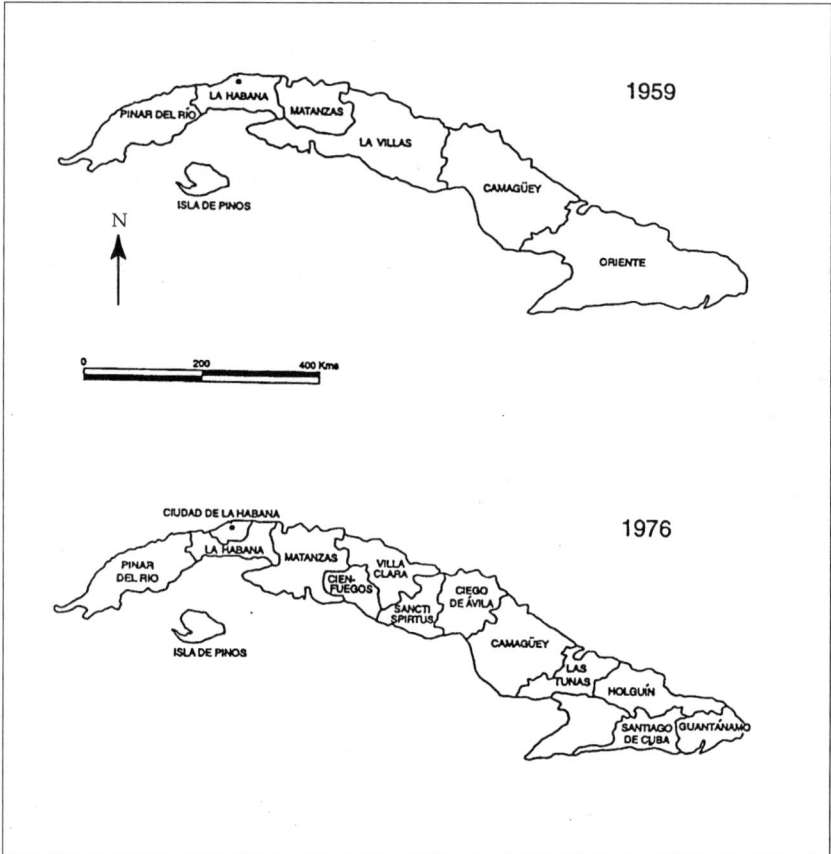

Figure 6.8 Cuban provinces before and after the 1976 jurisdictional re-organization

(*Source*: Scarpaci *et al.*, 2002)

As a result, in 1958, a new Master Plan was designed by Sert, Wiener, Schulz and Romañach, a team of North American and European planners. The new plan was based on the implementation of three main guiding principles:

- to avoid rigid structures that could halt Havana's physical transformation
- to maximise the city's tourist and recreational function
- to establish five main centres: (i) The civic square (today's Revolution Square); (ii) The University of Havana; (iii) The main waterfront; (iv) The economic centre, and (v) The Presidential Centre.

The Master Plan by Sert *et al* envisaged scenic settings for tourist activities in Havana. The city's transformation was to be centred around a re-design of the waterfront with high rise buildings and hotels and the replacement of the old colonial block of Old Havana with high rise offices and retail and hotel complexes. Figure 6.9 shows how Sert's plan foresaw the establishment of a great artificial island with hotels and casinos just off the shores of Centro Habana. There can be little doubt that Sert's plan would have radically and irreversibly altered Havana's profile had the revolution not succeeded in 1959.

Figure 6.9 Artificial island included in Havana's 1958 Master Plan

(*Source*: After Gonzalez, 1995)

Tourism in Revolutionary Cuba (1959–1989)

The victory of the revolution in 1959 meant a radical change and a re-organization of the tourism sector in Cuba. The new revolutionary government set out to eradicate the prostitution and drug trafficking that had flourished alongside tourism for over three decades. Thus, among the first measures adopted by the new government were the closing down of all gambling rooms and casinos, and the creation in February 1959 of the *Department of Beaches for the People* (*Departamiento de Playas para el Pueblo*). This Department's main objective was to warrant every Cuban citizen free access to any beach and private clubs and leisure resorts which formerly belonged to the affluent sectors of Cuban society.

After the revolution, the diplomatic relationships between Cuba and the USA deteriorated rapidly. In 1961, Cuba turned to the Soviet Union for economic and military support against the threats of a possible invasion by the USA. This led the US government to impose an economic blockage on Cuba. As a result, the nature of tourism flows to Cuba changed drastically. Visits from US citizens, which in 1958 had constituted 85 per cent of tourist arrivals, decreased by over 80 per cent in 1959 and a further 40 per cent in 1960 (Villalba, 1993). Tourist arrivals from Western countries also dropped drastically. As shown in Table 6.5, between 1963 and 1968, Cuba received fewer than 1,000 tourists per year from capitalist countries. Indeed, Cuba now entered a phase of isolation from the international tourist market that lasted for over a decade.

Table 6.5 Tourist arrivals from Western capitalist countries to Cuba, 1963–1972

Year	Tourist arrivals
1963	168
1964	189
1965	320
1966	266
1967	853
1968	1,771
1969	1,097
1970	1,634
1971	1,713
1972	1,950

(*Source*: Villalba, 1993)

In the aftermath of the revolution, the new government restructured the Cuban tourist sector by nationalizing all the tourist industries, from accommodation and catering to transport. New institutions were set up to implement an inward-oriented tourism development policy which mirrored the leadership's pursuit of social justice and equal opportunities for everyone. As a result, in 1959, the National Institute of the Tourism Industry (*Instituto Nacional de la Industria Turística*, INIT) was established in order to encourage the development of domestic tourism at the expense of international tourism. Indeed, INIT had to provide holidays for Worker Unions at exclusive cabarets and restaurants, luxurious hotels and expensive spas and health centres, previously belonging to a few aristocrats.

The development of domestic tourism entailed the broad division of Cuba into three main tourist areas: The Western Zone (*Zona Occidental*), the Central Zone (*Zona Central*) and the Eastern Zone (*Zona Oriental*). In each area a major city was designated to receive incoming tourists/workers and to provide logistical support for excursions to surrounding areas. These areas are illustrated in Figure 6.10 which shows how Havana City was the designated base-receiving city in the Western Zone; Cienfuegos was the main city in the Central Zone; and the Oriental Zone selected Santiago de Cuba as the main city.

Figure 6.10 Tourist regions in revolutionary Cuba

The promotion of national tourism continued until mid-1970s when two main events forced the Cuba leadership to re-think international tourism as a viable tool for national development. Firstly, in 1970 and 1973 poor sugar cane harvests revealed the vulnerability of the agricultural sector, hindering significantly Cuba's centralised planning. Secondly, the first Oil crisis generated more liquidity worldwide. This allowed Cuba better access to international credit and financial resources, which could be used for infrastructural upgrading.

As a result of the renewed interest in international tourism, the number of tourists to Cuba began to rise after 1973. Ayala (2001) reports that international tourist arrivals grew from 2,646 in 1972 to 96,652 in 1978. This increase included, however, tourists coming from other socialist countries through exchange programmes. Similarly, it is reported that, from 1975 to 1978, and from 1980 to 1981 a total of 19 hotels (accounting for 2,500 rooms) and 18 hotels (accounting for 4,900 rooms) were built or refurbished (Mincons, 1980). Other sources report that from 1976 to 1983 a total of 33 new hotels were built (Villalba, 1993).

The new tourism promotion strategy involved the institutional re-organization of the Cuban tourism sector. Thus, in 1976 the *National Tourism Institute (Instituto Nacional de Turismo,* INTUR) replaced INIT. The new institute was invested with reinforced planning and administrative powers and was flanked by new state firms such as Publicitur and Cubatur. These aimed to publicise tourism abroad and to organise trips to Cuba from sixteen European countries and Canada.

A few years later, two new state agencies were set up when the first signs of political change in Russia and the rest of the Soviet Bloc began to appear. In 1987, the Cubanacan Corporation was set up as a state holding (as discussed in chapter 3). This corporation took over nearly one-third of all properties belonging to state enterprises working under the INTUR umbrella. Its main objectives were to begin to attract foreign capital and encourage the modernization of the Cuban tourist sector (Ayala, 2001). In 1988, the Gaviota group was created in affiliation with the Cuban Army. The new group was immediately regarded as a well-established company of the armed forces which had gained experience in managing recreational centres for Soviet advisors back in the 1960s (Segre *et al.,* 1997). Similarly to Cubanacan, the Gaviota group was able to form associations with foreign investors in green tourism development projects. The new marketing campaign proved successful with international tourists growing steadily from 129,591 in 1980 to 326,300 in 1989, recording an average annual increase of over 15 per cent (Ayala, 2001).

Urban and Tourism Development in Havana During the 'Revolutionary Period'

At the end of 1958, Havana was a modern bustling metropolis in which most of the nation's economic, social and cultural activities were concentrated. Havana exhibited the typical attributes of a primate city, having a population three and half times as large as the combined population of the two next largest cities, that is, Santiago de Cuba and Camagüey (Diaz Briquets, 1994). The population density had increased constantly over the previous three decades, growing from 200 inhabitants per hectare in 1924 to 280 inhabitants per hectare in 1958. The city was ready to begin its expansion eastward of the Bay where cheap land and fine beaches represented strong incentives for housing investments.

Acosta and Hardoy (1973: 53) describe how the Revolutionary Government inherited a city that: (a) accounted for 52.8 per cent of the national industrial production by value; (b) handled 90 per cent of national port activity in its harbour; (c) contained the most shipyards and was the major fishing terminal; (d) was the sole centre for university education on the island and its unchallenged cultural centre; (e) had the bulk of government offices and the most important hospitals; (f) could boast the best shops and stores; (g) served as the principal centre of origin and destination for national travel and as the exclusive centre for international travel; and (h) attracted the largest percentage of housing investments.

The urban policy adopted by the Cuban leadership after 1959 has been comprehensively debated in the literature (see Acosta and Hardoy 1973, Diaz-Briquet 1994, Scarpaci, 2000a, Scarpaci *et al.*, 2002). From the outset, the newly established revolutionary government set out to reduce urban-rural imbalances that were hindering the economic and cultural development of Cuba's interior areas. In this context, Potter (2000: 73) notes that the Cuban government's policy aim was to ruralize the towns and to urbanize the countryside.

The functional integration between town and country aimed at redistributing social surplus product to rural areas by the provision of health and education facilities. On the one hand this anti-urban focus meant the reduction of Havana's urban primacy, although Acosta and Hardoy (1973) argue that, despite the development of other zones which had been promoted and achieved, Havana remained the indisputable centre of Cuba. On the other, it resulted in a significant decrease of funding for the further urbanization and infrastructural upgrading of Havana, with overall negative environmental impacts.

The anti-urban policy of the leadership was translated into two *Master Plans* for Havana that were devised in 1964 and 1971 respectively. Both plans recommended a reduction in population density in the central areas of Havana and the implementation of production-oriented, as opposed to consumption-oriented, infrastructural projects. Thus, throughout the 1960s and 1970s industrial zones and warehouses were developed in Berroa (East Havana) and La Lisa (West Havana) while the port and airport underwent major modernization works. Other significant agricultural, industrial and residential developments were carried out in Havana's southern areas. These were carried out with little forethought because they did not take into account the negative environmental impact that construction would have on the contamination of the Vento underground aquifer (Scarpaci *et al.*, 2002).

During these years, tourism disappeared from the agenda and Master Plans of the Havana-based planners. By the mid 1960s, all Havana's main tourist infrastructures including hotels and private clubs were nationalized. Some of these were deployed to lodge Cubans during their state-organized excursions to Havana while others historically related to gambling and prostitution, such as the Capri Hotel and the National Casino, were closed down.

Parallel to the anti-urban policy envisaged by the Cuban leadership, the promotion of domestic tourism aimed at decreasing Havana's primacy as the island's main tourist destination (Mincons, 1980). Throughout the 1970s, new tourist-oriented infrastructures were built mostly outside the capital. For example, Table 6.6 shows that between 1975 and 1981, a total of 29 hotels were built in Cuba. Of these, only three were located in Havana, accounting for 664 rooms (16 per cent of the total). The new facilities were predominantly located along the beaches of East Havana where Marazul and Santa Maria II hotels were opened together with the Megano beach recreational centre. Nonetheless, a few years later the Hotel Tritón was opened in Miramar in 1981. This was flanked by Hotel Neptuno in 1992 as part of a tourist complex which is regarded as the embryo of the current tourism redevelopment of Miramar (Coyula, 2002) and a driving force of the future urbanisation of West Havana.

Table 6.6 Hotels and rooms built in Cuba between 1975 and 1981

Province	Hotel	Rooms
Pinar del Rio	Pinar del Rio	136
Havana	Tritón	276
	Marazul	188
	Santa Maria II	200
Matanzas	Varadero I	136
	Varadero II	136
Villa Clara	Elguea	72
	Hanabanilla	128
Cienfuegos	Pasacaballos	180
	Rancho Luna	225
Sancti Spiritus	Zaza	128
	Ancón	183
	Costa Sur	72
Ciego de Ávila	Ciego de Ávila	136
	Morón	136
Camaguey	Camagüey	136
	Santa Lucia	225
	Nuevitas	72
	Florida	72
	Guáimaro	40
Holguin	Pernik	200
	Guardalavaca	200
	Moa	128
Granma	Bayamo	200
	Manzanillo	128
	Marea del Portillo	72
Santiago de Cuba	Tricontinental	68
	Balcón del Caribe	96
Guantánamo	Guantánamo	128
Total	29	4,097

(*Source*: De La Cueva, 2001)

In 1981, tourism was formally established as a principal development focus in Havana as stated in the Second Five Year Plan (1981–85), the basis of Cuban centralized planning. Indeed, a new Master Plan was devised in 1984 proposing an urban structure scheme for Havana where tourism and leisure had to play a significant role. The new plan envisaged the establishment of three east-west parallel strips running from the shoreline toward the south. The first strip would be devoted to recreation and tourism, the second to housing and the third to light industry, the Old City being the centre of this expansion (see Figure 6.11).

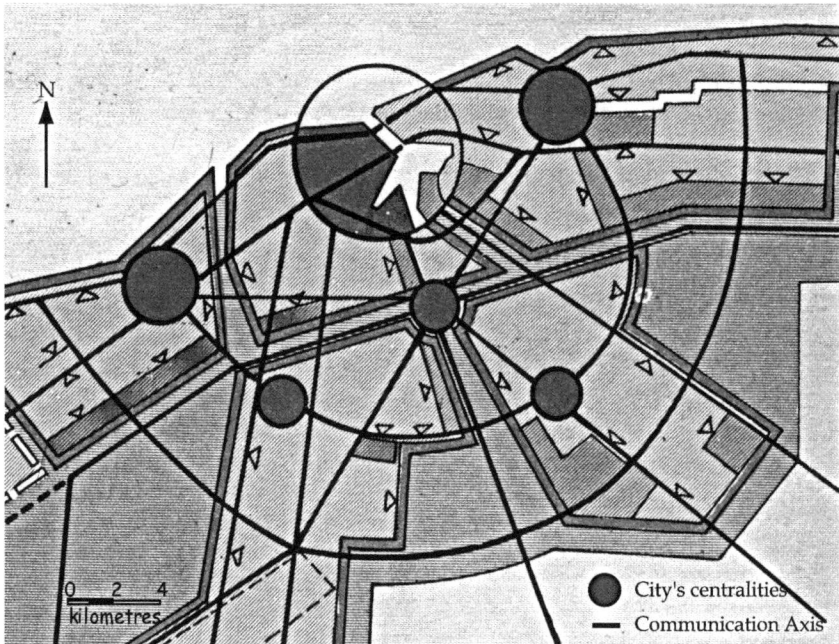

Figure 6.11 The 1984 Master Plan for Havana

(*Source*: After DPPF-CH, 1984)

The *1984 Master Plan*, containing ambitious development plans for Havana 2030, is also known for introducing two main novelties to Havana's urban planning (Gonzalez, 1995). Firstly, it established for the first time a system of jurisdictional and administrative norms and directives aimed at informing urban planning (see Fernandez, 1998 for a comprehensive review). Secondly, the plan had to be reviewed and approved by the Executive Committee of the Council of Ministries. This started a practice that indicates a new step toward further centralization of urban planning in Cuba. Indeed, in recent years the Cuban leadership has expressed growing concern for the future fate of Havana. As a consequence, the central government attempted to retain decision-making powers to control the rapid urban and tourism development of Havana in the Special Period which will be reviewed in the next section.

Tourism in the Special Period

As noted in chapter 1, in 1990 Castro announced the beginning of a Special Period for the island. The Cuban government was obliged to promote a series of economic and institutional reforms (which have been reviewed in chapter 3) to face the geo-political and economic change generated by the collapse of the Soviet Bloc. Tourism was identified as a crucial economic sector which could help to avoid the country's total breakdown. The promotion of international tourism was initially seen mainly as a temporary solution to the economic crises generated by the interruption of Soviet subsides in 1991 (Font, 1997; Foreign & Commonwealth Office, 1995). Nonetheless, by 1994 it became clear that tourism had acquired a driving role in Cuba's long-term development strategy.

Table 6.7 Tourist poles in Cuban provinces

Province	Poles	Potential Rooms
Pinar del Rio	10	2,032
Havana City	4	4,350
Havana Province	7	31,089
Matanzas	4	23,895
Villa Clara	7	8,935
Cienfuegos	5	3,120
Sancti Spiritus	8	5,408
Ciego de Avila	5	16,121
Camaguey	9	28,690
Las Tunas	2	6,500
Holguin	8	6,620
Granma	6	2,144
Santiago de Cuba	4	6,882
Guantanamo	2	984
Isla de la Juventud	4	6,297
Total	85	153,067

(*Source*: Mintur, 1996)

Between 1990 and 1995, a *National Plan for the Development of International Tourism* was devised by the National Institute of Physical Planning. The 1990–1995 study identified 67 'tourist poles' to be developed throughout the Cuban national territory. These were subsequently increased to 85 in 1997 and then to 93 in 2000 (Mena, 2001). The poles are listed in Table 6.7, which shows how the bigger poles in terms of proposed accommodation to are to be found in Havana province with a total of 31,089 rooms, Camagüey with 28,690 rooms, Matanzas with 23,895 and Ciego de Avila with 16,121.

As outlined in chapter 3, in light of the new tourism promotion strategy, tourist flows to Cuba grew consistently throughout the Special Period. Cuba became the most dynamic tourist market in the Caribbean. Table 6.8 shows how international arrivals in the Caribbean grew by nearly four per cent annually between 1990 and 2003. However, in the same period Cuba's share of tourist arrivals in the region grew from three per cent to 1990, eleven per cent.

Table 6.8 International tourist arrivals in Cuba, 1990–2003

Year	Tourist arrivals to Cuba (thousands)	Tourist arrivals to the Caribbean (thousands)	Cuba/Caribbean (percentage)
1990	340.3	11,400	3
1991	424.0	11,300	4
1992	460.6	11,700	4
1993	546.0	12,800	4
1994	619.2	13,700	5
1995	745.5	14,000	5
1996	1,004	14,300	7
1997	1,170	15,300	8
1998	1,416	15,900	9
1999	1,603	16,133	10
2000	1,774	17,200	10
2001	1,775	16,900	10
2002	1,656	16,100	10
2003	1,900	17,300	11

(*Source*: ONE, 2002; OTH, 2002b; WTO, 2003, Granma, 06/01/04)

Urban and Tourism Development in Havana During the Special Period

The 1990-1995 *National Plan for the Development of International Tourism* had forecast a key role to be played by Havana within the national tourism promotion strategy. Even so, in 1988, the DPPF-CH, Havana's office of the Institute of Physical Planning had already identified the areas of the city which offered great potential for tourism development. By 1996, these areas were formalized as Havana's 'tourist poles' (see chapter 4) and it soon became clear to Havana's planners that tourism had become a powerful force shaping Havana's urban growth outside the forecast contained in the 1984 Master Plan. Thus, in 1990 a new Master Plan was devised to acknowledge the change of international and economic settings brought about by the Special Period.

The new Master Plan thoroughly revised the previous one, drawing on its successes and failures over the previous seven years. The scheme sought a densification of Havana and suggested a 'filling in' of open spaces within the city's limits rather than extending its urban area. Unlike the previous plan, the scheme placed greater attention on smaller service centres and abandoned the theoretical division of Havana into east-west strips. Nonetheless, these small sub-centres failed to materialise due to the scarcity of financial resources brought about by the crisis and the lack of political will on the part of the central government (Gonzalez, 1995).

The *1990 Master Plan* was updated in 1992 in light of the unforeseen harshness of the economic crisis and the new institutional reforms that formally established the Popular Councils as municipal government entities (see chapter 10). The scarcity of financial resources and restricted access to international funding meant that urban development projects were concentrated in sectors that were able to generate hard currency and allow the economy to keep going. These were international sports events; scientific research; and real estate for foreigners and tourism. Thus, several sports facility centres were built, especially in East Havana, for the eleventh Pan-American games held in 1991. Similar efforts were concentrated on the construction of scientific research centres and pharmaceutical plants in West Havana, especially in what has come to be known as the 'Western Scientific Pole' where, for example, the vaccine for hepatitis B is produced. Lastly, as noted earlier, new hotels were built and old ones were remodelled within the urbanized zones of the coastal area after joint venture agreements were signed.

The concentration of urban development plans and infrastructural upgrading projects in dollar-oriented activities has generated some discontent among Havana's architects and planners alike. Several practitioners have unofficially raised concerns that, for example, too many financial resources are being used to build new hotels while the housing needs of local residents remain neglected. In this context, Coyula (2002) estimates that around 80 per cent of recent construction activity in Cuba is in some way connected to tourism.

Although no similar official figures or estimates exist for Havana, there can be little doubt that the real estate market for foreigners and tourism accounts for almost the totality of the city's construction activities in the Special Period. The

Cuban government's urban housing programme has slowed down significantly. For example, in 2002 alone Havana's housing stock decreased by 172 units with more than two houses collapsing per day (UNAIC, 2003). In addition, more than 100 hectares have been dedicated to the construction of condominiums (*inmobiliarias*) for foreigners (Scarpaci *et al.*, 2002). This construction process, however, has been slow until 2000 when the Cuban government decided not to sell these types of flat anymore.

Conclusions

This chapter has provided an historical account of the development of tourism in Havana and has shown how the city's fortunes have been entwined with the development of tourism activity. Indeed, throughout its history, most of Havana's urban development has been driven by the growth of tourism which, in turn, has been responsible for the city's socio-economic and spatial polarization and the encouragement of foreign domination. However, after 1959, the Revolutionary government set out to curb Havana's urban and tourist growth and to reduce income and environmental inequalities at the city and national levels.

Such socialist urban and development policies embraced by the Cuban leadership meant under-investment in Havana's urban utilities for over forty years. This led to the environmental and economic neglect of Havana until 1989, when the city began to experience new 'tourism splendour'. Several criticisms have been covertly or openly voiced against Havana's re-development as a tourist pole in the Special Period, in light of the city's recent history, as reviewed in this chapter. Thus, the next two chapters will assess the economic, social and environmental consequences of tourism on Havana, providing a critical evaluation of the main arguments in favour and against the re-emergence of tourism activities in the city. These are based on first hand fieldwork and interviews carried out by the first named author.

Chapter 7

Tourism and Socio-economic Change in Havana during the Special Period

Introduction

The promotion of tourism during the Special Period has generated a sharp economic and social impact on Cuban society. It is argued that the effects of the economic crisis and the development of tourism have generated income inequalities and growing socio-economic disparities. This, in turn, has prompted the embryonic stratification of the Cuban society, reversing many of the previous social accomplishments of the Cuban Revolution. On the other hand, the changes brought about by the 1990s reforms have not been entirely negative. As a matter of fact, the timid and zigzagging liberalization process reviewed in chapter 3 has also resulted in new civil society activities and the emergence of new interest groups.

In Havana, the economic effects of the opening up process and the growth of tourism have generally been positive, generating new employment opportunities, spurring the establishment of a small private sector and boosting hard currency revenues. However, critics of the tourism re-development strategy have pointed out three main areas of concern that are intrinsically linked to the new development model. Firstly, following the creation of jobs in tourism, ever more highly skilled professionals working in socially productive sectors, such as health care and education, have abandoned their State job for lower-skilled jobs in tourism. This has wasted human capital in Cuba. Secondly, the partial withdrawal of the State as the main employer has prompted the re-emergence of the informal economy and illegal activities such as crime and prostitution. Lastly, the economic benefits of tourism have been spatially limited to Havana's tourist poles and have generated inequalities in terms of employment opportunities among the city's various areas.

The main aim of the chapter is to identify and assess the economic and social impact of tourism on the Cuban society in the Special Period, with special reference to the socio-economic change undergone by Havana in recent years. The chapter is organized into four main parts. The first section investigates the relationship between the reforms and the appearance of civil activities during the Special Period. The second section reviews the growing social inequalities in Cuba following the flourishing development of the tourism-related dollar economy. The third section narrows down the analysis to Havana and considers the economic implications of the reforms on the Cuban capital. More specifically, the research examines the changing nature of Havana's economic structure as a direct outcome of the new economic opportunities generated by tourism. Section three of the chapter concludes with the appraisal of the spatial consequences of tourism development at the household, neighbourhood and city levels. In continuation, some conclusions concerning the socio-economic change in Havana during the Special Period will be drawn in the final part of the chapter.

It is important to highlight that this chapter is complemented by the findings presented in chapter 10 which focuses on the political consequences of the reforms on mechanisms of governance in Cuba.

The 1990s Reforms and the Emergence of Civil Activities

The social and political outcome of the 1990s reforms has been hotly debated in the literature. Leon (1997) argues that these reforms were reflected in new civil activities such as self-employment, *mensajeros*,[1] and collective theft from state-run companies. The development of such social practices is transforming socialist institutions while gaining wide acceptance within civil society. As a result, therefore, interest groups are emerging and acquiring 'a legitimate social identity as well as access to information regarding their numerical significance and function in the economy' (Leon, 1997: 46). The emergence of these groups is regarded as crucial to filling the political vacuum that may stem from the sudden dismantling of the Communist Party politics and to secure a peaceful transition for Cuba (Centeno, 1997).

Other authors have expressed more sceptical views concerning the emergence of civil activities in Cuba. Pérez-Stable (1999: 69) argues that 'mobilizational authoritarianism' is still the main motor of Cuban state communism. The reforms introduced in the 1990s are neither fostering the emergence of civil society nor are they embedded within a long-term programme that 'would require a new discourse designed to appeal to new constituencies and to guide old ones in new directions'. In her view, politics still represents an important factor within the Cuban model. Traditional and new institutionalism, therefore, can hardly provide a theoretical framework to analyze the dynamics generated by the 1990s reforms. They simply do not account for ideology and elites in their basic tenets.

There is, instead, general agreement that the opening up of the economy and the promotion of the external sector have led to the emergence of different interest groups and to an embryonic social stratification of the Cuban society (Eckstein, 1997; Font, 1997; Leon, 1997; Pérez-Stable, 1997). Monreal (1997) points out that the 1990s reforms appear to have been pursued by the government without a precise scheme. They would seem to have been dictated by the severity of the crisis, rather than a clear project or long-term plan for economic restructuring. A dual economy

---

1   Mensajeros are intermediaries between households and the official state apparatus who sell on the black market the portion of produces that the household did not consume (Leon, 1997).

in which the market-oriented external economic sector coexists with the domestic sector still under the planning system is the outcome of these measures.

The self-employed workers and black-market hustlers working in the market-oriented and informal segments (discussed later) of the Cuban economy are often deemed to be agents of future social and economic change in Cuba. Scarpaci (2002) argues that a possible political and economic paradigm shift in Cuba is likely to emerge from the action of agents who reside outside the traditional socialist institutions. In his view economic modernization brings democracy, hence:

> [T]he locus of empowered individual and household decision-making rests not in state-sanctioned grassroots organisation or the political apparatus but in a myriad of economic transactions – both legal and otherwise – that take place daily...[T]he seeds of political change and possible waves of democracy rest more in the demonstration effect generated by a tiny market (and a huge black market) and the presence of nearly two million tourists annually than in the extant system of governance (Scarpaci, 2002:164).

The assessment of Scarpaci's argument requires a closer examination of the nature of, and the role exerted by, Cuban grassroots organizations and civil society agencies such as national NGOs within Cuban socio-political and institutional settings. The existence of truly independent NGOs in Cuba has led to disagreement amongst scholars and has generated debate in the literature. Gunn (1995) documented approximately 2200 NGOs working in Cuba in the mid-1990s. Most of these started operating after 1989. She questions the true autonomy of many NGOs. According to her, the rising interest in NGOs is both top-down from the government and bottom-up from the population. On the one hand the state sought in NGOs a means to channel foreign funds to the state sector. On the other, many NGOs have been set up by popular and grassroots organizations to voice their calls for religious freedom and civil liberties to the state and international institutions.

An example of a Ministry-sponsored NGO is '*Pro-Naturaleza*', an environmental organization with some 5000 members, which was set up in 1993, the leadership of which is employed at the Ministry of the Environment, Science and Technology. The 'Felix Varela Centre' and the 'Pablo Milanès Foundation', however, were developed as independent cultural organizations. Both set up in 1990, their aims are respectively to provide recreational activities for child cancer patients and to support young Cuban artists.

A case of a Cuban NGO that refused to be coopted by governmental institutions is 'Habitat-Cuba'. This NGO was founded in 1974 to carry out housing and shelter-related projects. Since the end of the 1980s, Habitat-Cuba collaborated with several international NGOs such as OXFAM-Canada and the French CIMADE, receiving external funds. Despite its successes, which include the experimentation of the 'architect of the community',[2] Habitat-Cuba was closed down by the government in July 2001. This was largely because its members did not agree with the Cuban

---

2 The Architect of the Community is 'participative design method for structure modification of dwellings based on the tight relation between architect and the family-customer

National Institute of Housing to co-manage their founding, and the implementation of housing projects. In October 2001 the head of the National Institute of Housing was replaced by the government leadership.

The analytical division of Cuban NGOs into two categories does not do justice to the complexity of underlying social and financial factors that shape the identity of such civil society organisations. As Gunn (1995: 10) notes:

> The state frequently attempts to convert bottom-up NGOs into government instruments, while citizens occasionally try to re-shape top-down NGOs into grassroots organizations. The ideological lines between groups are also fluid. Bottom-up organizations are not necessarily anti-state, and top-down organizations are not necessarily anti-citizen empowerment.

Gunn's views concerning the complex nature of Cuban NGOs, are exemplified by the instance of the *Grupo para el Desarrollo Integral de la Capital* (Group for the Integrated Development of the Capital, GDIC), a quasi-NGO set up in Havana in 1987. The *Grupo* focuses on urban development and cooperates in the management of the city at a time when the government put an emphasis on new housing construction. The main aims of the *Grupo* are to avoid the sectoral implementation of investments in housing and to improve the image of urban areas by emphasizing Havana's urban and cultural values (Hernandez-Padron and Guerra-Benitez, 1997).

The institutional nature of the *Grupo* is rather controversial. Thus, Dilla-Alfonso *et al.* (1997) define it as a formal state institution while Gunn (1995: 10) points out that:

> the group has not yet been able to register as an NGO because it is not fully self-financing and remains officially connected with Havana City government. However, it acts as an NGO more than many registered organisations.

Tourism and Socio-economic Inequalities in Cuba

The promotion of tourism and the opening up of the economy have resulted in moderate increases in income inequality and other socio-economic disparities in Cuba during the 1990s. In a recent study by the University of Miami, Mesa Lago (2002) underlines that until 1989, Cuba had one of the most egalitarian economies and societies in Latin America. However, he goes on to assert that after the beginning of the Special Period eight main types of socio-economic disparities can be identified in Cuba. These inequalities can be categorized according to (i) income and wealth, (ii) taxes, (iii) provision of social services, (iv) regional imbalances, (v) racial inequality, (vi) discrimination vis-à-vis foreigners, (vii) satisfaction of basic needs, and (viii)

---

by means of a detailed study of the place and inquiries among the members of the family using psychoanalysis techniques', UNESCO (2003), http://www.unesco.org/most/centram2.htm.

poverty. For the purpose of this research, only categories number one, four and six will be investigated further because they are directly related to tourism development in the Special Period.

The first inequality (income and wealth) is linked to the rise of a small private sector in Cuba, following the legalisation of over hundred self-employed job categories through Decree Law 141 in 1993. Self-employed jobs can be found predominantly in services and tourism. Peters and Scarpaci (1998) note that self employed service categories include low-order retail activities such as beauty shops, shoe repair, massage therapy, spiritual advice, bed and breakfast (B&B) and home restaurants called *paladares*. These food establishments were once clandestine but mushroomed throughout Cuba after their legalisation in 1993. They exert a significant competition to State restaurants by offering a meal for 10-15 US$ against the 25-35 US$ meal served in tourist facilities.

At the national level, after the legalisation of self-employment, the number of small private entrepreneurs has increased steadily throughout the Special Period, growing from 121,000 in 1994 to 152,300 in 2001 (ONE, 2002; ECLAC, 2000). However, this growth has been positively correlated to an increase of income and wealth inequalities. Indeed, Mesa Lago (2002) maintains that, between 1990 and 2002, real average wages in the state sector shrank by 44 per cent, while extreme salary and income differences grew from 829 to one in 1995, to 12,500 to one in 2001.

This increase in income differences has been spurred by the rise of self-employment as revealed by a series of interviews conducted by Mesa Lago (2002) in Miami and Madrid with recent visitors and immigrants from Cuba. Indeed, while State employees continue to receive their fixed salary in pesos, the new entrepreneurs charge in US dollars without pre-established rates. As a result, the findings of his survey emphasise significant differences in income between State sector employees and the self employed in the private sector as reported in Table 7.1. It can be seen how, for example, in March-April 2002, the income of B&B or *paladar* owners were at least 15 times higher than that of a teacher or a police officer's earnings.

Similar results have been obtained by interview surveys conducted by other researchers. Peters (1997) and Peters and Scarpaci (1998) contend that the monthly earnings of a *paladar* owner in Vedado are roughly US$ 17.50. This figure is disproportionably lower than the US$ 12,500-50,000 estimated by Mesa Lago. However, the measurements are not comparable because they were conducted at different times and through different methodologies. Yet, both surveys would seem to agree on the fact that the Special Period has witnessed an increase of income inequalities between the public and private employment sector.

Table 7.1 Monthly income in Havana, Cuba (in Pesos and US$) March-April 2002

Occupations	Cuban Pesos	US Dollars (26 pesos = US $ 1)
State Sector		
Lowest pension	100	4
Lowest salary	100	4
Teacher (elementary and secondary)	200-400	8-15
University professor	300-560	12-22
Engineer, physician	300-650	12-25
Garbage collector	300-500	12-19
Policeman (regular)	200-500	8-19
Policeman (security for tourists)	700-800	27-31
Officer, armed forces	350-700	13-23
Cabinet minister	450-600	17-23
Private Sector		
Domestic servant		20-40
Private farmer	520-1,040	77-1,923
Transporter (truck with 20-60 seats)	2,000-50,000	385-770
Prostitute *(jinetera)*	10,000-20,000	240-1,400
Landlord of room, apartment, or home		250-4,000
Artist or musician (known abroad)		600-6,000
Owner of *paladar*		12,500-50,000

(*Source*: Mesa Lago, 2002)

Another factor which has played a crucial role in the increase of wealth inequalities in Cuba has been the rise of the informal sector, following the legalization of the dollar in 1994. According to ECLAC (2000), informal employment in Cuba represents 34 per cent of total employment, as shown in Table 7.2. This form of employment (see Lloyd Evans, 1994 for an in depth analysis of its main characteristics) is mostly concentrated in urban areas and normally reflects the proportion of excluded or underemployed workers. In Cuba, the informal sector is mainly composed of:

- would-be self-employed workers who have been denied a licence in the private sector and could not find employment in the public sector
- retirees who supplement their pension income, for example, by offering lifts by car- to tourist and selling refreshments on the street
- State employees who use materials and equipment from work to privately provide services ranging from building to maintenance work.

In recent years Havana has experience an exponential growth of the informal sector. The majority of informal activities are concentrated in the Bed and Breakfast and street vendors sectors, as will be explained in more details later on.

Table 7.2 Informal employment in selected Latin American countries

Countries	Year	Percentage of urban informal employment as to total employment
Argentina	1996	45
Brazil	1995	59
Chile	1996	37
Colombia	1996	46
Costa Rica	1995	42
Cuba	1996	34
Mexico	1995	48
Panama	1995	41
Peru	1995	55
Venezuela	1996	43

(*Source*: ECLAC, 2000)

The second inequality (discrimination vis-à-vis foreigners) stems from the growing social disparity that exists between foreigners and residents. As Mesa Lago (2002) points out, Cuban citizens experience discrimination in relation to foreigners in two main ways. Firstly, after the shrinking of public spending in health care, the best medical healthcare in Cuba can be now accessed mainly in US dollars. This has seriously prejudiced access to good medical facilities to Cubans who receive their wage in pesos in comparison to foreigners and tourists. Secondly, Cubans are prohibited from entering hotels and restaurants for international tourists and from using services, such as transport, which are available exclusively to foreign tourists. This form of discrimination was particularly true at the beginning of the 1990s. However, things have evolved in recent years. In fact, nowadays it is not uncommon to find wealthy Cuban families lodging in hotels aimed at international tourists.

The last type of inequality (regional imbalances) stems from diverging local development rates experienced by different Cuban regions. As emphasized in chapter 6, the reduction of socio-economic disparity among Cuban provinces has been a priority goal successfully pursued by the Cuban Leadership over the last forty years. Nonetheless, there are claims that the socio-economic homogeneity of the fourteen provinces has begun to crumble in the Special Period. For example, Mesa Lago (2002) calculated several indicators for four Cuban provinces (Havana City, Las Tunas, Guantanamo and Granma) in order to show a growing socio-economic division among these areas. He concludes that Havana has performed significantly better than the other regions in terms of several indicators, including urban population at social risk, the human development index, investment per capita and access to basic environmental health utilities.

Part of these growing regional differences can be ascribed to the spatially concentrated nature of the tourism development strategy pursued in the Special Period. As noted in chapter 6, the 1995 *National Plan for the Development of International Tourism* identified 67 'tourist poles' to be developed throughout Cuba. This Plan also established eight tourist priority areas to be developed at the national level. These areas, shown in Figure 7.1, were chosen according to their tourist development potential and the stock of natural resources, such as beaches and sea, they were endowed with. Priority efforts and investments involving foreign capital were therefore driven towards the infrastructural upgrading of such areas. As a result, the tourist priority regions were able to economically and socially develop faster than other Cuban territories.

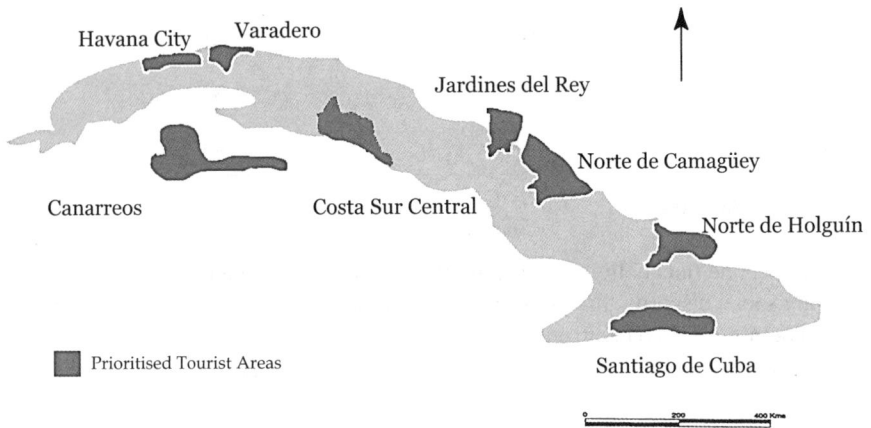

Figure 7.1 Prioritized tourist areas in Cuba during the Special Period

(*Source*: Chamber of Commerce of Cuba, 2002)

However, a different theory with a stronger political flavour can be put forward to explain the rationale beyond the selection of the tourist priority areas. Indeed, it could be argued that the concentration of tourism development in spatially self-contained coastal areas has been carefully planned by the Cuban Leadership in order to minimize or, at least, retain control over the cultural and political exchanges between international tourists and Cubans. This is especially true in inland areas where the effects of the revolution are more evident and Castro still enjoys wide popularity.

The Socio-economic Impact of Tourism in Havana During the Special Period

Tourism and Economic Development: The Shift Toward a Service Economy in Havana

It is arduous to assess the real economic impact of tourism in cities because of the methodological and measurement hurdles expressed in chapter 5. In the case of Havana, this task is complicated further by the paucity of publicly-disclosed disaggregated data on tourist expenditures, employment figures and social indicators. Nevertheless, the study of available data and sources allows the qualitative analysis of the changing nature of employment and new occupational opportunities generated by tourism.

It can be argued that the impact of tourism on employment in Havana during the Special Period has been significant in both quantitative and qualitative terms. At least two main trends can be identified in Havana's job market:

- the increase of jobs in tourism and services
- the rise of self-employment, mostly in accommodation and more generally in the dollar-oriented sector

The first feature is linked directly to the new employment opportunities generated in corporations and joint ventures infrastructures. The second one stems from the introduction of the 1990s reforms and indicates a change in the nature of employment opportunities that rely less on the State sector and increasingly on market mechanisms.

The increase of jobs in tourism and services – The number of jobs created in the tourist sector in Havana has increased throughout the 1990s. Figure 7.2 illustrates how the jobs provided by the tourist industry more than doubled between 1995 and 2002, growing from 13,210 to 32,962. After the collapse of economic sectors such as tobacco and sugar, the government has implemented programmes to re-train workers in declining economic sectors to emerging industries such as tourism (Cuban TV news, 22 August 2003). The increase of jobs in tourism can be framed within the broader shift of Havana's economic structure toward a service economy that has pragmatically being supported by the Cuban leadership.

In the absence of data on production by economic sector, evidence of the shift toward a service economy dominated by commerce and tourism is provided by an increase of investment and employment figures in services. Thus, Table 7.3 shows that between 1996 and 2001, State investment in sectors such as industry, construction and agriculture has proportionally decreased. As a matter of fact, it increased in absolute terms until 1999 but then decreased on average as a percentage of total investment. Indeed, in the 'productive sphere' of the economy,[3] only investments in trade infrastructure grew from CP 74.5 millions to CP 172.2 millions.

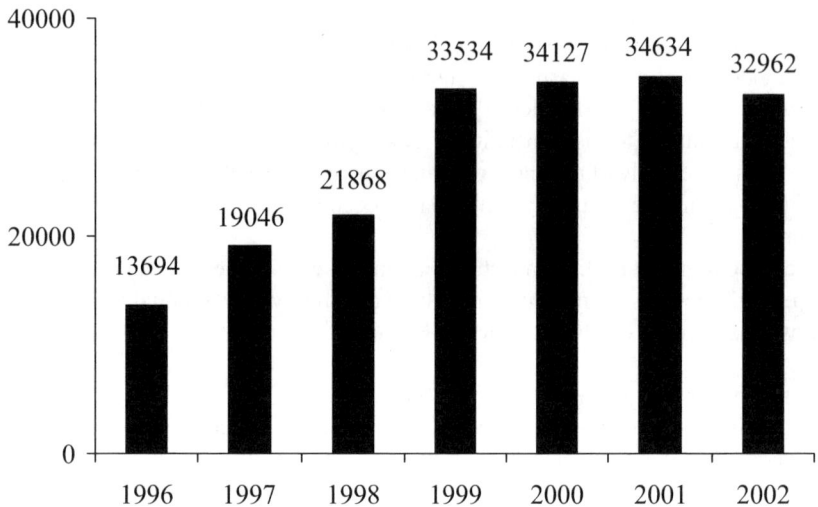

Figure 7.2 Jobs created in tourism in Havana during the Special Period

(*Source*: Mintur, 2001b; OTE, 2003)

The decrease of investment in the 'productive sphere' of the economy has been compensated by the increase of investments in 'non-productive' economic sectors, as defined by official Cuban statistics. Table 7.3 illustrates how investments in personal services and trade have increased nearly five-fold from CP 46.8 million in 1996 to CP 228.3 million in 2001. Likewise, investments in administration have tripled from CP 70.1 million to CP 217.8 million in the same period. These figures provide strong evidence for the claim that Havana's economic structure is undergoing structural transformation towards a service economy in the Special Period.

The figures reviewed above suggest that most of the local productive capacity upgrading, examined in chapter 3, has occurred outside Havana. It could be argued therefore that the Cuban leadership is trying to pre-empt an Import Substitution Industrialisation similar to the one that other Latin American countries embarked upon during the 1960s and 1970s. In these instances, the development policy was based on political and spatial concentration of the economic activities in a few major

---

3   Cuban economic data are based on Gross Social Product (GSP) that differs from Western Gross Domestic Product (GDP) in two main fashions. Firstly, the economic sectors are divided into 'productive' and 'non-productive' spheres. Secondly, the GDP includes value-added and non-productive services, while the GSP assesses gross value and excludes non-productive services.

cities. This, in turn, caused massive rural-urban migration and the escalation of social problems in the main Latin American capital cities.

Table 7.3 Investments distribution in Havana during the Special Period (million pesos)

Sector	1996	1997	1998	1999	2000	2001
Industry	169.1	116.8	204.7	354.2	265.8	151.1
Construction	27.2	14.4	21.8	40.6	25.2	12
Agriculture	3.4	4.8	5.9	4	3.8	1.9
Forestry	-	1.3	4.5	3.9	7.9	15.6
Transport	97.9	22.1	42.6	83.1	81.8	105.8
Communication	0.3	3.6	3.9	3.3	10.5	9.3
Commerce	74.5	58.4	67.9	56.3	117.5	172.2
Other Productive Activities	14.6	1.8	3	5.1	4.2	3.3
Service, Trade and Personal Services	46.8	17.5	49.1	88.3	128.7	228.3
Science and Technology	7.2	7.9	17.0	10.3	13.9	10.4
Art and Culture	13.7	6.6	8.4	20.4	21.7	62.2
Education	34.1	34.5	65	121.8	76.5	24.4
Public Health, Social Security, Sport	17	13.5	17.9	21	19.8	45.7
Finance and Insurance	0.7	0.1	11.4	1	12.3	45.7
Administration	70.1	115.2	62.8	122.6	90.2	217.8
Other Non-Productive Activities	0.5	8.5	16.2	8.1	17.2	30.7
Total	577.1	427	592.1	944	897	1136.4

(*Source*: OTE, 2002)

Despite the Cuban leadership's efforts to prevent the negative outcomes of the new development strategy, there can be little doubt that tourism, rather than industry and manufacturing, is prompting migratory flows towards Havana. There are claims that the employment generated by the tourist sector has been a major element that has prompted migration, especially of females toward the tourist poles (Oliveros, 2002).

Cuba registered an annual average of 12,000 city-ward migrants per annum throughout the 1980s (OTH, 2000). This figure more than tripled by the mid-1990s, with Havana registering a positive migratory flow of 28,000 people in 1996 (OTH, 2003a). The Government has since adopted measures to curb migration toward Havana, by means of intensifying existing policing activities and controls. As a result, migratory flows towards Havana decreased after 1995 although it could be argued that many in-migrants are now residing in Havana province, where migration has continued to increase. Evidence of this is discernible from the data contained in Table 7.4.

Table 7.4 Migratory ratio for Havana and Havana Province, 1990–2000

Province	In-migrants per 1,000 inhabitants by year				
	1990	1992	1995	1997	2000
Havana Province	3.4	1.6	7.1	8.8	6.3
Havana	6.3	5.7	12.9	-1.9	0.9
National total	-0.9	-0.6	-1.4	-1.1	-0.3

(*Source*: Oliveros, 2002)

Havana's economic shift toward a service economy has also been mirrored by employment figures, as reported in Table 7.5. It can be seen how workers in the productive sphere decreased from 432,750 in 1996 to 427,026 in 2001, while in the same period the number of workers in the non-productive sphere increased from 461,510 to 484,463. Table 7.5 is also useful in highlighting that within the service sector, tourism is taking away workers from other sectors with a high social function such as public health and sport. In official statistics, workers within these economic sectors are grouped under the category 'public health, sport and tourism'. Between 1996 and 2001, the workers employed in these sectors diminished from 89,618 to 85,746 while, as noted earlier, workers in the tourist industry increased in number. Broadly speaking, it could be concluded that tourism is draining human resources from two sectors on which the Revolution has historically placed a lot of emphasis, that is, health and sport.

There are multiple reasons for this draining of workers from social sectors towards tourism jobs, despite the fact that the vast majority of the newly created jobs in tourism are low-skilled and are mainly in the catering and lodging sector. Indeed, jobs in tourism have become attractive because of: (i) better working conditions; (ii) the prospect of better salary complemented by tips in dollars, and (iii) the possibility of using the corporation's car, a luxury commodity in Cuba. For example, while the average salary for a worker outside the tourist-hard currency sector is approximately US$ 12 per month, wages can increase up to US$ 100 in the State tourist industry (including tips).

Table 7.5 Employment in Havana during the Special Period

Sector	ca 1990*	1996	1997	1998	1999	2000	2001
Productive Sphere	500,900	432,750	440,161	412,770	405,612	431,539	427,026
Industry	211,600	184,949	185,846	149,815	145,608	138,779	142,480
Construction	82,200	61,960	69,231	61,183	55,564	59,616	54,390
Agriculture	90,000	11,447	11,266	17,193	11,702	32,210	27,443
Forestry	n/a	46	497	250	64	178	230
Transportation	1,300	45,695	34,771	40,090	42,194	45,681	46,623
Communication	n/a	6,485	7,460	10,331	10,303	10,989	10,762
Commerce	102,900	113,535	123,697	125,589	131,733	135,342	134,797
Other Productive Activities	13,000	8,633	7,393	8,319	8,444	8,744	10,301
Non Productive Sphere	438,500	461,510	479,006	476,487	499,354	472,457	484,463
Service, Trade and Personal Services	45,000	49,042	54,600	57,420	56,991	51,448	45,622
Science and Technology	20,100	18,500	17,946	17,975	17,748	17,045	17,755
Art and Culture	105,800	77,051	72,922	69,394	68,996	66,986	70,502
Education	n/a**	25,983	27,786	31,893	28,735	29,220	30,540
Public Health, Social Security, Sport, Tourism	67,800	89,618	84,740	84,720	84,829	84,165	85,746
Finance and Insurance	199,800	5,839	6,381	6,555	7,379	7,536	7,647
Administration	n/a***	182,691	181,511	174,264	51,416	25,197	29,687
Other Non-Productive Activities	n/a	12,786	32,220	34,266	183,260	190,860	196,964
Total	939,400	894,260	919,167	889,257	904,966	903,996	911,489

** included in Art and Culture figure above
*** included in Finance and Insurance

(*Source*: OTE, 2002 and *Scarpaci et al., 2002)

Self-employment and Tourism – Another important aspect which has characterized employment figures in Havana has been the rise of the private sector. Likewise, at the national level, the legalization of self employment has meant that thousands of city dwellers set up their own small businesses in Havana, ranging from agriculture to service provision. Table 7.6 shows how the number of self-employed workers increased steadily from 23,027 to 41,236 between 1996 and 2001. Furthermore, the significance of non-state employment including mixed enterprises and small business or private agriculture has risen in the same period as a whole. Table 7.6

illustrates that, while in 1996 the State employed directly or indirectly (for example through cooperatives and UBPC still linked to the state sector) around 97 per cent of Havana's working force, in 2001 it employed just over 91 per cent.

Table 7.6 Number of workers in Havana according to form of property

Sector	1996	1997	1998	1999	2000	2001
State Sector	894,260	919,167	889,257	904,966	903,996	911,489
Mixed Enterprises	4,246	5,125	8,820	7,545	13,334	13,629
Private Sector	25,275	38,449	48,418	69,599	66,587	67,510
Farmers cooperatives	185	224	286	3,777	4,434	853
Self-employed	23,027	31,942	30,231	41,454	41,435	41,236
Commerce	1,317	2,139	2,286	2,997	3,084	3,179
Associations and Foundations	1,789	2,101	2,294	3,322	2,063	2,301
Other	2,063	2,043	13,321	18,049	15,571	19,941
Total	894,260	919,167	889,257	904,966	903,996	911,489

(*Source*: OTE, 2002)

As noted earlier, self-employed jobs can be found predominantly in services and tourism, especially in *paladares* and B&Bs. No data are available on the historical evolution of *paladares* in Havana but there is general agreement that they flourished until 1997 then stabilized and decreased after 2000. Two different reasons for this decrease are provided by officials on the one hand and workers in the sector on the other. According to State officials, after 1996, state restaurants regained competitiveness against private restaurants by improving their service and food quality (Interview 7). This in turn forced many *paladares* out of the mixed market. By contrast, *paladar* workers argued in informal talks during fieldwork that many household restaurants were forced out of the market because the government raised taxes to an unsustainable level.

By contrast, the rise of B&Bs in Havana has been consistent throughout the second half on the 1990s. The number of B&Bs which are registered as tax payers in Havana tripled between 1998 and 2002 accounting for over 27 per cent of total national in 2002, as shown in Table 7.7. It has been estimated that in 1995, over seven per cent of individual tourists visiting Havana chose this kind of accommodation, whilst this proportion increased to 21 per cent in 1997 (Bohemia, 1997) and 23 per cent in 2002 (OTH, 2003b).

Table 7.7 Number of bed and breakfasts registered as tax payers (in US$)

Province	Year				
	1998	1999	2000	2001	2002
Havana	17*	2,284	2,568	2,705	2,730
Cuba	1,537	4,234	5,044	5,178	4,980

* According to experts this exceptional low value is due to counting mistakes by Havana's Office of National Revenue

(*Source*: ONAT, 2003)

The Socio-spatial Implications of Tourism Development in Havana

Along with the economic impact and structural changes described above, the worsening of the economic crisis and tourism re-development of the 1990s has been reflected in the rise of illegal activities and the informal economy in Havana. It is argued that tourism has generated a new wave of prostitution and street crime in Havana (Elinson, 1999) and created new actors and pressure groups that include *jineteras* (prostitutes); *chulos* (pimps); *maceteros* (money launderers) and *luchadores* (street hustlers offering guide service, cigars etc. to tourists).

Prior to the Special Period, Cubans approaching tourists and asking them for money or a gift was an uncommon occurrence, because they could be detained by the police. Throughout the Revolutionary period, the Cuban leadership managed to ameliorate the social living conditions in the capital and to change its negative pre-1959 image. As noted earlier, in the 'pseudo-republican' era, Havana and its hotels were advertised in tourism promotion campaigns as liberal and indulging places, as it can be seen in Figures 7.3 and 7.4. However, from 1990 onwards, petty theft and assaults were no longer infrequent in any part of Havana (Scarpaci *et al.*, 2002). Prostitution and street begging proliferated in the first half of the 1990s triggering the re-emergence of the type of anti social behaviour that had been virtually eliminated from the streets of Havana by the revolutionary government.

In the early 1990s, the rapid expansion of the sex trade and the adoption of prostitution as a survival strategy by many Cubans prompted serious health problems related to sexually transmitted diseases. In 1996, the leadership decided to crack down on prostitution in an attempt to stop the spread of such diseases. Notwithstanding governmental efforts, today it is still common to be stopped in the streets of Havana by male and female prostitutes who travel across the city to reach central tourist areas such as Vedado, especially 23rd Street and Malecón, and Old Havana. It is not easy to quantify the prostitution phenomenon in today's Havana. However, officials have acknowledged the existence of such problems, despite Fidel

Castro's claims that 'Cuban prostitutes are the best school educated prostitutes of the whole Latin American continent' (Stone, 2000).

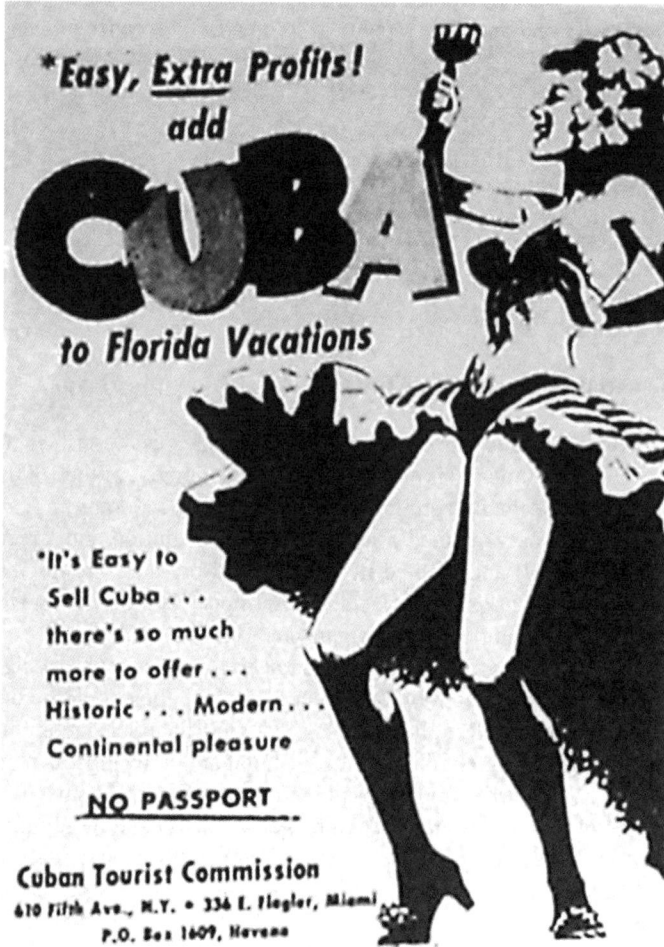

Figure 7.3 Pre-1959 tourism advertising campaign of Cuba

(*Source*: Villalba, 1993)

Figure 7.4 Pre-1959 tourism advertising campaign of Havana

(*Source*: Villalba, 1993)

The scarcity of financial resources and state employment has also contributed to the spread of the informal economy in Havana, especially in the private accommodation and street vendors sectors. For example, Coyula (2002) argues that in Havana 4,500 rooms are located in private residences which are registered and pay taxes. However, he estimates there are at least an equivalent number in the informal sector. Similarly, the number of informal vendors in the streets of Havana has visibly increased over the last few years (see Figure 7.5), although no data concerning such a phenomenon are available.

Figure 7.5 Informal street vendors in Havana

(*Source*: Photo by Andrea Colantonio)

The rise of the informal sector is engendering spatial changes at the household, neighbourhood and city levels. At the household level, family members often share rooms in order to be able to rent or use the space which is thereby freed-up. Moreover, families often modify their house design in order to rent out a room or create a work space. At the neighbourhood level, there are claims that city dwellers have begun to occupy common areas within buildings, portals, gardens and patios to carry out their activities, such as selling books and drinks. These new phenomena have been harshly criticised by municipal authorities and planners alike because they are introducing unauthorized commerce and affecting negatively Havana's urban culture.

At the city level, the concentration of authorized and informal B&Bs within coastal municipalities is creating an economic divide in Havana. Garcia Jimenez (2000) pinpoints that the majority of B&Bs in Havana are located in the northern municipalities of Plaza (36.7 per cent), Playa (32.1 per cent) and East Havana (22.7 per cent). There can be little doubt that the remaining are located in Old Havana and Centro Havana while they are virtually absent from southern areas. This is contributing to the economic polarisation of Havana where coastal areas are *de facto* benefiting from new economic opportunities generated by tourism in the private sector, while southern municipalities are left behind.

The analysis of two life-case studies exemplifies the impacts and the implications of the socio-economic and spatial changes brought about by the Special Period in Havana. The first author carried out two separate interviews with Ana and Maria[4] in which these impacts can be clearly discerned. Ana (Interview 9), is a doctor in her forties who works at a central clinic in Vedado. As many doctors of her generation, she studied medicine during the mid-1970s because being a doctor at that time in Cuba was considered as a prestigious and well-paid profession. Further, doctors benefited from some privileges such as paid holidays in the best nationalized Cuban hotels. After the economic crisis hit Cuba, Ana learnt how to cut hair to become a hairdresser (without a licence) at weekends and in the evenings. Further, she and her husband modernized one room in their flat facing the Malecón in order to rent it out illegally for US$ 10 per night. As a result, they were forced to move to live in the same room with Ana's mother.

Maria (Interview 8) is an 18 year-old who lives with her mother in Miramar and has just enrolled on a two year course to train in the catering sector. In 1997, Maria moved into her mother's room because they subdivided her large room into two smaller rooms without any building or modification permissions in order to rent them. Maria and her cousin, who lives in Cerro Municipality and would like to move to Miramar because of better economic opportunities, hope one day to visit their Mexican relatives and to take up a job in Cancun. They are currently looking for a job in tourism and have been illegally asked to pay US $ 300 in exchange of a job as receptionist in one of Havana's best hotels.

Urban Tourism Enclaves in Havana

Another important socio-spatial change in Havana has occurred in the construction of the city's leisure spaces. Indeed, as a result of the tourism development strategy, Havana has experienced a moderate increase in the supply of entertaining facilities. Nonetheless, the best recreational and nightlife facilities, oriented to both tourists and residents, are being built within Havana's new and refurbished hotels rather than

---

4   Pseudonyms will be used throughout.

in the city at large. The rationale underpinning such a strategy is unclear although two main explanations have been suggested.

As noted earlier, the first explanation holds that the Cuban leadership aims at controlling and minimising interactions between tourists and Cubans. According to this argument, tourists can cause the transfer of social behaviours based on consumerism, materialism and drug consumption, especially when it comes to night life, which are still relatively unknown to Cubans. Further, tourists can encourage the transfer of new ideas and ideals to Cubans that portray the current stage of the Cuban socialist experiment in a negative light. The second explanation contends that tourism decision-making in Havana is currently permeated by non-integrated and insular planning as will be examined in chapter 10 in greater depth.

Many hotels for international tourism in Havana have built their own discothéque and piano bars inside their premises, the most famous ones being the 'Turquino' discotheque inside Hotel Habana Libre and 'Cohiba' discotheque within the Hotel Meliá Cohiba complex. Night clubs like these are often the only ones allowed to stay open until late throughout the week and therefore attract Havana's young residents seeking amusements or entertainment during the week. Nonetheless, the entrance to these clubs is expensive and is exclusively in convertible pesos or dollars (usually US$ 10-20) or, in many instances, is limited to tourists only. Havana's inhabitants earnings in pesos are *de facto* precluded to enter these night clubs as they are often beyond their financial limits.

Such spaces can be considered to be *urban tourism enclaves* that prejudice local residents' recreational needs. They serve to increase the cultural and social isolation and differences between urban dwellers and tourists through the establishment of spaces that are destined for tourist consumption only. The isolating effect of urban tourism enclaves is less divisive than their rural counterpart, because of the nature of urban life. In fact, the interactions between residents and tourists in urban environments are not limited to night life but continue throughout the day through a variety of economic, social and cultural transactions which are embedded in daily activities.

Conclusions

Tourism development and the economic opening up of the Special Period have been associated with the emergence of new actors and interest group in Havana and Cuba as a whole. It is not clear what role civil society groups and private and informal sector workers will play in promoting political and economic change in Cuba but there can be little doubt that the Cuban Leadership has cracked down on them on at least two occasions, and with different instruments. Both in 1996 and at the beginning of 2003, the Cuban government commanded strict policing controls against illegal self-employed workers with a special focus on taxi drivers, *paladares* restaurants, Bed and Breakfast owners, and *jineteros*.

Similarly, by the mid-1990s, the government increased taxation levels for the private sector forcing many *paladares* and Bed and Breakfast establishments to close down. This anti-private sector policy was more effective in smaller and medium tourist areas, such as Trinidad and Cienfuegos, but yielded modest result in Havana where groups and civil movements are still active with more or less covert political agendas and economic sectoral interest.

Public and urban development policies would also seem to have failed in preventing the emergence of socio-economic disparities at different spatial scales, ranging from the household to national levels. In Havana, the Special Period has spurred a change in the city's economic structure which, in turn, has been associated with the materialization of an economic divide between Southern and Northern municipalities. The next chapter will demonstrate how this polarisation of Havana has not only been socio-economic, but environmental too, because the environmental improvements generated have not spread outside the city's tourist poles.

Chapter 8

Tourism and Environment in Havana during the Special Period

Introduction

The account thus far has showed how urban tourism has prompted significant social and economic change in Cuba at the local and national levels. This change is bringing the country 'back to the future' in social and economic terms as tourism is prompting a new socio-economic stratification of the Cuban society that recalls pre-1959 memories. However, the impact of tourism has not been exclusively social and economic but environmental also. At the national level, the promotion of tourism has occurred at a high environmental cost, while in Havana the rapid increase of tourist inflows and tourism development projects are testing the city's dilapidated infrastructural network, such as the water and sewerage systems and transport services.

More specifically, it is argued that urban tourism is prompting diverging environmental conditions within Havana's neighbourhoods. This, in turn, is increasing the socio-economic divide between northern and southern city districts, described in chapter 6. Indeed, works by the *Grupo para el Desarrollo de la Capital*, point out that the city is developing along its coastline while inland areas are not benefiting from the process of urban change that is stemming from the development of tourism (GDIC, 2002). Further, the *Grupo* goes on to argue that the promotion of tourism in Havana is actually prompting the emergence of new policy-related issues at the neighbourhood and pole levels (GDIC, 2002).

The main aim of this chapter is to assess selected dimensions of the environmental impact of tourism on Havana by employing the methodology and the variables identified in Chapter 5. Great emphasis will be placed upon the impact of tourism on the city's urban utilities and the provision of environmental health services, while the effect of tourism on natural features will only be touched upon here. This assessment exercise, coupled with the findings of chapter 7, is vital to demonstrate the broad re-emergence of patterns of urban duality within Havana's urban fabric outlined in the aims of this book.

The chapter is thus organised in four main parts. It begins with a critical overview of the 1990s restructuring of institutions and governing mechanisms involved with environmental matters in Cuba and its implications for Havana. The second part reviews the salient socio-environmental characteristics of Havana's municipalities, highlighting how northern coastal neighbourhoods currently display better living conditions than southern areas. This will be followed by the examination of the impact that tourism is exerting on Havana's main urban utilities. The main objective of this section is to test whether the current tourism development strategy represents a major driver for urban environmental stresses or not. Lastly, the main findings of the chapter will be summarized in the concluding section of the chapter.

Environmental Reforms and Tourism in the Special Period

The economic crisis has yielded two conflicting trends in the environmental policies of Cuba. On the one hand, the need for hard currency has increased the pressure to marginalize environmental protection. Thus, environmentalist groups claim that many recent development projects have been carried out with little or no consideration for the environment, such as the recent tourist re-development in Varadero (in Matanzas province, see Figure 5.8). On the other hand, the Cuban government has included the achievement of 'sustainable development' objectives in its policies, hoping to obtain international political approval and the support of national environmentalists. As a result, there is no general agreement on whether the recent 'greening' of Cuba, based on the promotion of organic agriculture, the use of bicycles as the principal means of transport, the rediscovery of traditional medicine and other measures, has been prompted by the scarcity of resources rather than any ideological shift within the leadership (Eckstein, 1997).

By the mid-1990s, the Cuban government's efforts towards environmental protection had led to the restructuring of institutions and governing mechanisms involved with the environmental management and natural resource planning in Cuba. Thus, in 1994 the government created the *Ministry of Science, Technology and Environment* (*Ministerio de Ciencia Tecnología y Medio Ambiente*, CITMA); in 1997 it enforced an innovative and integrated Environmental Law; and in 1998 it set up the *National Committee of Trade and Environment* to prevent negative effects of trade on the environment. The country is also developing a decentralization process based on methodological procedures for environmental control and management at the municipality level (CITMA, 2000).

Until recently, the *National Commission for the Protection of the Environment and the Rational Use of Natural Resources* (*Comisión Nacional de Protecion de Medio Ambiente y del Uso Racional de los Recursos Naturales*, COMARNA) was the central mechanism through which all matters having environmental implications were passed (Collis, 1995). COMARNA was the co-ordinator responsible for incorporating over twenty ministries and institutions in the environmental decision-process, but lacked any real decision-making power.

Referring to the tourist sector Collis (1995) notes:

Foreign investors wishing to build hotels in Cuba had to present their ideas to the Institute of Physical Planning which suggested a site and, in most cases, had an environmental impact study performed. The proposed location of the site, the environmental impact study and construction plans were presented to COMARNA, which reviewed the documents in consultation with environmental experts. Finally, COMARNA called together a meeting of all relevant ministries and institutions to discuss the project. If all groups agreed on the final proposal, it was approved by Physical Planning and the work began. If there were any insurmountable disagreements between the parties the decision was deferred to the Council of Ministries. In light of Cuba's economic situation, the Council of Ministries at times may have been more concerned with development than with environmental protection (Collis 1995:1).

In 1994, COMARNA was replaced by the CITMA. The highly bureaucratic Cuban governmental system was becoming incompatible with the environmental issues linked to the opening up of the economy. New elements such as corporate environmental economics and international environmental benchmarking practices forced the government to reduce a large and slow disconnected bureaucracy into a single ministry.

Further, in 1997, CITMA passed *Law 81, the Law of the Environment* replacing the old Law 33 of 1981. The new law is ambitious in its goals and its details to the point that Rey Santos (1999) claims it has been adopted as a model in the elaboration of environmental laws in other Latin American countries such as Panama and El Salvador. In addition, CITMA developed a National Environmental Strategy that is considered the clearest expression of Cuban environmental policy within which its main projections and directives are shaped. The strategy encompasses five major aspects of environmental policy-making in Cuba. These are:

i.   the principles underpinning the Cuban environmental strategy;
ii. recommendations on Cuba's socially sustainable economic development;
iii. the identification of the main actors responsible for implementing the environmental policy;
iv. the assessment of the main national environmental problems, and
v.   the definition of the main instruments to implement the national strategy.

Another novelty introduced by Law 81 has been the obligatory requirement of an Environmental Impact Assessment and the concession of an Environmental Licence as pre-requisites to new investments that impinge or could have effects on the environment. Within this context, Houck (1999) points out that the National Environmental Strategy and the Law of the Environment empower CITMA in ways new to Cuba. First, it elevates to the status of law an environmental impact review process managed by CITMA. Second, it makes compulsory, by advancing it to the status of law, an environmental licence required by CITMA for specific proposals affecting the environment. Thus, Houck concludes that 'environmental impact assessment in Cuba, as in many developing countries, has a strong substantive element; it is not, as in the United States and Europe, a purely procedural requirement' (Houck, 1999:5).

Despite these good intentions expressed by the Cuban Leadership, there is general agreement that tourism development in the first half of the 1990s has led to serious environmental disruption in Cuba (Díaz-Briquets and Pérez-López, 2000). This was especially true during the early construction of tourism infrastructure, such as roads, airports and electric grids, in the pristine environments of the numerous Cuban cays. For example, Díaz-Briquets and Pérez-López (2000) note that *Coco Cay* and *Guillermo Cay* (see Figure 8.1) did not have any public or tourist infrastructures until 1993. After four years, they had over 1,500 rooms, an airport, over 200 kilometres of roads, several electricity generating units and 100 kilometres of pipes to supply water from the mainland.

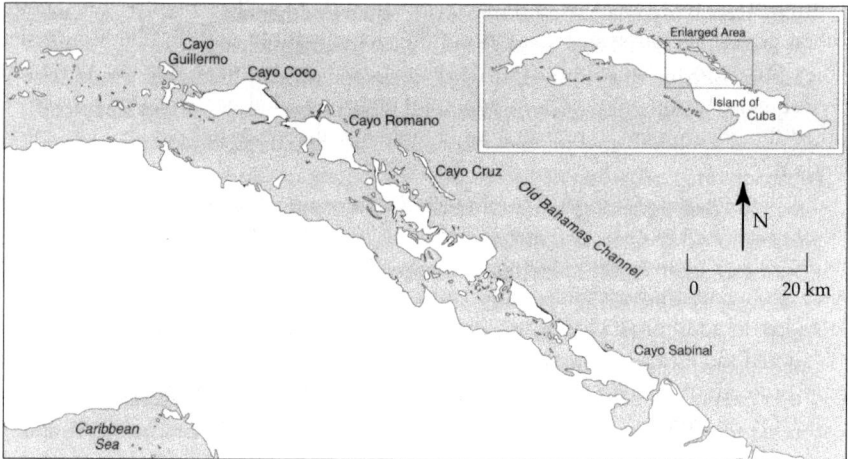

Figure 8.1 Most important Cuban cays

(*Source*: Díaz-Briquets and Pérez-López, 2000)

The in-depth analysis of the environmental impact of tourism in rural areas is outside the scope of this monograph. Here, it suffices to underline that Cuban authorities have partially acknowledged the environmental damage caused by tourism (Convención de Medioambiente, 2003). However, they have also pointed out that the future growth of tourism will continue to rely not only on the availability of large-scale tourism-oriented facilities but also on the implementation of more environmentally friendly development plans. This is essential to preserve the country's natural resources which are a primary asset on which most of the tourist industry depends (Convención de Medioambiente, 2003) In this light, it can be noted that the Law of the Environment and the National Environmental Strategy are relatively new and reflect important challenges that the government will have to face in the future for the protection of the environment in Cuba.

The Effects of the Environmental Reforms on Havana

The most tangible and direct outcome of the 1990s environmental management decentralisation process for Havana has been the elaboration in 1998 of the

Environmental Strategy for Havana by CITMA. This document epitomizes governmental authorities' growing concerns for Havana's environmental problems and is divided into two parts. The first one provides a review of the city's main environmental problems, while the second part lists a series of short- medium- and long-term objectives to address them.

The Environmental Strategy (CITMA-CH, 1998) identifies seven main categories of environmental issues currently characterizing Havana. These are:

- inadequate management of solid waste
- hospital waste management
- inadequate treatment and disposal of liquid waste
- water provision through an obsolete system
- air pollution
- noise pollution
- deforestation

The first four issues are related to urban utilities and will be addressed in the next section of this chapter. The remainder of this section will review the remaining ones, namely, air and noise pollution and deforestation.

Havana does not display a high concentration of industrial plants. However, industrial pollution is high because of obsolete Russian and East European production equipment as well as the old age of the facilities. Lezcano (1994) reports that 100 industrial plants located within Havana are heavy air polluters, 53 per cent of which cannot be retrofitted to reduce air pollution and would have to be shut down in order to reduce pollution. The heaviest polluters are electric power plants, metalworking shops, gas production plants and oil refineries. According to Lezcano (1994) air pollution in the form of smoke, dust, and industrial gases is most prevalent in the municipalities of 10 de Octubre, Marianao, Cerro, La Lisa, Regla, Havana Vieja and Centro Havana.

Most of the polluting industries are located around the La Habana Bay, such as the 'Ñico López' refinery (see Figure 8.2) and the electric power plant 'Antonio Maceo' in the Regla municipality. Some 100 other polluting industries are located in more than seven municipalities along three rivers that flow directly into the Bay: the Luyanó, Martín Pérez and Arroyo Tadeo rivers (GTE Bahia Habana, 2003). Many years of untreated disposal of liquid and solid waste into these rivers and the Bay have transformed the latter into one of the most polluted bodies of water in the world (Rodriguez Cruz, 1996). However, since the 1970s the UN Development Programme and the Cuban government have intensified their efforts to clean up the bay with unclear results. For example, while Diaz-Briquets and Pérez-López (2000) cast doubt on the outcome of such efforts, Rodriguez Cruz (1996) contends that forms of organic life can increasingly be found in the Bay again once more.

Noise pollution is another environmental issue identified by the Environmental Strategy as associated with obsolete industrial equipment and airport activities. No statistics are publicly available concerning noise contamination levels in Havana.

Nonetheless, during unofficial discussions with CITMA officials it emerged that in the past local residents have complained about the high noise and smell associated with industrial activities in the Cotorro, Regla and Boyeros municipalities. Further, other residents located near the airport have complained about the noise associated with night flights, while residents of central areas of Havana raised concerns about the noise pollution stemming from the air conditioning systems of hotels and loud music played in bars to attract the attention of tourists.

Figure 8.2 Ñico López refinery in Havana Bay

(*Source*: Photo by Andrea Colantonio)

The last problem identified in the strategy is deforestation which affects most of Havana's peripheral urban areas. This problem has also been examined by a recent research project titled CAESAR (2003) carried out jointly by the University of Havana, the Autonomous National University of Mexico, the University of Munich and the Autonomous University of Madrid. The preliminary research of the CAESAR investigation team indicates that urban agricultural initiatives can be deemed responsible for much of the deforestation that has occurred in Havana in recent years. Urban agriculture has also coupled with ill-conceived land use in Havana's peri-urban interface, such as sugar cane plantations and urban agricultural gardens, leading to further deforestation. This in turn, has engendered an alteration of natural drainage and hydrological systems in much of the green belt that was established around Havana in the 1960s.

Tourism, Urban Infrastructure and Dualities in Havana

Havana's environmental problems are not only linked to the environmental features reviewed above but also to malfunctioning and unequally distributed urban infrastructure among the city's areas. As was unveiled in a recent conference on urban planning held in Havana in October 2002 (GDIC, 2002), the main failure of the revolutionary government's efforts has been the inability to reduce environmental and social differences between Havana's southern and northern neighbourhoods in terms of housing conditions and infrastructural provision. Throughout the conference it was also highlighted that in recent years this division has been exacerbated by the implementation of urban development policies grounded on tourism promotion. As a result, the socio-economic and environmental gap amongst Havana's areas is widening rather than getting smaller, as will be exemplified in the next section.

Socio-Environmental Mapping of Havana

Havana City province is composed of 15 municipalities that were created after the 1976 jurisdictional re-organization of Cuban provinces. Table 8.1 (see also Figure 8.1) shows how the biggest municipality is Habana del Este (East Havana) with 144.9 square kilometres, followed by Boyeros (134.2 square kilometres) and Guanabacoa (127.4 square kilometres) both located in southern areas. The smallest municipalities are Centro Havana and Havana Vieja with 3.5 and 4.5 square kilometres respectively. Both municipalities are located in the historic centre of Havana and exhibit the highest population density, that is, 43,107 inhabitants per square kilometre and 21,103 inhabitants per square kilometre respectively. The least densely populated municipality is Guanabacoa with 834 inhabitants per square kilometre.

The spectrum of economic activities carried out in Havana's municipalities is wide and largely diversified. With the exception of extractive industry, a representative sample of Cuba's main economic productions can be found in Havana. Thus, the city's economic activities encompass tourism, sugar cane production, cigars and pharmaceutical products amongst many others. As outlined in chapter 6, tourism is a vital economic sector in coastal municipalities, while it is absent in the economic structure of municipalities located in southern areas. Similarly, light and heavy industries are located around the Bay in the southern municipalities of Regla, Cotorro, Boyeros and Cerro, while they are virtually absent in the northern neighbourhoods.

Table 8.1 The main physical and economic characteristics of Havana's municipalities

Municipality	Population	Area*	Density**	Main economic activities and productions
Playa	181,843	36.2	5,023	Tourism, pharmaceutical, paper, diary products
Plaza de la Revolución	172,045	11.8	14,580	Tourism, beer, mechanics, University, hospitals, State administration, shoes, tobacco
Centro Habana	150,877	3.5	43,107	Tourism, State administration, tobacco
Habana Vieja	94,966	4.5	21,103	Tourism, Power industry, fishing, meat, port, tobacco
Regla	42,390	9.2	4,607	Petrol refinery, Power industry, fertilizers, fishing, wheat mill, comestible oils
Habana del Este	185,468	144.9	1,279	Tourism, shoes, fridges, chemicals
Guanabacoa	106,374	127.4	834	Diary products, gas, metallurgic, warehouses
San Miguel del Padrón	154,323	25.7	6,004	Plastics, mechanics, metallurgic, pharmaceutical
Diez de Octubre	229,626	12.1	18,977	Distillery, meat, mechanics, hospitals
Cerro	135,261	10.3	13,132	Metallurgic, food processing, beauty products, chemicals, comestible oils, pharmaceutical, sport, hospitals
Marianao	138,107	21.3	6,483	Sugar, tourism, paper, electronics, University
La Lisa	127,669	37.5	3,404	Pharmaceutical and bio-technology, mechanics, glass, food processing
Boyeros	188,286	134.2	1,403	Airport, oxygen, paper, concrete, plastic, perfumes, ice-cream, hospitals, textile
Arroyo Naranjo	199,720	83.1	2,403	Diary products, textiles, rum, hospitals
Cotorro	74,580	65.7	1,135	Metallurgic, diary products, paper, textile, beer, pharmaceutical
Total	2,181,535	727.4	3000	

*   Square kilometres
** Inhabitants per square kilometre

(*Source*: Calculated from Asamblea Municipal Ciudad de la Habana, 1988; ONE, 2002; INRH, 1997a)

The polarization of economic activities in Havana is reflected in environmental contrasts between the northern and southern urban areas. In this context, two scholars have provided an in-depth and comprehensive analysis of the socio-environmental differentiation amongst Havana's municipalities that can be used to describe Havana's current (re)dualization process. González Rego (2000) has employed sets of indicators recorded by Havana's municipalities by the mid-1990s in order to portray the city's social and environmental spatial-territorial differences. In his methodology González Rego (2000) looks at three main 'statuses' of Havana's municipalities, that is, socio-demographic status, socio-residential status and socio-laboural status.

The first status is defined by a set of indicators that includes: migration rate, ageing index, racial composition, educational level, social security services, mortality rate, infant mortality rate, abortion numbers, birth rate, divorce numbers, teenage pregnancy rate and sexually transmitted disease. The second set of indicators that describe the socio-residential status considers residential heterogeneity, population density, housing conditions, *ciudadelas* (estates in extremely poor living condition) and overcrowding. Lastly, the third status entailed the study of employment level, employment characteristics and the self-employed.

The findings of González Rego (2000) are summarized in Table 8.2 which categorises the social municipalities' risk level for each 'status' domain. Thus, it can be seen that the municipalities of Centro Habana, Habana Vieja, Arroyo Naranjo, Cotorro, Cerro and Regla are characterised by a moderate or high social risk in every status. In contrast, the municipalities of Playa, Plaza de la Revolución and Habana del Este are more often associated with low or very low social risk levels. González Rego's (2000) conclusions can be embraced here to cast light on the crystallized socio-economic conditions between southern and northern areas that underlie Havana's current spatial and social duality.

A second influential author writing on environmental differences in Havana is Pérez Rodriguez (1995). In her study, she places a strong emphasis on socio-environmental criteria to differentiate Havana's areas. Indeed, she divides Havana into several areas according to the city's various phases of urbanization, establishing a correlation between the latter and local environmental problems. Her subdivision includes 143 areas grouped into 5 sets that range from Old Havana as the original colonial city centre to urbanization projects in East Havana carried out by the revolutionary government in recent years. For each area she examines a set of environmental variables that include flooding, ground water contamination, water provision, housing, the condition of urban infrastructure, air pollution and lack of green areas.

Pérez Rodriguez (1995) concludes that areas urbanized before the revolution between the 1930s and 1950s display better environmental features because of newer and better functioning urban infrastructures coupled with better housing conditions. These areas include Vedado, Miramar and parts of East Havana and can be found along the coastal west-east urban development axis that came to a halt after the revolution (as described in chapter 6). The remaining areas are situated around the south of the Bay. They display less favourable socio-environmental living conditions linked mostly to poor housing conditions and obsolete and malfunctioning urban infrastructures whose upgrade has been neglected by the revolutionary government for four decades.

Table 8.2 Social and environmental differentiation amongst Havana's municipalities

Level of social risk according to socio-demographic status*	Municipality
VHR	Marianao, Arroyo Naranjo, Centro Habana
HR	Habana Vieja,
MR	La Lisa, Cotorro, San Miguel del Padrón, Guanabacoa, Boyeros, Playa, Habana del Este
LR	Cerro, Diez de Octubre
VLR	Regla, Plaza de la Revolución

Level of social risk according to socio-residential status	
VHR	Habana Vieja, Centro Habana, Diez de Octubre, Cerro
HR	San Miguel del Padrón, Arroyo Naranjo, Marianao, Plaza de la Revolución, Guanabacoa, La lisa, Regla
MR	Playa, Cotorro
LR	Boyeros
VLR	Habana del Este

Level of social risk according to socio-occupational status	
VHR	Cotorro, Diez de Octubre, Regla
HR	Arroyo Naranjo, Marianao, San Miguel del Padrón, Habana Vieja, Centro Habana
MR	Guanabacoa
LR	Playa, Habana del Este, Boyeros
VLR	La Lisa, Cerro, Plaza de la Revolución

(*Source*: After Gonzalez-Rego, 2000)

* VHR   = Very High Risk
  HR   = High Risk
  MR   = Moderate Risk
  LR   = Low Risk
  VLR = Very Low Risk

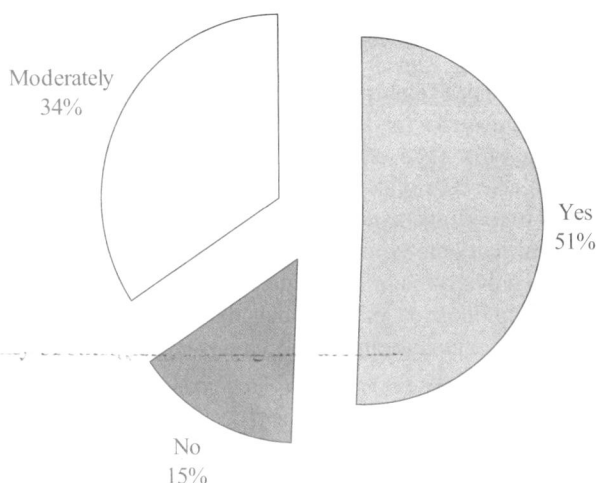

Figure 9.10 Residents' views as to whether they would like to see more
tourism development in their area (percentage)

Table 9.5 Residents' views as to whether they would like to see more **tourism**
development in their area

Question	Frequencies (n)				
	Old Havana	Montebarreto	East Havana	Vedado	Total
Yes	24	9	27	18	78
No	3	13	5	2	23
Moderately	11	18	6	18	53

If the preceding perceptions concerning the overall intensity of tourism impact
and changes brought by tourism are analyzed together, they highlight that tourism
has become an important vector of change in each of the tourist poles which is
engendering a positive economic impact at the local level. The majority of residents
think that the impact of tourism has been positive and would like to see more tourism
in their area with the exception of residents of Montebarreto. The latter have shown
some reservations concerning future increases. Indeed, it could be argued that the
business-oriented and high-expenditure-based tourism being promoted in Playa
municipality is certainly not giving residents of Montebarreto an equitable share
in the environmental and economic gains that stem from tourism. Furthermore,
local shops and *botegas* (corner grocery stores) are increasingly being replaced by
expensive tourism-oriented shops and *diplotiendas*. The latter are dollar-based shops

which serve the diplomats of an increasing number of embassies that are relocating from Vedado to this area because of the new centrality being promoted in this area of the city.

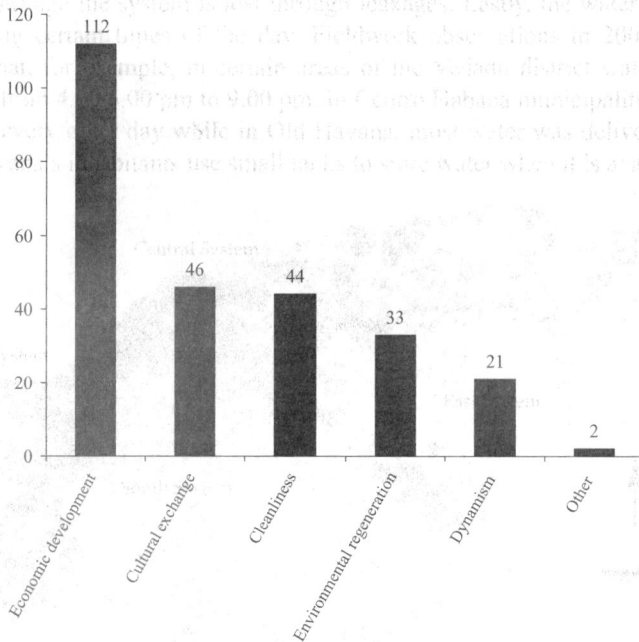

Figure 9.11 Residents' views as to why they would like to see more tourism development in their area

Perceptions Concerning the Relationship between Tourists and Residents

The analysis of the tourist-resident relationship and the subsequent residents' 'irritation' level caused by tourist activities (see Doxey's 'irrindex', 1975, for a description) has been carried out through (i) a question asking residents to rank their level of happiness with regard to tourism development in their area, and (ii) a series of statements against which residents' attitudes were measured.

Interviewees were asked to weight their level of satisfaction with regard to current tourist development in their area on a scale from 0 to 10, where 0 indicated a complete lack of satisfaction and 10 maximum satisfaction. The findings are summarized in Figure 9.12 which shows how 52 per cent of respondents expressed a level of satisfaction between 6 and 10 while the majority of respondents ranked their level of satisfaction at 5. The response at the pole level would seem to confirm the results at the city-aggregate level and to indicate that those residents who are mostly dissatisfied about the development of tourism can be found in Montebarreto, while the most satisfied are concentrated in Vedado.

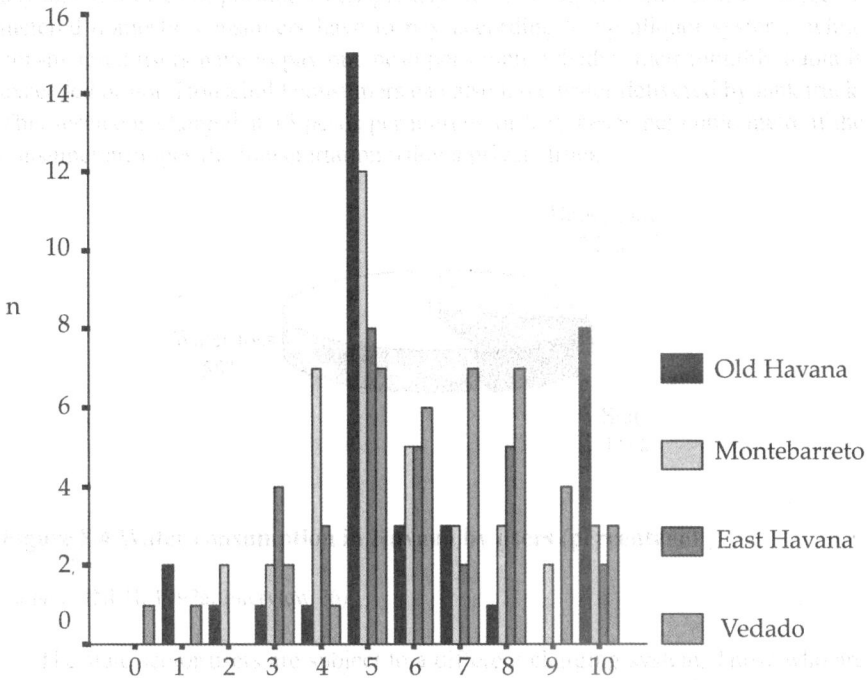

Figure 9.12 Tourist poles residents' level of satisfaction concerning tourism development in their area (ranked from 0 to 10 where 0 = no satisfaction and 10 = maximum satisfaction)

Similar results are confirmed by residents' response to the statement that 'Local residents welcome the presence of tourists in this area'. Table 9.6 confirms that one third of respondents are in favour of tourists and agree or strongly agree with the statement. However, residents of Vedado have more neutral views on this issue or do not agree with the claim.[14] Such findings are interesting if compared with the preceding results summarised in Figure 9.12. Indeed, it could be argued that the residents of Vedado are complacent with the level of tourism development in their area but are not too enthusiastic about tourists. This leads to the paradoxical conclusion that residents welcome 'tourism without tourists'. In other words, residents are satisfied with the economic and physical regeneration of their area brought by tourism but feel the presence of tourists is less than positive.

Tourism is often criticised for generating the overcrowding of tourist destinations. This in turn creates a host-visitor conflict in terms of resource use and space sharing. As regards the overcrowding impact of tourism, the survey findings do not allow

---

14 See footnote 3.

unequivocal conclusions to be reached, with the exception of Old Havana.[15] More specifically, in Montebarreto, East Havana and Vedado the negative and positive residents' attitudes toward the statement that tourism is responsible for overcrowding are approximately balanced. However, over half of respondents of Old Havana believe that tourists are contributing to local congestion problems. As noted earlier, this result can easily be understood because in old colonial centres and heritage areas tourists and residents are forced to share a limited physical space, generating overcrowding effects.

Lastly, the relationship between tourists and residents is also commonly influenced by the struggle for the use of existing facilities such as shops and other retailing activities. The survey suggests that tourism is not considered to make shopping more unpleasant in Havana's tourist areas.[16] The only exceptions are represented by Montebarreto and Old Havana, where over one third of respondents believe that their shopping opportunities have deteriorated because of tourists. As indicated earlier, the shopping problem in Montebarreto can be linked to the excessive promotion of tourism-oriented shops rather than to the actual shopping activity. However, in Old Havana the high concentration of commercial and tourism facilities in a limited space may create host-tourist frictions when it comes to shopping.

Perceptions Concerning Tourism's Displacement of, and Interference with, Residents' Activities

The displacement effect of tourism has been widely discussed in the literature (Shaw and Williams, 1994; Hultkrantz, 1998; Gilderbloom, 1998). The responses of Havana city dwellers indicate that over two thirds of respondents perceived the tourism industry as displacing their daily activities and meeting places, as shown in Table 9.7. Answers also suggest that primarily hotels (n = 78), bars and restaurants (n = 70) and, to a lesser extent, squares and public spaces (hotel 5) are perceived to have become inaccessible to residents because of tourism. The analysis at the tourism pole level confirms that the displacement effect is perceived with almost the same degree of intensity in each pole. Old Havana, however, is the city area where residents showed the most concern. This particular impact of tourism in Old Havana will be considered in greater depth later on in the case study of the impacts of tourism on Havana's colonial district.

---

15 See footnote 3.
16 See footnote 3.

Table 9.6 Residents' responses to statements concerning the relationship between tourists and residents expressed by percentage

The relationship between tourists and residents	Percentage of respondents in each tourism pole stating a given level of agreement																			
	Old Havana					Montebarreto					East Havana					Vedado				
	SA	A	N	D	SD	SA	A	N	D	SD	SA	A	N	D	SD	SA	A	N	D	SD
1 Local residents welcome the presence of tourists in this area	33	36	22	6	3	14	39	19	8	19	46	43	6	3	3	19	38	43	-	-
2 The presence of tourists does make shopping more unpleasant	8	24	11	54	3	5	30	11	32	22	8	14	38	32	8	0	16	27	35	22
3 The presence of tourists is not responsible for overcrowding this area	20	20	9	49	3	8	22	32	14	24	29	24	21	24	3	18	31	3	36	10

Key: SA = Strongly Agree
A = Agree
N = Neutral
D = Disagree
SD = Strongly Disagree

Table 9.7 Residents' answers to questions concerning tourism's displacement of, and interference with, residents' activities

Displacement of, and interference with, residents' activities	Percentage							
	Old Havana		Montebarreto		East Havana		Vedado	
	Yes	No	Yes	No	Yes	No	Yes	No
1 Is there any place where you used to go which has been converted into tourist infrastructure?	84	16	67	33	68	32	72	28

A second negative impact which has been associated with tourism development strategies is the interference of tourists with residents' activities. In Havana, in spite of the preceding belief, it was found that the tourists' interference with residents' activities is still considered low. Indeed, less than one quarter of respondents think that tourists interfere with their daily activities. The responses at the city and individual tourist pole level show similar percentages, indicating no major differences between poles.[17] If this result is examined in conjunction with the findings of the question on the displacement effect of tourism, the analysis would seem to suggest that there is a low level of interference between tourists and residents because different spaces and circuits are being created for the activities of each group of users. This means that more hotels, bars and restaurants are being aimed towards tourism consumption and fewer towards local residents' needs.

Perceptions Concerning the Danger of Investments in Facilities and Services which Primarily Serve Tourists

The danger of investments biased towards primarily meeting tourists' needs is the last impact which is often ascribed to tourism promotion policies and will be examined here. Residents' attitudes relating to this danger were measured against a series of statements revolving around this issue. The responses are summarized in Table 9.8 and indicate that over 80 per cent of respondents maintained that local residents are not benefiting from the newly built tourism facilities in their area or have a neutral view. This clearly suggests a perceived bias in infrastructural investments towards tourism.

---

17 See footnote 3.

Table 9.8 Residents' responses to statements concerning the danger of investments in facilities and services which primarily serve tourists and the extent of public participation in planning expressed by percentage

The danger of investments in facilities and services which serve primarily tourists and the extent of public participation in planning	Percentage of respondents in each tourism pole stating a given level of agreement																			
	Old Havana					Montebarreto					East Havana					Vedado				
	SA	A	N	D	SD	SA	A	N	D	SD	SA	A	N	D	SD	SA	A	N	D	SD
1 Local residents are benefiting from the new tourism facilities built in this area	15	10	31	28	15	5	11	27	27	30	5	8	46	27	14	3	11	30	35	22
2 Local residents have better shopping opportunities because of tourism	3	6	32	19	44	3	3	22	11	35	-	11	16	35	19	-	-	5	24	39
3 Tourism has brought availability of more produces which are available in pesos	6	17	17	40	20	3	11	31	17	39	14	14	23	14	34	-	-	9	57	34
4 Tourism has contributed to the increase of prices	33	41	11	10	5	53	17	21	9	-	66	24	10	-	-	34	31	13	8	14
5 Local residents are always audited directly or via delegates about tourist development plans	13	18	18	28	23	14	5	8	32	41	11	8	11	24	47	3	3	10	31	56

Key: SA = Strongly Agree
A = Agree
N = Neutral
D = Disagree
SD = Strongly Disagree

Along similar lines, there is generally agreement among respondents within all the poles that residents do not have better shopping opportunities because of tourism.[18] Although new shops and small supermarkets offering a wider range of produce have opened in Havana in the Special Period, these are aimed to increase hard currency revenues. As noted in chapter 3, after 1994 local production began to be channelled to the TRDs, which constitute the local US dollar market where goods can be bought in US dollars. In 2004, the circulation of the US dollar was halted, nonetheless, this has led to a general increase in prices, even of basic needs items, which has also been highlighted by residents' responses.

In this respect, the vast majority of respondents do not think that tourism has resulted in the availability of more produce available in pesos.[19] For example, in Vedado, no responding resident believes that the economic benefits of tourism have been translated into greater availability of produce in pesos. These polarized views may well be due to many of the shops that opened in the Special Period being geared towards tourists rather than residents. On several occasions, interviewees in Vedado complained that the local *bodegas* are often empty or closing down. As a result, residents are forced to buy food at local supermarkets or farmers' markets where prices are ten times higher than state shops.

The findings relating to the four statements above would seem to suggest that, once again, the newly built tourism-oriented infrastructures are destined for exclusive tourism consumption only while local residents are not benefiting from them. Moreover, although residents perceive tourism as a driver of local economic development in their area, they also admit that tourism is contributing little to meeting residents' shopping needs. It can be argued that tourism, and more generally the external sector, has triggered the availability of a wider variety of goods in Havana's main shopping malls such as the Cohiba (or Galeria Paseo) and Carlos III centres. On the other hand, such shopping centres are dollar-operated and are accessible more to dollars earners than to everyone.

The concerns about the risk in investment bias toward tourism have also emerged from the answers to the question which asked residents to indicate what services or infrastructures they would like to see in their area to make the most of their free time. This question was aimed at assessing how local urban settings could be improved to meet inhabitants' and tourist recreational needs alike avoiding skewed promotion policies. The choice of answers provided to respond to the question included a broad range of leisure-oriented infrastructures ranging from personal care to cultural facilities. The order in which services and facilities were listed by residents is reported in Figure 9.13. The results show that gymnasia, restaurants and dance saloons are among the most recurrent items in the answers.

If these responses are examined in conjunction with previous findings, they would seem to validate the claim voiced by some Havana-based planners (Interview 14) that many new recreational and leisure infrastructures are being built within

18 See footnote 3.
19 See footnote 3.

hotels and tourism-oriented facilities. Hence, they are not serving the population at large. Havana's inhabitants used to have unlimited access to such facilities until the late 1980s when the Special Period brought about financial austerity and a division of international and domestic tourism circuits. This division is *de facto* prejudicing Havana residents' access to such facilities and undermining their right to leisure and entertainment. This issue will be re-examined in more detail in the next chapter.

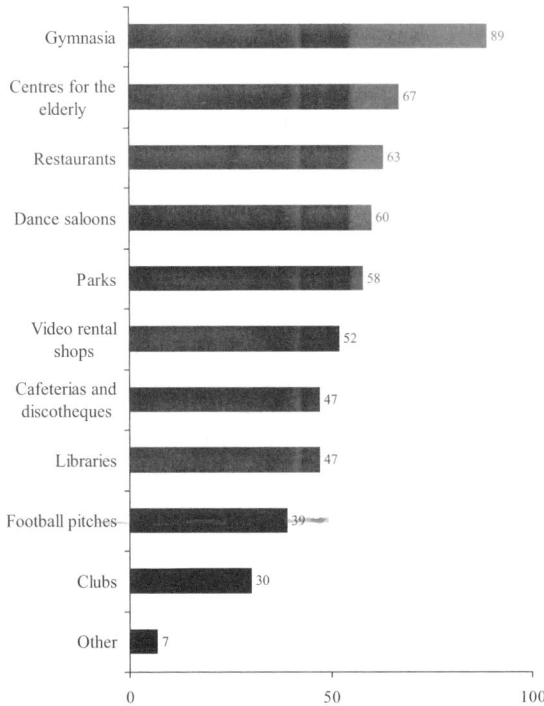

Figure 9.13 Services and infrastructures that respondents would like to see in their area to make the most of their free time

Perceptions Concerning Public Participation in Tourism Planning

The last important objective of the survey was to assess the extent to which the input from residents' and the community feeds through the tourism planning and decision-making processes. This is a crucial element in avoiding the occurrence of the negative impacts of tourism reviewed above and in improving ill-conceived development plans. The city-level survey results indicate that over two thirds of respondents did not agree with the statement 'Local residents are always audited directly or via delegates about tourist development plans'. Just over 10 per cent of respondents had neutral views, while the remaining one tenth agreed with the statement. At the pole level,[20] the survey response shows that Vedado is the city area where more interviewees did not agree, while residents of Old Havana mostly perceived that they were consulted and informed with regards to tourism development plans in their area.

According to survey findings it can be concluded that residents' involvement in urban tourism management is still far from satisfactory despite the Cuban leadership's rhetorical claims stating otherwise. Participatory planning in tourism in Havana is still imperfect due to weak participation by an important stakeholder of the tourism industry, namely, local residents (Colantonio, 2004). More 'inclusiveness' in planning would be instrumental in acknowledging that Havana's dwellers have become *de facto* an important 'stakeholder' of the tourism industry, whether they want to be or not.

However, in order to understand the rationale and the modalities of public participation in planning in socialist models of governance it is important to look at the role played by institutions in such societies. In the context of communist countries, it is argued that the institutional framework is often designed to subordinate state and civil society to the communist party. In Cuba, for example, Article 5 of the Constitution states that the official party is '[the] organised vanguard of society'. Thus, Meurs (1992: 231), reviewing Marx's writings, notes that:

> within Marxist theory, popular control has usually been seen as involving some kind of hierarchical structure. Direct participation through community and/or workplace organisations is expected to feed into a pyramid of representative institutions at the level of regional and national government.

Within institutions, elected or non-elected community representatives, or key informers such as medics, teachers and community leaders, play a crucial representative role in representing the local communities' main needs. It is clear, therefore, that public participation in communist models of governance can hardly be assessed according to the paradigm devised for liberal democracies. Rather, it requires an in-depth analysis of the representational role of mass and grassroots organizations.

The Impacts of Tourism: The Case Study of Old Havana

The historic centre of Havana, or *Habana Vieja*, despite covering only a small part of the city's total area, houses the largest collection of preserved Spanish colonial buildings in the world and was declared a World Heritage Site by UNESCO in 1982. Since 1990, Old Havana has played a key role in promotional campaigns for tourism in Cuba and has experienced a significant increase of tourists visits.[21] As a result,

---

20 See footnote 3.

21 It is estimated that over 80 per cent of tourists who travel to Havana visit Old Havana (Interview 20).

several impacts of tourism, both positive and negative, have begun to unfold during the last decade. This section provides an overview of the main effects of tourism in the old colonial centre. The latter has been chosen as a case study because it clearly epitomizes several quandaries that the planners of Havana are currently facing in terms of minimising the negative impacts of tourism while maximising the economic revenues of the sector.

For more than four decades the *Oficina del Historiador* (Office of the City Historian), has contributed to the refurbishment of decaying buildings, the rehabilitation of the housing stock and to providing solutions to overcrowding problems in Old Havana. In 1995, the Office of the City Historian designed and began to implement the *Master Plan for Old Havana's Regeneration* with a strong focus on tourist development. As preparation for the Master Plan, the Council of State created *Habaguanex* within the *Oficina*: a unique public entity which has total economic independence from the government budget. It manages dollar-operated facilities without remitting profits to the main legislative body and negotiates historic preservation and new construction projects directly with foreign investors and NGOs (Scarpaci, 2000b). The use of foreign financial resources by *Habaguanex* and the strong emphasis on tourist redevelopment in Old Havana is creating tensions amongst several actors and investors' interests in the Municipality.

Firstly, politicians and state institutions insist on the promotion of 'social tourism'. This is tourism in line with the achievement of objectives stemming from the socialist paradigm, such as the equal redistribution of economic benefits and the avoidance of profiteering. Secondly, foreign investors are concerned about the financial returns on their investments especially in the remodelling of old buildings into hotels and the provision of other tourist services and facilities. Thirdly, tourists are mainly interested in nightlife and other recreational activities. They perceive the historic centre as a place of consumption, relaxation and leisure. Lastly, local residents are concerned about the influence of tourism in displacing other activities.

Gilderboolm (1998) notes that many of Old Havana's best houses have been converted into tourist hotels and offices. Much of the local population has therefore been relocated to other areas within the historic centre, because they were considered squatters. Scarpaci *et al.* (2002) argue that at least 200 residents have been displaced and relocated in East Havana, across the bay. According to Scarpaci (2000b), planners insist that only half of the roughly 85,000 residents occupying Old Havana should reside there. This is because of the very poor housing stock and overcrowding conditions that characterize the area.

However, the revitalisation process and the tourism re-development of the Special Period have brought significant environmental health benefits for local residents. For example, in 2000, *Aguas Habana* was set up as a joint venture between 'Aqueduct of Havana', the company responsible for water provision and system maintenance in Havana, and 'Aguas de Barcelona', a Catalan firm. The new joint venture represents a novelty in the Cuban urban services provision sector, which has traditionally been run entirely by Cuban governmental authorities. Although the utility company began to adopt self-financing criteria and to charge for water provision, *Aguas Habana* is believed to have greatly improved Old Havana' water system to the extent that by the end of 2005 the delivery of water to residents by trunk will be unnecessary (Interview 12).

Further, the regeneration of the area by the *Oficina* has also meant an integral upgrade of the sewerage and drainage systems in Havana's old district. The *Plan Maestro* is currently eliminating local residents' illegal connections to such systems which have led to the flooding of sewerage waste from gully-holes. This has significantly reduced the risk of airborne contagious diseases in the area (Interview 26).

The review of these impacts highlights how future challenges for Old Havana, and more generally for Havana and Cuba as a whole, revolve around finding a balance between historic and political preservation, tourism and economic restructuring. Further, as Scarpaci (2000b: 737) notes '[S]tate restructuring is evident on every corner [of Old Havana]'. Indeed, *Habaguanex*'s primary responsibilities to generate dollars and seek foreign capital within Cuba's current state structures embody the 'third way' notion introduced in chapter 1. This peculiar Cuban mix of market-based and centrally planned forms of economic and political governance offers great potential to minimize displacement effects from dominant foreign interests and to avoid the economic and social exclusion that may stem from processes of urban revitalization. However, its outcomes remain to be seen.

Conclusions

This chapter has reported the findings of a questionnaire survey designed to assess the perceptions of the inhabitants of Havana's various tourist poles concerning the impacts of tourism in their neighbourhood. Taken as a complete entity, the findings of the questionnaires confirm the results of chapter 7 and 8 on the multidimensional impacts of tourism. Nonetheless, important specifications can still be made for each individual impact.

The findings have indicated that tourism is perceived by hosts as generating a positive economic impact that translates into more employment and the improvement of local living standards. Further, an increasing number of Havana's residents would like to work in tourism not only for economic reasons but also to have more opportunities to meet tourists and have a closer encounter with the outside world. Nonetheless, broadly speaking, the social impact of tourism is believed to be negative, mainly because of the widespread re-emergence of prostitution and crime across Havana. By contrast, the cultural impact of tourism would seem positive only in those areas where tourism segments other than 'sun and beaches' have been promoted.

The questionnaire provided little evidence to suggest any perceived serious negative environmental impact of tourism, apart from litter and poor cleanliness which could be ascribed to deficient waste management infrastructure in Havana. In most respects, it could be argued that tourism is perceived as a catalyst for environmental regeneration in Old Havana and Vedado. However, this regeneration process is perceived, in turn, to have widened environmental differences amongst the various areas of the city. Lastly, the questionnaire has underlined a perceived lack of public participation in tourism planning in Havana. This problem will be addressed in more detail in the next chapter, which focuses on the changes in planning and governance practices brought about by the Special Period in Havana, and their relation to tourism.

residents' perception on the impacts of tourism on Havana. This has never been done before in Havana and constitutes a fundamental objective of this book, highlighting the importance of public participation in the urban governance and planning processes in relation to tourism development.

PART III
Tourism and Governance in Havana:
Concluding Perspectives

Chapter 10

Tourism Planning and Governance in Havana during the Special Period

Introduction

Part II of the book has examined the plethora of impacts that tourism has had on Havana after 1990. This Part focuses on the policy implications of such impacts in the Special Period with a special emphasis on changes in decision-making and planning practices that have been determined *de facto* by pressures and activities carried out by local, national and foreign forces in tourism and the external sector. Broadly speaking, the decentralization of state institutions and economic reforms promoted in the early 1990s are often said to indicate a shift in Cuban politics towards more democratic practices, the fostering of public participation and more interactive governance. On the one hand, there are claims that the institutional redesign and economic reforms carried out in the 1990s by the government are fostering real public involvement in governance at the national and municipal levels. On the other hand, it is argued that the reforms of the 1990s are simply recasting the socialist rhetoric of centralized governance in new clothes.

The aims of this chapter are twofold. The first is to review how fundamental principles and practices underpinning Cuban socialist planning mechanisms have changed in the Special Period and to assess how strategies formulated for more locality-based and decentralized planning (not limited to the tourist sector) have translated into concrete realities. The second is to argue that the current institutional strengthening process embarked upon by the Cuban leadership to yield more 'inclusiveness' in the decision-making process, has been largely flawed. This ineffectiveness is due to a lack of political will for a radical shift that is able to blend together the tenets of socialist doctrine with market economy individualism.

The chapter is composed of three sections. The first reviews the historic development and the implementation of physical development planning in Cuba. Particular attention will be dedicated to the changes in the main planning practices and mechanisms that occurred in the Special Period and the main pitfalls associated with them. In this context, the aim of the section is to highlight that old planning practices are becoming increasingly incompatible with new tourism project procedures and are in general need of thorough modernising. The second part of the chapter endeavours to delineate the actors and stakeholders involved in Havana's city governance and highlights the importance of tourism planning for the city's overarching future urban development. The last section will draw some conclusions concerning tourism planning and city governance in Havana during the Special Period.

Planning in the Special Period

Planning has been a milestone of Cuban socialism and it has been taken seriously by the Cuban Leadership since the triumph of the revolution. In 1960, the Central Planning Council (*Junta Central de Planificación*, JUCEPLAN) was established to fix, orient, supervise, and coordinate the economic policies of the various state agencies (Acosta and Hardoy, 1973), and more generally to promote national and local economic development according to goals established by the Cuban Leadership. At least four different stages characterized the activity of planning after 1959. These were: (i) the 1960s thrusts toward collectivization and moral incentive; (ii) the post-1970 'institutionalization' and liberalization; (iii) the Rectification Process of 1986 and (iv) the crisis and reforms of 1990s (see Colantonio and Potter, 2003; and Font, 1997 for a review). Each phase reflected the political and economic vicissitudes that accompanied the Cuban socialist experiment since its onset. However, there is general agreement that planning and decision-making in Cuba have been centralized and characterized by a vertical and paternalistic approach.

National, local and sectoral development plans were centrally formulated by the Technical Secretariat of JUCEPLAN following directives from the government. In the early 1960s, it became apparent that national and central planning would need a broader base of regional data on natural resources, local infrastructures, community problems and human resources (Acosta and Hardoy, 1973). Thus, the government set out to organize a system of regional planning that permitted the systematic integration of economic activities and regional-physical elements that provided a territorial dimension to development.

In 1962, the National Institute of Physical Planning (*Instituto de Planificación Física*, IPF, originally created in 1955 and called the National Council of Physical Planning) was integrated into JUCEPLAN and granted greater independence and authority. Since 1994, the IPF has been appointed to the Ministry of Economy and Planning as the leading state agency in territorial planning. The Institute is responsible for accomplishing, directing and controlling the policy devised by the government concerning the use of land, the spatial organization of the socio-economic activities and the management of human settlements (IPF, 1998).

The IPF is at the top of a hierarchical system of institutional structures that incorporates Provincial Offices of Physical Planning (*Dirección Provincial de Planificación Física*, DPPFs) and Departments of Architecture and Urbanism (*Departamentos de Arquitectura y Urbanismo*, DAUs) in the 14 provinces and 169 municipal offices of the country (for diagrammatic representation refer back to Figure 5.9). These offices exercise control over construction, gathering information and statistics. Furthermore, their goal is to adjust centrally-taken decisions to meet local conditions. Both DPPFs and DAUs are technically subordinated to the IPF but functionally and administratively depend on local government. They epitomize the Cuban government's recent efforts to decentralize the decision-making process at the local level. However, informal discussions with various members of Havana's Office of Physical Planning have highlighted how such efforts have yielded mixed results (Interview 10, 18). For example, it is argued that the power of IPF municipal offices is limited to the gathering of statistical data, while the provincial offices have often had a mere consultative function.

The main instruments used by the IPF for physical planning in Cuba are summarized in Figure 10.1, which points out how each dimension of physical planning relies on the use of specific tools and mechanisms. These are schemes, plans and detailed studies which are the basis of planning; inspections and land regulations upon which the control sphere of planning relies; and Construction permits and Macro- and Micro-certificates that constitute the management dimension of planning. The review of all these instruments and tools is outside the scope of this work, and only the significance of Schemes, Plans and Macro- and Micro-certificates will be reviewed here.

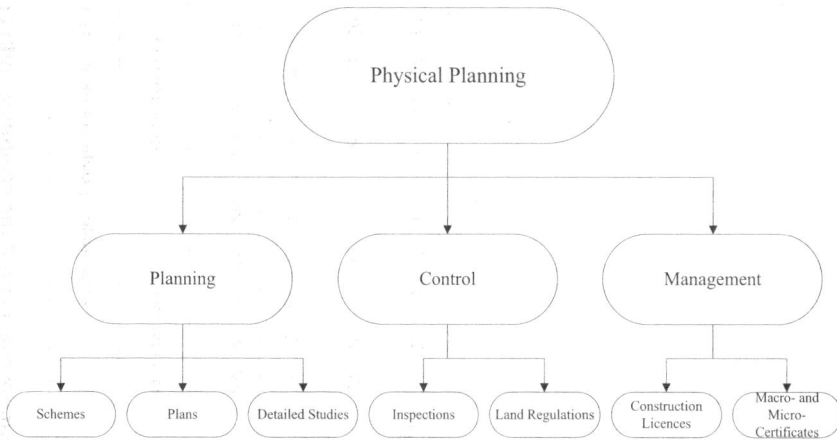

Figure 10.1 Instruments and tools of physical planning in Cuba

Schemes and Plans for territorial development exist at the national, provincial and municipal levels. Schemes can be short, medium and long term-oriented while plans are of two kinds: general or partial. The main difference between the two instruments lies in their functional applications. While schemes have a mainly strategic planning function, plans are more oriented towards achieving tactic-operational goals. Macro- and Micro-certificates are also of crucial importance within the planning process. In recent years they have both been required by CITMA to grant environmental licences and authorization to begin construction work for new or refurbished economic activities (see chapter 3).

Baroni (1991) notes that Macro- and Micro-certificates are the first legal requirements to be met by investment proposals. Indeed, national and foreign investors are required to present their investment project to IPF which, subsequently, identifies the national area most suitable to receive the new investment (Macro-localization or *Macrolocalización*). Once the Macro-localization has been agreed, the investor has to consult the Provincial Offices of Physical Planning to obtain the Micro-localization (*Microlocalización*) for the investment proposal, that is, the specific location of the project.

The Special Period has brought about three main changes in planning mechanisms and practices. These are:

- A shift from medium- and long-term plans to short-term ones.
- The Macro-localization process is increasingly being ignored by investors.
- Fines in pesos against illegal constructions and activities are ever less effective because of the increase in purchase power of dollar-earners determined by the legalization of the dollar (Interview 4).

Firstly, planners of the IPF have highlighted how the scarcity of financial resources determined by the Special Period has increased uncertainty which, in turn, impedes the establishment of medium- and long-term development plans. As a consequence, development strategies and plans are increasingly short-term in their orientation (Interview 1).

Secondly, in the late 1990s there emerged a tendency on the part of national and joint-venture investors to approach DPPFs directly with punctual investment proposals that skipped the Macro-localization process. González (2001), for example, reports how a Canadian group approached directly Havana's DFFP for a Micro-localization permit to open a bank and a shopping centre in a disused green area just off 23rd Avenue and L Street corner. The investment proposal was initially taken into consideration but subsequently rejected. Despite its negative outcome, this instance highlights that foreign investors' market-driven choices are becoming ever more incompatible with the Macro-localization plans by Cuban planners.

Lastly, fines against private illegal or unauthorised constructions are often in pesos and their effectiveness has been undermined by the legalization of the dollar. Such fines can easily be paid by newly enriched private small entrepreneurs who earn in dollars. This, in turn, is transforming fines into an ineffective controlling instrument of planning. According to a planner (Interview 4) based at Havana's DPPF the average fine for an unauthorized extension of a private house is 1,500 pesos (roughly US$ 58). While such a fine could deter a peso earner worker from ignoring construction permissions it is clearly not sufficient to dissuade dollar earners.

Planning and Tourism: Pitfalls of the Special Period

The economic reforms and the planning adjustments introduced in the Special Period have been characterized by the appearance of an environmental component

in the planning realm. Investment proposals by national and foreign investors
have to comply with procedures and requirements unknown before 1989. The
most innovative planning change is perhaps the integration of Macro- and Micro-
localization certificates with an Environmental Impact Assessment (EIA) to obtain
the Environmental Licence by CITMA.

Figure 10.2 summarizes the three main elements that are required by CITMA
to concede the Environmental Licence for the development of a tourism-oriented
project in urban and rural areas. It can be seen how the EIA, along with Macro-
and Micro- certificates, has become a pre-requisite to begin any construction work,
especially in the tourism sector as it has been deemed responsible for much of the
new wave of environmental disruption in Cuba (see Chapter 3). Indeed, the investor
has to present an EIA of the proposed development plan to the local DPPF along
with a list of measures to be adopted to mitigate or prevent negative impacts that may
stem from the project itself. Finally, CITMA reviews the documents and eventually
decides whether or not to concede the environmental licence.

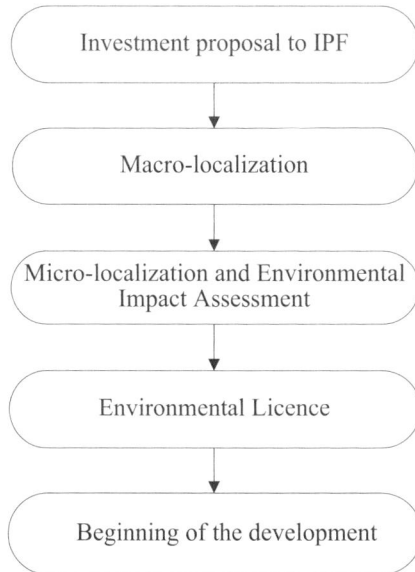

Investment proposal to IPF

↓

Macro-localization

↓

Micro-localization and Environmental
Impact Assessment

↓

Environmental Licence

↓

Beginning of the development

**Figure 10.2 Planning requirements for the implementation of a tourist
development project**

The new planning mechanism represents, at least in theory, a step forward
towards more environmental concern in Cuba. However, its translation into practice
has not been exempt from criticisms. Officials dealing with environmental issues
have highlighted that the majority of the investors are more concerned with the
technical and economic details of the construction plan (architectural style and
economic budgets of hotels for example) than with its EIA since they do not consider

it a priority. In practice, the EIA is conducted only after other expensive and time-consuming legislative requirements are met by the investor to obtain Macro- and Micro-localization permits. Thus, CITMA personnel often receive project proposals that have negative implications for the environment and have to face the dilemma of whether to grant the Environmental Licence or not.

The denial of the Environmental Licence means that the whole Micro-localization process has to be carried out anew in order to generate less negative environmental impacts. This, in turn, implies new additional costs for national firms and the risk that the foreign investor abandons the project if the proposing firm is a joint venture. CITMA is aware of the country's need for foreign investment and the economic loss that may stem from a denial of the environmental licence. Thus, in a few instances, CITMA officials have turned a blind eye to an environmentally unsound tourism development project (Interview 19). In this context, it can be argued that the Environmental Licence concession problem could be avoided if the EIA was carried out before the Micro-localization, or even before the Macro-localization process began and was subject to prior review.

A second main criticism voiced against the changes occurring to the planning process in the Special Period, especially for urban areas, concerns power redistribution in the urban decision-making process and ineffective inter-institutional consultations for tourism investments approval. While the first aspect will be examined in more detail in the next section on urban governance, here the analysis focuses on the study of the physical planning processes involved in tourism projects in urban areas.

Tourism development is the outcome of planning interactions between MINTUR, State Holdings, DPPF, and a variety of state agencies ranging from the National Institute of Hydraulic Resources to the Centre for Environmental Control and Inspection (*Centro de Inspección y Control Ambiental*, CICA) which are responsible for finalising construction details and approvals. Although Figure 10.2 has exemplified the implementation of a tourism project as a linear process, the planning process is often untidy, non-linear and involves other components flanking the concession of the Environmental Licence. There are at least two other elements which are deemed essential to tourism planning. These are: (i) the Schemes of Tourism Territorial Development (*Esquema de Ordenamiento Territorial Turismo*, EOTT) devised by the local DPPFs and (ii) the consultation process that DPPFs[1] initiate with other state agencies to grant Micro-localization certificates.

The EOTTs are framed within the wider context of a City Scheme of Territorial Development and aim at forecasting and guiding spatial transformations and land use related to tourism projects. They are updated every four years. For example, Havana's EOTT was devised in 1997 and subsequently updated in 2001. DPPFs

---

1   DPPFs in Cuba also carry out (i) Study for the Feasibility of Urban Projects (*Estudio de Factibilidad Urbanística*) and (ii) Area Studies (*Estudio de Área*) for land use concession. Both activities are of a consultative rather than strategic planning nature and require consultations with other state agencies, for example on infrastructural requirements and environmental authorizations before the final approval of development licences.

have also to consult a variety of State agencies to forecast the infrastructural needs of Micro-localization projects and obtain environmental endorsement by CITMA. During the fieldwork, an interview with a CICA specialist underlined that the consultation process lasts three days which is often not sufficient time for an accurate technical study of the new tourist project requirements (Interview, 17). As a result of this hasty inter-institutional consultation process, approvals for investment projects often do not forecast adequately the infrastructural and environmental demands that stem from new development projects.

City Governance and Participatory Planning in Havana and Cuba

The state and economic reforms promoted in Cuba during the Special Period are yielding a shift in the modalities of the country's governance and planning practice. There are two main peculiarities of Cuban Socialism that need to be taken into account to understand the rationale underpinning the 1990s reforms and their impact on the evolution of models of governance in Cuba. Firstly, the Cuban revolution was not driven by a Marxist ideological belief nor was it planned with the aim of establishing a communist regime to curb the expansion of the capitalist world. Its main design was, in reality, the expulsion of the USA from the island.

Thus, many authors point out that the Cuban revolution represented a reaction to the overwhelming dominance of the USA in the island's political and social life (Pérez-Stable 1997, Kilmister 1992). In this context, Hill (1990) argues that Cuba is, first of all part of Latin America and secondly, part of the communist world. This distinction is essential in order to understand the reason why Cuba developed its own form of communist rule and adapted Marxist principles to its reality rather than passively importing them from other models.

Secondly, the policy shift of the 1986 Rectification Process (see Colantonio and Potter, 2003) clearly unravels two main key features of revolutionary Cuba:

- the political vitality of Cuban communism never depended on the Soviet Union. Rather, Cuban politics were permeated by Fidel Castro's ideas and those of the revolutionary leadership (Centeno, 1997);
- ideology has historically played a central role in the Cuban model (Pérez-Stable, 1999). The revolution is a milestone in the cultural and social identity of the Cuban peoples. On many occasions the government has used the revolution's achievements to rally the people around the defence of *La Patria* (the homeland), to legitimize tough economic measures or the suspension of democratic liberties.

In this context, it is easy to understand how, even before embracing the Soviet model of centralized planning and governance, Castro and the Revolutionary Leadership set out to eliminate Havana's primacy and dismantle the municipal government institutions that the U.S. military had imported from the mainland.

Indeed, after 1959, Castro abolished Havana's mayoral office and replaced nation-wide the U.S.-imposed model of the city mayor's office with national, provincial and municipal-level planning councils. In Scarpaci's (2002: 175) words:

> Local government in Castro's Cuba became a potpourri of committees, organisations and commissions whose duties overlapped at the local, provincial and sometimes even the national level.

Two key aspects of local government and administration in revolutionary Cuba were: the establishment in 1966 of Local Power (*Poder Local*), and the enactment of the 1976 Constitution that led to the institutionalization of People's Power (*Poder Popular*) in 1977. *Poder Local* represented the first attempt to decentralise State institutions at local level within a Marxist-Leninist framework. *Poder Local*'s aim was to strengthen the role of mass organization and it was made up of an executive committee, a president, two secretaries, and ten delegates who were elected by community meetings of the population. There is no general agreement on the results achieved by this decentralization attempt in terms of broadening community inputs into the decision-making process. Scarpaci (2002: 177) notes that the Cuban Communist Party chose the president of each *Poder Local*. This set of political institutions:

> could be seen [instead] as eroding the access points for popular inputs into the democratic process and therefore would constitute implementation of the second reverse wave of authoritarianism.

The 1976 Constitution was enforced within the context of the post-1975 institutionalization process. It served to consolidate a new legal structure and the establishment of trade unions and to legislate other societal norms of conduct such as a family code. The Constitution was linked to the formation of a system of Cuban local government structure, the People's Power. Greenwood and Lambie (1999) argue that the People's Power system was designed as a new organ of popular participation to balance the centralized planning system with the revolution's social and participative ethics. *Poder Popular* consists of both locally elected delegates[2] and an administrative element. It is structured on the geographical division of the national territory into fourteen provinces. The provinces are divided into 169 municipalities, and in turn, these are articulated into wards (*circunscripciones*).

---

2   Since 1976, elections are competitive at the local level. By law, there must be at least two candidates and there is no official party slate. At least half of the representatives of the national assembly are composed of delegates directly elected to municipal assemblies (Scarpaci *et al*, 2002). In practice, the candidates list is prepared by a candidates' commission consisting of the Central Organization of Cuba Trade Unions, the Federation of Cuban Women, the Committees for the Defense of the Revolution and so on, which are subject to substantial Communist Cuban Party's influence (Greenwood and Lambie, 1999).

The National Assembly is the highest level of the People's Power structure. Before 1992, the year in which the first constitution was heavily amended, representatives from each municipality were elected to the Municipal Assemblies. The Municipal Assembly then elected one representative to both the Provincial and National Assemblies amongst its members (Meurs, 1992). Since 1992, the Provincial and National Assemblies have been elected directly. Municipal Assemblies, however, must still approve candidates before they are submitted to the popular vote (Greenwood and Lambie, 1999). Although Municipal and Provincial Assemblies are required to meet twice per year, it is argued that public participation in Municipal Assemblies is substantial. Popular control over the development and administration of local development plans occurs through weekly and monthly meetings between electors and delegates. Thus, citizens can bring requests and complaints to their delegates in weekly surgeries (*despachos*). Further, every six months a *circumscription* meeting is held, where electors report their views and receive response from their delegates (Greenwood and Lambie, 1999).

Unfortunately, *Poder Popular* assemblies do not formulate development plans for their respective territories. They can only discuss and approve or suggest amendments to the decisions taken by the Provincial Planning Departments (Scarpaci *et al.*, 2002). Meurs (1992) argues that, once the plan is in place, representatives are often ineffective in meeting the daily needs of the population, since they do not have sufficient authority to actually solve problems. In practice, much of the work of municipal and provincial government is carried out by an appointed Management Council (*Consejo de Administración*), which has executive power. Assemblies must approve the membership of the *Consejo*, but otherwise have little direct control over them (Greenwood and Lambie, 1999). It is clear therefore that People Power assemblies generate a confusion between elected government and executive responsibility (Pérez-Hernandez and Prieto-Valdes 1996).

In 1992, the Popular Councils (*Consejos Populares*) were formed to give more decision-making to local communities. These councils are composed of delegates from the same neighbourhood electoral district, along with representatives from local retailing, manufacturing, and grassroots and mass organizations, such as the Cuban Federation of Women (FMC) and the Committees for the Defence of the Revolution (CDRs), as well as government offices (Scarpaci *et al*, 2002). Greenwood and Lambie (1999) argue that, although they are not integrated into the institutional framework of municipal government, the Popular Councils provide a neighbourhood-based forum for popular expression and debate. Further, they represent another means by which municipal authorities are made aware of popular local feeling.

As described in chapter 3, throughout the Special Period, the government restructured institutions and the governing mechanisms involved with economic and physical planning activity. In 1994, it carried out a bureaucratic reorganization under the terms of *Decree Law 147* of April 22. The Decree abolished several state committees and national institutes formerly belonging to the Council of Ministers and subsumed their operations under existing or new ministries. A total of seven new ministries were created, while the organizational category of 'state committee' was abolished and the number of national institutes was reduced. The newly established ministries are those of Economy and Planning; Finances and Prices; Foreign Investment and Economic Cooperation; Labour and Social Security; Metallurgy and Electronics Industry; Science, Technology, and the Environment; and Tourism.

There is no general agreement on the underlying philosophies behind these decentralizing state and government reforms. Brohman (1997) distinguishes two types of decentralization measures: administrative where the change of institutions may not involve a shift of political power; and political which entails the empowerment of new political actors in governance. Pérez-Stable (1999) argues that the 1990s decentralization measures in Cuba were merely administrative, and consequently the state and party institutions are not generating the interactions between state, market and society that could guarantee more participatory policy making procedures. The new institutions have been re-designed to manage the changes in governance towards a different form of totalitarianism that still concentrates decision-making power in the Communist Party's hands.

Similarly, Fonts (1997) points out that the new decentralizing measures exert a control mechanism, since interest groups and citizens lack the possibility of formally generating and negotiating proposals. The members of groups within civil society are given the opportunity to voice their opinions and generate proposals only at the local level. At the regional and national levels, the National Assembly constitutes a bottle-neck mechanism to filter proposals and enforce state policy measures.

In contrast to these criticisms, many Cuban authors argue that the decentralization process is reducing the centralist and paternalistic Communist state's approach to planning (Herranz-Gonzalez, 1997). Further, they allow co-ordination between popular participation and community interests (Prieto-Valdes, 1997) and secure coherence, continuity and unity between national and local objectives of governance (Vasques-Penales and Davalos-Dominguez, 1997). The process therefore is strengthening civil mechanisms of interactive governance while broadening public participation. The most evident examples of this are the Popular Councils' role in promoting the Workshop for Neighbourhood Change since 1988 (see Colantonio and Potter 2003 for a review of this) and the state's support for the implementation of such experiments in interactive governance involving state and local communities in urban areas.

Tourism Planning in Havana: Peculiarities, Risks and Opportunities

Previous sections and chapters have highlighted Havana's growing tourism function and have singled out the major impacts that tourism is generating on Havana's environments and its social fabric. The planning of the tourist sector is therefore crucial to minimize risks and create opportunities for environmental, social and economic gains associated with such impacts. Indeed, many Cuban authors and officials have already acknowledged the importance of an adequate tourism planning system for Havana (Ledo, 1999; Pérez-Fernandez and Garzia-Zamora, 1999; Lanza,

1999). Urban and tourism planning in Cuba presents at least four main peculiarities and structural elements that make planning in Cuba a unique process and difficult to fit within planning models and systems elaborated by authors and practitioners in the literature.

The first peculiarity consists of a strong and growing Cuban military presence in tourism. Gaviota is a well-established company of the armed forces that gained experience in managing recreational centres for Soviet advisors back in the 1960s (Scarpaci *et al*, 2002). Gaviota today runs nearly 8 per cent of Havana's total hotel rooms. The ownership of Gaviota increased in excess of fourfold in seven years, jumping from 203 rooms in 1996 to 946 in 2002 (OTH, 2003a). Moreover, Gaviota now operates bus tours, marinas, and a large fleet of taxis and airline flights. The end of the Cold War era and involvement in many wars in Africa, have meant shrinking funds for military operations. The Cuban army therefore has increased its presence in the tourist industry hoping to achieve a certain degree of financial independence from the government budget and the rest of the economy. The army still represents an important interest group in Cuba and its plans for tourist development may not easily be included within the urban planning process of Havana.

The second peculiarity stems from the monopolistic nature of the Cuban tourist sector where all the firms involved in the offer of tourism products have been state-owned for the last thirty years and are now operating as State holdings. Such ownership may present administrative hurdles in terms of compliance with planning procedures and control mechanisms by the tourism industries and more generally by State holdings. For example, Houck (1999) in discussing the effects of the new Environmental Law (see chapter 8) in Cuba, argues that government ownership of the totality of economic activities could pose problems for CITMA to bring state-owned enterprises into compliance with environmental requirements. On the one hand, in recent years CITMA has been empowered with tools and instruments to encourage good environmental performance and best practice by government industries. On the other, officials of CITMA are aware of the scarcity of financial resources that many firms are experiencing. They understand that closing down State economic activities will damage the national economy as a whole.

The third structural element stems from the nature and operational model of joint ventures that can, at least theoretically, pose structural problem for the planning process of tourism. As seen in chapter 3, joint venture firms act as a single company with a legal status which is different from the participating firms. Both participants put up a certain amount of capital or equity for the new company. At present, there are eight foreign firms operating in Havana which manage ten hotels through the establishment of joint venture or management contracts as listed in Table 10.1. Nuñez (1995) argues that the lack of financial resources has forced many Cuban firms to consider the use of urban land as their main contribution to the joint venture. In his view, urban land has often been used as 'simple input in the investment process' by the Cuban counterpart (Nuñez, 1995:3). However, the lack of any land market in Cuba makes it difficult for both Cuban and foreign firms to establish an appropriate valuation of Havana's land, complicating the planning process.

**Table 10.1 Hotels owned by joint ventures or under foreign management
        contracts in Havana**

Hotel	State Holding	Number of rooms	Administration
Deauville	Horizontes	144	Hotetur
Club Arenal	Horizontes	166	Blau
Parque Central	Cubanacán	279	Golden Tulip
Melía Cohiba	Cubanacán	462	Sol Melía
Melía Habana	Cubanacán	413	Sol Melía
Novotel Miramar	Gaviota	427	Accor
LTI Panorama	Gaviota	317	LTI
Habana Libre	Gran Caribe	572	Sol Melía
Presidente	Gran Caribe	158	Hoteles C
Sevilla	Gran Caribe	190	Accor
Total		3128	

(*Source*: OTH, 2003c)

Moreover, foreign firms, whilst possessing better financial resources and technical facilities, normally contribute to the joint venture in terms of the design and the construction plan of the tourist development project. It may happen, therefore, that decisions affecting the type of project to be developed are taken at considerable distances from Cuba with the proponent being unaware of the local environmental and social conditions. In Havana, for example, the construction of high-rise hotels in the 1990s, such as the Hotel Panorama LTI in Miramar, shown in Figure 10.3, has been criticised by some architects for clashing with the characteristic low-rise architecture of Havana and to a lesser extent that of Miramar. Hotels of this kind, which are not uncommon in Cuba, are built to meet the taste of many international visitors and often have glass facades. This architectural solution is not regarded as optimal since in the Caribbean there are many hours of sun per day. The glass absorbs solar heat more quickly than other materials and requires, therefore, a higher use of air conditioning systems.

The last peculiarity of the Cuban planning system is embedded in the nature of the Cuban political system which can offer the necessary continuity to achieve long term planning and management objectives. In many cities the planning process is often embroiled in urban politics. Plans for development or environmental management, therefore, may last as long as the mandate of a municipal authority, that is, four or five years. From this perspective, Havana's governmental authorities and the central government may offer with their stability a potential advantage to guarantee the long-term political support to the planning process and to achieve pre-established objectives.

Figure 10.3 Hotel Panorama in Miramar
not including Hotel Naco... and Hotel Ve...
(*Source*: Photo by Andrea Colantonio)

The current tourism development strategy that is being pursued for Havana, despite helping the city to economically and environmentally revitalize some of its districts, has not been exempt from criticisms. Tourism infrastructures currently being developed in Havana reveal how the tourism industry's efforts are skewed towards the promotion of the accommodation sector while, for example, nightlife and shopping dimensions associated with tourism are still highly neglected or located within Havana's best hotels.

Table 10.2 elucidates how out of 771 tourism-oriented facilities classified as such by Havana's Tourist Board (OTH, 2002b), there are only three discothèques and three party-venues (*salon de fiesta*). In contrast, the number of hotels has increased and the number of rooms available has tripled between 1988 and 2002, growing from 4,682 rooms to 12,002 respectively, as shown in chapter 4. Moreover, Table 10.2 shows figures for both national and international tourism. For example, the 169 *cafeterias*, 119 shops and 22 night clubs listed, are likely to include small and run-down facilities, which are used by Cubans only and are unknown to the majority of international tourists. Hence, the number of recreational and night life facilities is likely to be smaller than the one suggested by the Havana Tourism Board.

Table 10.2 Tourism facilities and infrastructures in Havana

Activity	Corporation												Total
	Cubanacán	Horizontes	Islazul	Gran Caribe	Habaguanex	Gaviota	Rumbos Oeste	Rumbos Este	Caracol	Transtur	Pertosol	OTH	
Hotels	11	13	16	11	15	4	1	1	-	-	1	-	73
Cafeterias	59	-	14	-	28	2	25	41	-	-	-	-	169
Cabaret	2	-	3	1	-	-	-	-	-	-	-	-	6
Night Centres	8	-	8	-	-	-	4	1	-	-	1	-	22
Karaoke	1	-	1	-	-	-	-	-	-	-	-	-	2
Discotheques	-	-	1	-	-	-	2	-	-	-	-	-	3
Restaurants	8	-	1	1	18	-	-	5	-	-	-	-	33
Venues for parties	1	-	1	1	-	-	-	-	-	-	-	-	3
Shops	97	-	-	-	9	11	-	-	119	-	-	-	236
Bar restaurants	-	-	-	1	4	-	-	-	-	-	-	-	5
Cafés	-	-	1	-	2	-	-	-	-	-	-	-	3
Markets	-	-	-	-	10	-	-	-	-	-	-	-	10
Shopping centres	-	-	2	-	11	-	-	1	-	-	-	-	14
Recreational parks	1	-	1	-	-	-	-	-	-	-	-	-	2
Shopping points	-	-	4	-	-	-	3	38	-	-	-	-	45
Bars	-	-	1	-	-	-	-	-	-	-	-	-	1
Snack bars	-	-	-	-	-	-	-	1	-	-	-	-	1
Tourism centres	-	-	-	-	-	2	-	2	-	-	-	-	4
Clubs	-	-	-	-	-	-	1	-	-	-	-	-	2
Thematic clubs	-	-	-	-	-	-	-	1	-	-	-	-	1
Infotur	-	-	-	-	-	-	-	-	-	-	-	9	9
Photo shops	-	-	-	-	1	-	-	-	-	-	-	-	1
Car rental points	28	-	-	-	-	13	-	-	-	85	-	-	126
Total	217	13	55	15	98	32	36	91	119	85	2	9	771

(*Source*: OTH, 2002a)

As chapter 7 has highlighted, many hotels for international tourism in Havana have built their own discothéque and piano bar inside their premises which are *de facto* precluded to Havana's residents and create urban tourism enclaves. This skewed development of recreational facilities exclusively within hotels is also linked to the criticism that tourism decision-making in Havana is currently permeated by non-integrated and insular planning. According to an official of the *Oficina del Historiador*, tourism planning in the majority of Havana's new tourist poles suffers from short-sightedness and profiteering interests by tourism State holdings (Interview 13). In his view, MINTUR holdings' investment projects are still made on an individual basis and are limited to the construction plan of each facility. Investments do not take into account the organic development of the area where such tourism infrastructures are found. Hence, investment plans lack a wider spatial, functional and cross-sectoral vision concerning the overall growth of the city area and its multifaceted dimensions.

A second criticism directed towards Havana's current tourism development strategy concerns the underdevelopment of the city's shopping facilities and the limited presence of small retailing that is deemed a vital element of the tourism industry. Indeed retailing in Havana is still based on large state shops: the TRDs which were described in chapter 3. These shops often offer a limited variety of goods and are overstaffed. In other words, they display low productivity and marginal profitability. TRDs contribute guaranteed employment to a large sector of the population, but they under-perform in term of maximising the potential revenues that could stem from the tourist sector. Old Havana is currently the only successful example of small retailing promotion. Here, officials of the *Oficina del Historiador* have correctly assessed the importance of tourism expenditures and local residents remittances which have become Cuba's second source of hard currency. The *Oficina* has encouraged small retailing in the Old Colonial city streets, ranging from family souvenir shops and hand made arts and crafts to catering, that attract hard currency from tourists and Cubans alike.

Conclusions

This chapter has underlined several key features and planning issues concerning the future development of tourism in Havana. Firstly, the Special Period has brought changes in planning mechanisms and practices in Cuba. Planning activity has slowly moved from high level national government to both the municipal and neighbourhood levels. If, on the one hand, this has allowed a more place-based planning, on the other, it has limited the negotiating power of emerging interest groups at the local level. Secondly, the current Cuban legal framework would seem to be a further element hindering public involvement in planning activity. Until local communities are able to set up their own organizations, they will lack the legal institutional identity necessary to be significant in any negotiation process.

Thirdly, there has been a pragmatic shift toward short-term planning determined by the scarcity of financial resources of the 1990s. As a result, development plans are increasingly short-sighted and often driven by economic criteria. This, in turn, leads to non-integrated and insular planning in urban areas. Fourthly, at the city level, the strategic planning of tourism ought to aim at developing more recreational and nightlife facilities outside hotels and other tourism-oriented facilities. This will help to meet the leisure needs of tourists and Havana residents alike. Lastly, tourism promotion has thus far been primarily based on the construction of new accommodation. In the future, Havana's tourism industry should increase and diversify the supply of tourism services and facilities outside the accommodation segment.

Chapter 11

Conclusions

Introduction

Tourism is now of central importance within Havana and indeed, within Cuba's urban environments and landscapes. Throughout the Special Period, tourism has played a crucial role in transforming Havana's main functions and its environmental, economic and social fabric. Chapter 6 documented how tourism has been a powerful force in shaping Havana's urban development during the 1990s, contributing to the city's socio-economic and spatial polarization. Indeed, the Cuban capital is developing along its coastline according to urban growth patterns that resemble pre-revolutionary ones. This, in turn, is triggering the emergence of economic, social and environmental dualities in Havana, as shown at various points in this book.

Chapter 7 provided evidence that tourism has generated income inequalities and growing socio-economic disparities in Cuba. It has also given rise to socio-economic changes at the household and neighbourhood levels, and re-introduced negative social phenomena such as prostitution and crime that stem from the new economic opportunities associated with tourist inflows. On the other hand, tourism has generated new employment opportunities and prompted the emergence of new interest groups and civil society activities. The economic opening up and the growth of the external sector have determined the embryonic establishment of a small private sector and has brought about new 'stakeholders' and civil society groups within Havana. This, in turn, has created new areas of concern for Havana's municipal and planning authorities, who will have to accommodate the growing variety of interests and cross-sectoral agendas of old and new actors.

The environmental impact of tourism on Havana was discussed in chapter 8. The latter chapter concluded that the effect of tourism on Havana's environment has been mixed. While in some instances tourism has indirectly prompted environmental improvement, such as the upgrade of the local water and sewerage systems, in others it has been responsible for increasing flooding problems, for example, in Havana's western districts. Nonetheless, the present study would seem to suggest that *current* levels of tourism development cannot *yet* be considered as a driver for serious urban environmental stresses in Havana or, at least, that tourism is not engendering a significantly negative impact on the city's infrastructures and urban services.

The conclusions presented on the basis of chapters 6, 7 and 8 have been corroborated by the findings of the questionnaire survey conducted concerning residents' perceptions of several aspects of tourism development in Havana. These were presented in chapter 9. The questionnaire survey underlined several planning concerns which need to be addressed by municipal authorities at the city- and the tourism pole-levels. At the city level, the responses of Havana residents have highlighted how the strategic planning of tourism ought to aim at developing more recreational and nightlife facilities outside hotels and other tourism-oriented facilities. Further, tourism promotion thus far has been primarily based on the construction of new accommodation. Hence, there is the need to increase and diversify the supply of tourism services and facilities outside the accommodation segment in order to match the increase in rooms. At the pole level, the study identified several planning issues peculiar to each of Havana's tourist areas. These will be discussed in the remainder of this section.

In Old Havana, the high concentration of newly refurbished hotels is exerting extra pressure on the city's old water and sewerage systems, creating a use conflict with local residents. Recent studies have shown that the water system loses almost 50 per cent of the water it processes because of leakages, while almost 90 per cent of its pipes have passed their designed lifespan. The sewage system that serves the central area was built between 1908 and 1915 for a population of 600,000. Today the same system is serving a population of almost 1,000,000. Further, the future planning of tourism development in Old Havana will need to take into account the displacement effect of tourism on local residents' daily activities and recreational meeting venues.

In Montebarreto the problems associated with tourism are different. CITMA's officials hinted (Interview 2, 6) that new hotel development is linked with the flooding of the 3rd Avenue area, as building work has obstructed natural underground channels that drained rain water to the sea. It is argued, however, that the local municipal authority, the Popular Council of Playa, managed to build a consensus among the various hotel chains to upgrade urban infrastructures, such as the local drainage, water and road system with great benefit for local residents. This is a clear step forward which demonstrates how revenues stemming from tourism can be re-invested locally to carry out the upgrade of major utilities, as long as the political will exists to do so.

On the other hand, Coyula (2002) argues that the development pattern of Montebarreto has been short-sighted for two main reasons. Firstly, four high-rise business and conference tourism-oriented hotels (Triton, Neptuno, Melia Havana, and Panorama) have been built parallel to the shore line, leaving pedestrians and the rest of the new buildings without a view of the sea. Secondly, development plans for this tourism complex forecast the construction of 18 buildings making up the Miramar Trade Centre with 1.9 million square feet for offices and shops, plus 750,000 square feet for parking 2000 cars. As Coyula (2002: 4) notes: 'the whole complex of more than 100 acres is dollar-oriented with no room for a badly needed mixed urban development that would include other urban functions and different levels of income and social strata.' Broadly speaking, it could be argued that the promotion of a new centrality in Montebarreto, with an emphasis on economic activities linked to the external sector and the tourist industry, risks creating a divide between residents and newcomers in terms of the provision of services and access to urban facilities.

East Havana is the pole of the city facing the most obstacles to its development. Despite good economic forecasts and expectations by municipal planners, this area is failing to fulfil its full development potential because it lacks almost all basic urban facilities. Unlike in Montebarreto, the municipal authorities have failed to persuade hotels and other tourist infrastructure developers, including State holdings and joint ventures, to share equally the financial and operational burden of building urban utilities such as sewerage, drainage, water and road systems. Further, after 11 September 2001, the few negotiations for the development of this area which were still ongoing came to a complete standstill. It could be argued therefore that the main challenge ahead for this area, and arguably for the rest of Havana, is the financing of environmental utilities.

Lastly, Vedado has historically been an important and privileged commercial, recreational and administrative centre of Havana. As outlined in chapters 8 and 9, throughout the Special Period, this neighbourhood has again become a contested space among several forces and interest groups. Many foreign investors would like to start new economic activities in the booming La Rampa district between 23rd Street and L Avenue. Tourists are attracted by the good shopping and entertainment facilities in the area. Street hustlers travel across the city in order to meet tourists along the Malecón. As a consequence, the struggle for space is negatively affecting the social life of Vedado residents, who appreciate the economic and physical regeneration brought by tourism but feel the presence of so many tourists is perhaps excessive. Thus, one of the municipal authorities' main objectives should be to decongest the area and promote new centralities in the Cuban capital. However, this process needs to avoid the social and spatial polarization which, for example, is being created in Montebarreto.

Tourism Development, Globalization and Dependency: The Cuban Approach

International tourism and the external sector are playing a crucial role in Cuba's re-insertion into the global capitalist economy and the country's economic and institutional restructuring. However, this is not happening without contradictions and tensions between the differing objectives of the forces of socialism, modernization and globalization. As outlined in Chapter 1, the main tension remains between the centripetal internal force exerted by the Cuban government on the one side and centrifugal exogenous forces driven by the global economy on the other.

The analysis of the dynamics between these diverging forces has revealed how the Cuban leadership's determination to maintain political stability under the Communist Party has so far failed to find an appropriate mix of traditional socialist governance, modern culture, which comes together with tourism, and the market place. It could be argued that the 1990s reforms appear to have been pursued by the government without a precise framework in mind. The governmental actions seem to have been dictated by the extreme severity of the crisis rather than a clear project with a long-term plan for economic and political restructuring.

The outcome of these measures was a dual economy in which the market-oriented external economic sector coexisted with the domestic sector, still under the planning system. According to Monreal (1997), the fact that the term 'economic reforms' appeared only recently in the official debate on economic policies underlies the difficulties of defining a political and ideological context within which to frame them. In other words, the government has realized the long-term non-sustainability of the present model of economic governance and has tried to redefine its aims and objectives without radically changing them.

On the other hand, the 1990s tourism-led development strategy introduced two important changes to the political economy in Cuba. Firstly, against all odds, Cuba has embarked upon an Imports-substitution policy centred on international tourism in order to avoid excessive foreign dependency and the replication of vicious circles of post-colonial polarization. Chapter 3 illustrated how the new development policy focused on the promotion of the domestic productive capacity and the creation of local linkages in order to spread the benefit of growth in social, sectoral and regional terms. However, despite the efforts to reduce the 'leakages' normally associated with outward-oriented growth, the results of the 1990s development policy remain unclear.

Secondly, both the re-establishment of the tourist industry and the scarcity of financial resources have generated a shift from medium- and long-term to short-term planning in Cuba. Indeed, the profiteering nature of the tourist industry and the economic uncertainty determined by the Special Period are increasingly impeding the establishment of long-term development plans. As a consequence, development strategies and plans have become progressively more short-term in their orientation.

Another important aspect of Cuba's re-insertion into the world economy has been the introduction of managerial-capitalist planning principles which are epitomized by the setting up of State corporations and the institutional restructuring of the external sector. Indeed, since 1992, Cuba has endorsed an aggressive campaign to attract FDI and to modernize the functioning of the external sector. These endeavours culminated in the enactment of *Law 77* of 1995, *the Foreign Investments Law* and the establishment of State holdings which now operate with foreign currency and enjoy some autonomy from the State in terms of decision making.

The nature of the new State corporations blends together elements of capitalist entrepreneurialism with centralized decision-making. Since their establishment, State holdings have formed numerous joint ventures with foreign capital, especially in the tourism sector. Nonetheless, Chapter 10 highlighted that the nature and current operational model of joint ventures in Cuba pose structural problem for the planning process and have increased Cuban firms' vulnerability to the commercial power held by foreign enterprises. Indeed, the lack of financial resources has forced many Cuban corporations to consider the use of urban land as their main contribution to the joint venture. This mechanism reduces risk-sharing in the partnership, but it has some disadvantages which reinforce core-periphery dependency in three main fashions. Firstly, it does not provide Cuban firms with guarantees against possibly unfavourable contracts due to their limited bargaining power. Secondly, it does not allow the Cuban counterpart significant control over the joint venture's finance, management and planning operations. Lastly, the agreements of cooperation often do not include the valuable transfer of knowledge, skills and technology.

Lessons for Tourism-led Development in the South

As reviewed in Chapter 3, tourism has developed as the leading economic sector of many developing peripheral regions. Nonetheless, the consequences and impacts of this difficult-to-regulate industry have been problematic (Potter *et al.,* 2004b). Indeed, there are a number of common problems that have been linked to international tourism in developing countries. These include socio-economic and spatial polarization, environmental destruction, cultural alienation, and the loss of social control and identity among host communities (Brohman, 1996). The case study of urban tourism in Havana reveals at least five main key features from which we can draw important lessons concerning the risks and opportunities of tourism-led development strategies for developing countries.

Firstly, the promotion of international tourism often symbolizes the opening up of a country to external scrutiny. In socialist states, where environmental resources have often been traded off for economic development, this process has meant greater accountability to the international community and the inclusion of environmental awareness in the development agenda. Chapter 8 argued that the economic crisis has yielded two conflicting trends in the environmental policies of Cuba. On the one hand, the need for hard currency has led the Cuban government to implement recent development projects with little or no consideration for the environment. On the other hand, the Cuban government has included the achievement of 'sustainable development' objectives in its policies, hoping to obtain international political approval and more hard currency through conservation and environmental awareness programmes funded by international donors and NGOs.

By the mid-1990s the government restructured the institutions and governing mechanisms involved with environmental management and natural resource planning in Cuba. There is no general agreement on whether the recent 'greening' of Cuba has been prompted by a shift in ideological values rather than pragmatic reasons. However, it could be argued that the environmental reforms of the 1990s were encouraged by Cuba's re-insertion into the world system and the wave of environmentalism that has become a core element of globalization and economic modernization since the 1970s.

In addition, over the last decade, there has been an increased interest in 'voluntary initiatives' and 'corporate self-regulation' as a contribution by the national and international tourist industry to the sustainability discourse. Despite the fact that these initiatives are often viewed with scepticism (see Utting, 2002 for a review), in Cuba there have been a few instances in which FDI and joint ventures have proved to be important vectors for the transfer of good environmental practices. For example, almost all joint ventures or management contracts established between Cubanacan and Sol Melía have led Cubanacan to share corporate environmental strategies and management systems devised by Sol Melía's mother branch.

Secondly, in many countries in the South, tourism enclaves have acted to reinforce longstanding neo-colonial patterns of socio-economic and spatial polarization (Brohman, 1996). Cuba has not been exempt from this phenomenon and current tourism development patterns would seem to have turned the clock back to pre-1959. Coastal and urban tourism enclaves have generated a spatial dichotomy between a privileged (tourist and elite) space along the coastline, such as Miramar and Vedado in Havana, and a less-privileged space in the interior rural and urban areas. Tourism has also re-proposed spatial disparities between areas with, and areas without, tourism resources. The main goal of national governments should be to drive the localization of foreign capital toward less advantaged areas through economic incentives and tax breaks while decongesting high-density tourist areas.

Thirdly, international tourism has important implications for the patterns of urbanization in socialist countries at two different levels. At the urban development level, tourism played a major role in Havana's urban growth. Indeed, at the beginning of the Special Period the national and foreign tourist industry sought to capitalise on Havana's world class heritage and good transport infrastructure, concentrating most of its activity in the Cuban capital. This led to the partial neglect of other tourist areas and Havana's rapid economic and urban development. As a consequence, Havana regained its primacy as the most important Cuban city despite the Cuban government's anti-urban focus.

At a fundamental level, however, tourism development has not changed the main characteristic of Cuban socialist cities. Such cities still serve mainly as functional-administrative centres with few amenities and a neglected recreational function. In this context, the present work has documented that tourism promotion in Havana was primarily based on the construction of new accommodation, with the limited promotion of shopping and nightlife facilities outside hotels and other tourism-oriented infrastructures. For this reason, Chapter 10 argued that Havana's tourism industry should increase and diversify the supply of tourism services and facilities outside the accommodation segment in the future. This will help to meet the leisure needs of tourists and Havana's residents alike.

Fourthly, a potential problem for economies in transition is the absence of tourism SMEs. Despite their lack of legitimacy in Cuba, these enterprises are deemed essential to broaden the economic and employment benefits of tourism to other sectors of the economy. The development of small and family businesses is a pre-condition, a *sine qua non*, necessary to spread the economic benefits of tourism at household level. However, in transitional economies the vacuum left by large state-run enterprise has only been filled with difficulty by SMEs in the provision of services. Small entrepreneurs have often lacked access to financial capital to start an economic business because priority has been given to the privatization of large State enterprises. Until this hindrance is eliminated, for example, by the setting up of special *ad hoc* lending programmes by international financial institutions or donors, the development of household business will be replaced by the service provision offered by large foreign corporations.

Lastly, tourism can be positive for local communities in economic, social, environmental and political terms. This benefit is likely to be proportional to the extent of the community's input into the decision-making process. Chapters 8 and 9 have illustrated how host communities are *de facto* stakeholders of the tourism industry. For this reason, institutional mechanisms to broaden popular participation should be created according to local conditions, needs and interests. These new institutional arrangements should transcend the state-versus-market dichotomy. As Brohman (1996: 61) points out:

> The problem is to find the correct mixture of market orientation and state intervention, given divergent development conditions in individual countries, and then devise a set of institutional and organisational arrangements that are compatible with this particular mixture. Neither the State nor markets are neutral institutions; both can work for good or ill. The question for tourism strategies should be under what conditions states and markets can work to serve broad development objectives and how to bring these conditions.

Brohman's remarks underline the crucial importance of mechanisms and institutions of participatory governance in achieving development goals. This is especially true in socialist states where governance systems are often designed to subordinate state and civil society to the communist leadership. As Chapter 5 has emphasized, communist parties deemed this democratic gap instrumental by to achieve the prescriptions of the communist paradigm of development. This gap has impeded broad popular participation in government and decision-making. However, international tourism has often acted as a catalyst for social change and has been able to spur demands by local residents in less democratic societies for democratization. Thus, the next section reviews the impact of international tourism, and more generally the economic opening up, on the extent of popular participation in Cuba's political and economic governance.

Popular Participation and Governance in Cuba

Since the beginning of the Special Period, three main components have sustained the Cuban regime and its model of governance. These are the high value placed on the Revolution, Castro's leadership, and popular faith in, and love of, the homeland (Leon, 1997). The Revolution was a milestone in the cultural and social identity of the Cuban people. The government has frequently appealed to the revolution and its achievements to legitimize the undertaking of tough measures for the stability of the system. In 1991, for example, a party congress was organized on the 123rd anniversary of the start of the Ten Years War of Independence from Spain (1868–1878) in order to establish a parallel between today's revolutionaries and those who fought for Cuba's independence (Pérez-Stable, 1997).

Castro's charismatic leadership has also played a crucial role in Cuba's system of governance. Castro is the uncontested leader of the regime after forty-five years of communist rule and is still the major figure responsible for the main political and economical decisions. Centeno (1997) argues that, because of his personality, it is not likely that Castro will retire from the Cuban political scene, accepting a gradual diminution of his power and an ideological shift from his values. The stability of his government has been ensured by the absence of democratic elections and the impossibility of a military coup: his brother Raul is the chief of the army and there is no rivalry between them (Hennessy, 1990). Cuban leaders have also never contradicted Castro's politics. Indeed, the Communist leadership managed to keep a long-standing pattern of governance by favouring mobility within its ranks and reconfiguring itself without major changes of politicians during the 1990s (Pérez-Stable, 1997).

Finally, their faith in, and love of, the homeland helped Cubans to face the financial problems arising from the crisis without dangerous grievances. The Cuban leadership is aware of this love and has leveraged this patriotism in order to guarantee volunteer works on several occasions. However, since 1989, appeals for new sacrifices in the name of the Revolution and the homeland have become less frequent and the government was forced to make room for a series of economic reforms, which were reviewed in chapter 3.

Nonetheless, the state and tourism-led economic reforms promoted in Cuba in the 1990s are yielding a timid shift in the modalities of the country's governance and planning practices in both rural and urban contexts. There can be little doubt that new social relationships, institutions, actors and processes are gradually emerging at national and local levels. A variety of methodologies and general models have been offered to explain the transformation underway since the mid-1980s in Cuba and its capital. Thus, institutionalists focus on the analysis of the structure of political power and the underlying causes of the decentralization process embarked on by the Cuban leadership. Others suggest that political culture may be decisive, due to Fidel Castro's charismatic leadership and the peculiarities of Cuban communism. Social theorists analyze the emerging pressure for change from below within civil society and the effects of interest groups on the fabric of Cuban society.

Chapter 7 has argued that the seeds of political change in Cuba may rest in the self-employed workers and black-market hustlers working in the market-oriented and tourism-related segments of the economy. For this reason, the Cuban Leadership cracked down on them in 1996 and at the beginning of 2003. This anti-private sector policy was more effective in smaller and medium urban tourism areas, such as Trinidad and Cienfuegos, but yielded modest result in Havana where groups and civil movements are still active with more or less covert political agendas and economic sectorial interest.

The concentration of tourism development in spatially self-contained coastal areas has allowed the Cuban Leadership to minimize or, at least, retain control over the cultural and political exchanges between international tourists and Cubans. This is especially true in inland areas where the effects of the revolution are more evident and Castro still enjoys wide popularity. However, it is in Havana that the economic and societal changes brought about by urban tourism in the Special Period are more visible than in the rest of Cuba. Havana therefore is likely to play a central role in Cuba's transition towards a new political and economic path of development in a post-Castro Cuba.

Tourism in Havana is perceived to be a profitable economic sector within which to work, not only because it offers better working conditions than state jobs, but also because it provides more opportunities to meet tourists and has a closer encounter with the outside world. This perception clearly reveals the important role that tourism could play as a catalyst for socio-political change in Cuba. However, the economic and social modernization that could stem from tourism is currently hindered by the Cuban legal framework which prevents new actors and pressure groups from setting up their own organizations. Until this framework is modified, emerging social groups will lack the legal-institutional identity necessary to be significant in any negotiation process or participatory governance system.

Avoiding excessively ideological positions, chapter 9 raised questions about the disengagement of Cuban socialism from popular participation and argued that the 1990s state and institutional restructuring process has failed to guarantee more 'inclusiveness' in decision-making. This ineffectiveness is due to a lack of political will for a radical shift which would require an overarching new 'way of doing things' based on (i) a change of mandates and the *modus operandi* of existing institutions; (ii) more transparency and sharing of information in the decision-making process; and (iii) a modification of legal and administrative frameworks to legitimize the negotiating power of new interest groups.

Although chapters 1 and 9 have underlined the danger of easy comparisons between the transitions of former socialist states, it is useful to identify possible future scenarios for Cuba's transition according to the model of governance embraced by former and continuing socialist states after 1989.

Scenarios for Cuba's Transition and Final Recommendations

During the mid-1980s, the problems associated with the communist model of governance became clear to most ruling groups within the communist world. After the Soviet Bloc began to show the first signs of its almost inevitable collapse, two different behavioural patterns can be identified among communist countries in reaction to the imminent geo-political change that would stem from the dismantling of the USSR. While in East Europe the first steps towards a market economy and democratic rule were made, in Asian communist countries the leadership allowed subtle market-oriented reforms while reaffirming a clear single-party government.

East European countries such as Poland, Hungary and Czechoslovakia began a process of economic decentralization that enabled the emergence of a second society within the authoritarian regime (Pérez-Stable, 1997). Thus, once the communist parties of these countries abdicated, the already constituted civil society made a smooth transition towards a new institutionalized model possible. In Cuba there is no such legal political opposition able to take over the country if the communist leadership were to call a democratic election or Castro should suddenly disappear from the Cuban political scene. Moreover, it is unlikely that the transition will begin from below. Although the economic reforms have produced a partial stratification of society and the emergence of distinct interest groups, they do not seem to have had the wider impact they had in the case of the East European countries.

Two further examples of East European transitions can be ruled out for Cuba. These are the stagnation of Romania and Yugoslavia's ethnic-regional war. In Romania, the severe economic crisis and the abandoning of social welfare mechanisms led to violent riots which were followed by a period of severe stagnation. As far as Cuba is concerned, the social welfare achieved by the Revolution and the partial recovery of the economy after 1993 led to the exclusion of this scenario. In Yugoslavia the disappearance of the communist party caused a sharpening of regional contrasts and ethnic conflicts that eventually resulted in civil war. This scenario can also be excluded for Cuba because of the absence of regional frictions within the State.

By contrast, Asian communist countries did not abandon the communist model of governance after the Soviet Bloc's collapse. Rather, they adapted it to the new post-Cold War international scene. Pérez-Stable (1997) contends that this has been possible because in China, Vietnam and North Korea, the communist regimes originated from genuine revolutions and were not imposed from outside. Before the collapse of their Soviet ideological progenitor, the single ruling party of these countries undertook a programme of economic liberalization and managed to retain control over everyday aspects of society.

Centeno (1997) points out that the new established Chinese model could appear attractive to Cuba. The Chinese government has managed to attract foreign investment and to create a dynamic private entrepreneurship whilst maintaining much of the public sector. The feasibility of the model was made possible by a wide agricultural sector that has provided food security to the urban population and cheap labour to compensate for the inefficient public sector. However, Cuba has a smaller agricultural system and serious problems of food provision. Thus, the Chinese model seems a difficult path to follow for Cuba.

It can be argued that a credible scenario for Cuba's transition could be the sudden disappearance of Fidel Castro from Cuba's political arena. This could be followed by a rapid regime change in which the USA government and the Cuban expatriates' lobby based in Miami might play a crucial role in filling the leadership and institutional vacuum left by Castro. The USA embargo would eventually be lifted and Cuba could again become a favourite destination for millions of Americans. As a result, the increase of tourists to Cuba would be dramatic, posing serious social and environmental threats to the island. For example, it is estimated that as many as one million private boats could visit Cuba from the USA if the embargo were to be lifted (GDIC, 2003).

Whatever happens to Cuba in the years to come, the strategic planning of future tourism development in Havana is crucial to ensure that the urban environment will not be sacrificed for short-term economic benefit and local residents' lives will not be affected negatively in environmental and social terms by the FDI and tourists influx. Havana's tourism development strategy ought not to be aimed simply at increasing tourist numbers or revenues. It is essential that municipal authorities, the industry and urban communities assess and predict what the environmental demands and social impacts on Havana's resources will be as a result of various levels, scales and types of tourism development.

Future research should focus on forecasting the pressure that sharp increases in tourism could exert on Cuba's rural and urban areas in order to pre-empt the negative outcomes of tourism-led development strategies which have characterized other Caribbean countries. Further, it is important to assess what role small-scale businesses and informal sector workers in the tourism sector can play in a Post-Castro Cuba. These small-scale private sector initiatives exert a very useful development role in helping to direct and promote the entrepreneurial drives of the local population. The growth of an indigenous management and entrepreneurial class will be crucial to continue the current government's efforts to reduce future foreign dependency and to promote a fair development for all Cubans.

Appendices

Appendices

Questionnaire Survey Concerning Local Residents' Perceptions of Tourism Activities in Havana's Tourist Poles

Q1: How long have you been living in this area (Old Havana, Montebarreto, East Havana and Vedado)?

1 ( ) Less than 1 year   4 ( ) 11-15 years
2 ( ) 1-5 years   5 ( ) 16-20 years
3 ( ) 6-10 years   6 ( ) More than 20 years

Q2: Level of education

1 ( ) None   4 ( ) Pre-University
2 ( ) Primary school   5 ( ) Higher Education
3 ( ) Secondary school   6 ( ) Postgraduate

Q3: Employment

1 ( ) Student   5 ( ) Retired
2 ( ) State employee   6 ( ) Unable to work
3 ( ) Self-employed   7 ( ) Other
4 ( ) House wife

Q4: In what sector do you work?

1 ( ) Retailing   6 ( ) Health
2 ( ) Industry   7 ( ) Tourism
3 ( ) Public Administration 8 ( ) Services
4 ( ) Construction   9 ( ) None
5 ( ) Education   10 ( ) Other_____

Q5: Is your activity in this area?

1 ( ) Yes   2 ( ) No   3 ( ) Partially

Q6: Have you got any working relationship with tourism?

1 ( ) Directly   2 ( ) Indirectly   3 ( ) None

Q7: Do you have access to remittances?

1 ( ) Yes   2 ( ) No   3 ( ) Prefer not to say

Q8: Would you like to work in tourism?

1 ( ) Yes   2 ( ) No
If yes go to Q9:

Q9: Why would you like to work in tourism?

1 ( ) Economic advantages
2 ( ) Cultural interchange
3 ( ) To meet people from abroad
4 ( ) To have a possibility to leave the country

5 ( ) Improve language skills
6 ( ) Better working conditions
7 ( ) Other_____
8 ( ) Do not know/not answering

Q10: What could you bring to tourism?

1 ( ) Work
2 ( ) Ideas/proposals
3 ( ) Culture

4 ( ) Nothing
5 ( ) Other
6 ( ) Do not know/not answering

Q11: What do you think are the benefits that tourism has brought and is bringing to this area?

1 ( ) Economic benefits
2 ( ) Generation of employment opportunities
3 ( ) Strengthening of local culture
4 ( ) Promotion of Cuban culture abroad
5 ( ) Vitality/dynamism to the area

6 ( ) Cleanliness
7 ( ) Funding/Donations
8 ( ) Nothing
9 ( ) Other_____
10 ( ) Do not know

Q12: What do you think are the main negative effects of tourism in this area?

1 ( ) Price increase
2 ( ) Weakening of local culture
3 ( ) Change of local cultural tradition
4 ( ) Interference of tourists with local residence activities
5 ( ) Traffic congestion
6 ( ) Damage to architecture
7 ( ) Difference of opportunities between nationals and tourists

8 ( ) Changes in food/diets
9 ( ) Different opportunities between Nationals and foreigners
10 ( ) Prostitution/*Jineteras* (young Cubans harassing tourists for sexual purposes)
11 ( ) Less personal security/crime
12 ( ) Increase of illegal activities
13 ( ) Nothing
14 ( ) Other
15 ( ) Do not know

Q13: Do you think tourism has improved ( ) or worsened ( ) Havana's current social and environmental conditions?

Q14: Is there any place where you used to go which has been converted into tourist infrastructure?

1 ( ) Yes   2 ( ) No

What is this place?

1 ( ) The whole area
2 ( ) Public space such as squares, monuments
3 ( ) Bars/Restaurants

4 ( ) Hotels
5 ( ) Other _____

Q15: Is there any place where tourists interfere with your daily activities?

1 ( ) Yes   2 ( ) No

Q16: What is this place?

1 ( ) The whole area   4 ( ) Hotels
2 ( ) Public space such as squares, monuments   5 ( ) Other
3 ( ) Bars/Restaurants

Q17: Is there any place whose characteristics or conditions have been positively changed by tourism?

1 ( ) Yes   2 ( ) No

Q18: What is this place?

1 ( ) The whole area   4 ( ) Hotels
2 ( ) Public space such as squares, monuments   5 ( ) Other _____
3 ( ) Bars/Restaurants

Q19: Has the change brought by tourism been positive ( ) or negative ( )? Why?

1 ( ) Economic development   5 ( ) Population displacement
2 ( ) Cultural and social revitalisation   6 ( ) Personal insecurity/
3 ( ) Environmental revitalisation   crime increase
4 ( ) Dynamism   7 ( ) Other_____
                                             8 ( ) Do not know

Q20: What is the impact of tourism on your neighbourhood?

1 ( ) Positive   2 ( ) Negative   3 ( ) Little impact   4 ( ) No impact

Q21: Would you like to see more tourism development of your area?

1 ( ) Yes   2 ( ) No   3 ( ) Moderate increase

If Yes go to Q22

Q22: Why would you like to see more tourism development in this area?

1 ( ) Prosperity/economic development
2 ( ) Cultural exchange with tourists
3 ( ) Vitality/dynamism
4 ( ) Environmental revitalisation

5 ( ) Cleanliness
6 ( ) Other _____
7 ( ) Do not know/No answer

Q23: Do you have relatives who live abroad and visit you whenever they can?

1 ( ) Yes   2 ( ) No

Q24: Do you feel you are benefiting from current tourism development?

1 ( ) Yes   2 ( ) No   3 ( ) Partially

Q25: What aspect of tourism in Havana would you change if you could?

1 ( ) Equal opportunities between tourists and residents
2 ( ) Promote development of non-tourism projects
3 ( ) Reduce crime
4 ( ) Control of 'jineterismo'
5 ( ) Better employment opportunities for residents

6 ( ) Better retailing capacity
7 ( ) Training of local employees
8 ( ) Development of more infrastructures for national tourism
9 ( ) Other _____
10 ( ) Do not know/No answer

Q26: What do you think could be done to improve tourists' visits to this area?

1 ( ) Encourage home business/art craft
2 ( ) Eliminate crime
3 ( ) Eliminate 'jineterismo'
4 ( ) Cleanliness
5 ( ) Improve tourist infrastructures and services

6 ( ) Promote cultural exchange between tourists and residents
7 ( ) Better freedom for tourists
8 ( ) Improved customer care towards tourists
9 ( ) Other _____
10 ( ) Do not know/No answer

Q27: What do you think could be done to improve the benefits that tourism is bringing to this area?

1 ( ) Better employment
opportunities for locals
2 ( ) Improved promotion
3 ( ) Increase the length of visit to this area
4 ( ) Allow local community to
re- invest locally revenues from tourism

5 ( ) Increase tourists number
6 ( ) Other _____
7 ( ) Do not know/No answer

Q28: What are the major changes occurring in this area?

1 ( ) Physical environment linked to the
construction of tourism infrastructures
(hotels, museums etc)
2 ( ) Less attention to the housing
needs of local residents
3 ( ) More night life, leisure and cultural facilities
4 ( ) Less options for locals (specify which)
5 ( ) Change in local costumes, traditions
and relationships between people

6 ( ) Worsening
social behaviours
7 ( ) More attention to the
needs of local residents
8 ( ) Other.
Which?_____
9 ( ) Do not know/
No answer

Q29: What services or infrastructures would you like to see in this area to make the most of your free time?

1 ( ) Football pitch
2 ( ) Parks
3 ( ) Gyms
4 ( ) Cafes
5 ( ) Restaurants
6 ( ) Clubs

7 ( ) Discos
8 ( ) Video rental
9 ( ) Cinema
10 ( ) Libraries
11 ( ) Areas for dancing
12 ( ) Centres for elderly people
13 ( ) Other. What?

Q30: On a scale from 0 to 10 how happy are you with regard to current tourist development on this area? (0 = minimum satisfaction ; 10 = maximum satisfaction)

0 1 2 3 4 5 6 7 8 9 10

Q31: Please tell us if you agree with the following:
1 Strongly Agree
2 Agree
3 Neutral (or Do not know)
4 Disagree
5 Strongly Disagree

	1	2	3	4	5
Tourism has created greater employment opportunities (including self employment)					
Tourism has contributed to increased living standards in this area					
Tourism has contributed to the increase in prices					
Tourism has brought availability of more produce which is available in pesos					
Local residents benefit from the revenue brought from tourists to this area					
Local residents have better shopping opportunities because of tourism					
The presence of tourism does make shopping more unpleasant					
Local residents welcome the presence of tourists in this area					
The presence of tourism is responsible for increased crime in this area					
The presence of tourists is not responsible for overcrowding this area					
The quality of life of residents has improved because of tourists					
Tourism has a positive effect on the cultural life of this area					
Local residents are benefiting from the new tourism facilities built in this area					
This area experienced more litter problems because of tourists					
Tourists do not greatly add to traffic problems in this area					
The new tourism infrastructures have prompted physical regeneration of the area					
The new tourism development is increasing environmental differences between this and other city areas					
The provision of water has worsened since the tourist development began					
The provision of gas has worsened since the tourist development began					
The provision of electricity has worsened since the tourist development began					
Local people are always audited directly or via delegates about tourist development plans in this area					

Personal data

Age_____   Sex   (M)   (F)

The questions were translated in Spanish by the researcher.

Andrea Colantonio, April 2003

Appendix 2

Main Institutional and Economic Reforms in Cuba during the 1990s

Dimension	Year	Reforms/framework shift
Institutional	1992	Constitutional Reform • Decentralization of state monopoly on external trade • Establishment of mixed property and land usufruct
	1994	Reorganization of main State administrative organs
Economic opening up	1995	Law 77 on Foreign Direct Investments Decree Law 165 on creation of Free Export Zones
New organizations	1993	Establishment of producer co-operatives (UBPCs) Introduction of entrepreneurial self-financing schemes for State-run companies
	1998	Law 187 on Entrepreneurial excellence
New economic spaces	1993	Decree Law 140 on the legalization of US dollar Decree Law 141 on authorization of self employment
	1994	Introduction of new currency: the convertible peso Decree Laws 191 and 192 on the formation of agricultural produces and art craft markets
	1995	Establishment of currency exchange shops (Cadeca)
	1997	Decree Law 171 on authorization of Bed and Breakfasts
	2004	Circulation of the US dollar halted
Financial	1997	Decree Law 172 on the setting up of Central Bank of Cuba Law 73 on Fiscal System
	2005	Revaluation of convertible pesos against US dollar

(*Source*: Adapted from BNC, 2001; Ferriol and Carriazo, 1998)

Appendix 3

Trip Index for Havana

$$\textbf{Trip index} \; = \; \frac{\textbf{Number of tourist days spent in a given city}}{\textbf{Total number of tourist days of the whole trip}}$$

$$\begin{array}{l}\text{Trip index} \\ \text{for Havana}\end{array} = \frac{\text{tourist arrivals in Cuba x \% of tourists who visited Havana x average length of the visit (days)}}{\text{tourist arrivals in Cuba x average length of the visit in days}}$$

Tourist arrivals in Cuba in 1998 = 1,514,832

Percentage of tourists who visited Havana = 0.5

Average length of visit in days = 4

Trip index for Havana = 2,831,664/17,731,068 =

$$= 0.159$$

Bibliography

Acosta, M. and Hardoy, J.E., (1973), *Urban Reform in Revolutionary Cuba*, Antilles Research Program, Yale University

Agrawal, A. and Gibson, C.C., (1999), Enchantment and Disenchantment: The Role of Community in Natural Resource Conservation, *World Development* 27 (4): 629-649

Aguas de la Habana, (2003), *Una Empresa a Servicio de los Habaneros*, Havana

Aguilar Tamayo, R., (1996), 'El Taller de Atares Como Centro de Transformación Integral de Barrio' in Vàsquez-Penelas A. and Davalos Dominguez R (eds), *Partecipacion Social. Desarrollo Urbano y Comunitario*, Universidad de La Habana, 93-105

Andersen Consulting, (1990), *Plan estratégico para la revitalización del Bilbao Metropolitano*. Fase I: Exploración del entorno e identificación de temas críticos. Fase II: metas, objetivos y estrategias. Fase IV: Plan de accion, Bilbao

Arquitectura Cuba, (1974), Transformación Urbana en Cuba: La Habana, *Arquitectura Cuba* 341: (2)

Asamblea Municipal Ciudad de la Habana, (1988), *Ciudad de la Habana. Datos de Interés*, SAD, Havana

Ashworth, G.J., (1989), 'Urban Tourism: An Imbalance in Attention' in Cooper C.P. (ed.), *Progress in Tourism, Recreation and Hospitality Management*, Belhaven, 33-54

Ashworth, G.J., (2003), Urban Tourism: Still an Unbalance in Attention? in Cooper C. P. (ed.) *Classic Reviews in Tourism*, Channel View Publications

Ashworth, G.J. and Tunbridge, J.E., (1990), *The Tourist Historic City*, Belhaven Press, London

Asiedu, E., (2002), 'On the Determinants of Foreign Direct Investment to Developing Countries: Is Africa Different?', *World Development*, 30 (1): 107-119

Ayala, H., (2001), *Medio Siglo de Transformaciones del Turismo en Cuba*, Facultad de Contabilidad y Finanzas Gestion Hoteleras y Turismo, University of Havana

Baroni, S., (1991), 'Planificacion Fisica en Cuba: Experiencias y Perspectivas', in *Hacia una Cultura del Territorio*, in Ponce de Leon E. (2003) (ed.), Habana Ecopolis and GDIC, Havana

Barriball, K.L. and White, A., (1994) 'Collecting data using a semi-structured interview: A discussion paper', *Journal of Advanced Nursing* 19(2): 328-335

Becken, S. and Simmons, D.G., (2002), 'Understanding Energy Consumption Patterns of Tourist Attractions and Activities in New Zealand', *Tourism Management*, (23): 343-354

BNC, Banco Nacional de Cuba, (1989-2002), *Economic Report*, various years,

Havana
BNC, Banco Nacional de Cuba, (2001), *La Economía Cubana en el Periodo Especial 1990-2000*, Havana
Bohemia, (1997), *El Turismo en la Habana*, Havana
Böröcz, J., (1990), 'Hungary as a Destination 1960-1984', *Annals of Tourism Research*, (17): 19-35
Boyden, J. and Ennew, J., (eds) (1997) *Children in Focus: A manual for participatory research with children*, Stockholm, Grafisk Press
Bradley, A., Hall T., and Harrison, M., (2002), 'Selling Cities Promoting New Images for Meetings Tourism', *Cities*, 19 (1): 61-70
Briassoulis, H., (1992), 'Environmental impacts of tourism: a framework for the analysis and evaluation' in Briassoulis, H. and Van der Straaten, J. (eds), *Tourism and the Environment. Regional, Economic and Policy Issues*, Kluwer Academic Publisher, Dordrecht
Britton, S.G., (1982), 'The Political Economy of Tourism in the Third World', *Annals of Tourism Research*, 9 (3): 331-358
Britton, S.G., (1991), 'Tourism, Capital and Place: Towards a Critical Geography of Tourism', *Environment and Planning D: Society and Space*, 9 (4): 451-478
Brockington, D. and Sullivan, S., (2003), 'Qualitative Research' in *Development Fieldwork. A Practical Guide*, (eds) Scheyvens R. and Storey D., Sage Publications, London
Brohman, J., (1996), 'New Directions in Tourism for Third World Development', *Annals of Tourism Research*, 23 (1): 48-70
Brohman, J., (1997), *Popular Development: Rethinking the Theory and Practice of Development*, Blackwell Press, Oxford
Brundenius, C., (2002), *Tourism as an Engine of Growth. Reflections on Cuba's New Development Strategy*, Centre for Development Research, Copenhagen
Bull, A., (1995), *The Economics of Travel and Tourism*, Longman
Burtenshaw, D., Bateman, M. and Ashworth, G., (1991), *The European City: Western Perspective*, London: Fulton
Butler, R.W., (1980), 'The Concept of a Tourist Area Cycle of Evolution; Implications for the Management of the Resources', *Canadian Geographer* 24 (1): 5-12
Butler, R.W., (1981), *Tourist Development*, Longman, New York
Butler, R.W., (1993), 'Pre and post-impact assessment of tourism development' in Pearce, D. and Butler, R.W. (eds.), *Tourism Research: Critiques and Challenges*, Routledge
Butler, R.W., (1999), 'Problems and Issues of Integrating Tourism Development' in Pearce D.G. and Butler R.W. (eds), *Contemporary Issues in Tourism Development*, Routledge
CAESAR, (2003), *La Sostenibilidad mediante la Gestión Ambiental de los Recursos Hídrico y el Uso de la Tierra en Áreas Urbanas Periféricas de América Latina: Un Proyecto Cooperado de Universidades Latinoamericanas y Europeas*, University of Havana.
Cardoso, F.H. and Faletto, E., (1970), *Dependency and Development*, University of

California Press, Berkeley

Castro, F., (2001), Introduction, *Informe a la Asamblea Nacional del Poder Popular*, Internal document, Havana, 1-2

Cater, E., (1997), 'Ecotourism in the Third World- Problems and Prospects for Sustainability' in France L. (ed) *The Earthscan Reader in Sustainable Tourism*, Earthscan Publications, London

Centeno, M.A. and Font, M., (1997), Introduction, in Centeno, M.A. and Font, M. (eds), *Toward a New Cuba? Legacy of a Revolution*, Lynne Rienner Publisher, London, 1-9

Centeno, M.A., (1997), 'Cuba's Search for Alternatives' in Centeno, M. A. and Font, M. (eds), *Toward a New Cuba? Legacy of a Revolution*, Lynne Rienner Publisher, London, 9-25

CES, Centro de Estudios Turísticos, (1981), *La Historia del Turismo en Cuba*, Havana

CICA, Centre for Environmental Control and Information, (2001), *Application of Law- Decree on Environmental Regulation Violations Report*, Havana

CITMA-CH, Ministry of Environment, Science and Technology Ciudad de la Habana, (1998), *Estrategia Ambiental Provincial*, Havana

CITMA, Ministry of Environment, Science and Technology, (2002), *Cuba. Environment and Sustainable Development 10 Years After Rio de Janeiro Summit "Rio+10"*, Havana

CITMA-CH, (2003), *Evolución e Historia del Proceso de Urbanización de Ciudad de La Habana*, internal document, Havana

Coccossis, H. and Parpairis, A., (1992), 'Tourism and the environment: some observations on the concept of carrying capacity' in Briassoulis, H. and Van der Straaten, J. (eds), *Tourism and the Environment. Regional, Economic and Policy Issues*, Kluwer Academic Publisher

Colantonio, A., (2000), *The Environmental Impact of Tourism in Latin American Cities: The Case Study of Havana*, MA thesis, Institute of Latin American Studies, University of London

Colantonio, A., (2004), *"Tourism in Havana During the Special Period: Impacts, Residents' Perceptions and Planning Issues"*, (2004), Paper presented to the Association for the Study of the Cuban Economy (ASCE) Conference, Miami

Colantonio, A. and Potter, R.B., (2002), *Participatory Planning in 'Special Period' Cuba: The Experience of Three Workshops For Neighborhood Change In Havana*, CEDAR Research Paper 36, Royal Holloway, University of London

Colantonio, A. and Potter, R.B., (2003), 'Participatory and Collaborative Planning in "Special Period" Cuba' in Pugh, J. and Potter, R.B. (eds), *Participatory and Communicative Planning in the Caribbean: Lessons from practice*, Ashgate Press, Aldershot and Burlington, 68-97

Collis, D., (1995), Environmental Implications of Cuba's Economic Crisis, http://www.georgetown.edu/sfs/programs/clas/Caribe/bp8.htm accessed 12/06/00

CONAS, (1995), *Cuba. Inversiones y Negocios 1994-1995*, Consultores Asociados

S.A. Havana

Convención de Medioambiente, (2003), *IV Convención Internacional Sobre Medio Ambiente y Desarrollo*, Conference Proceedings, Havana

Conway, D., (1998), 'Microstates in a Macroworld' in Klak, T., (ed), *Globalization and Neoliberalism. The Caribbean Context*, Rowman & Littlefield Publishers Inc, 51-64

Coyula, M. (2002), 'City, Tourism and Preservation. The Old Havana Way', *ReVista: Harvard Review of Latin America*, Harvard University, available at http://drclas. fas.harvard.edu/publications/revista/Tourism/coyula.html

Crick, M., (1989), 'Representations of International Tourism in the Social Sciences: Sun, Sex, Sights, Savings and Servility', *Annual Review of Anthropology*, (18): 307-344

Cuban Chamber of Commerce (2002), *Foreign Trade*, (2), Havana

Cuban Constitution (1992) at http://www.cubapolidata.com/gpc/gpc_constitution _1992.html, accessed on 08/12/01

D'Amore, L.J., (1982), 'Guidelines to planning in harmony with the host community' in Murphy, P. (ed.), *Tourism in Canada: Selected Issues and Options*, Univeristy of Victoria, Canada

Davalos Domínguez, R. and Basail Rodríguez, A., (1997), 'Presentacion' in Davalos Domínguez, R. and Basail Rodríguez, A., (eds) *Desarrollo Urbano: Proyectos y Experiencias de Trabajo*, Universidad de La Habana, iii-vii

De La Cueva J., (1997), 'Los Hoteles en la Cuba Colonial' in *Obras* 1:(2)

De La Cueva J., (2001), *500 Años de Construcciones en Cuba*, Chavin, Havana

De Lacy, T., Battig, M., Moore S. and Noakes, S., (2002), *Public-Private Partnerships For Sustainable Tourism*, APEC

De Leuchsenring, E. R., (1952 circa), *Transformacion en Medio Siglo (1902-1952)*, cyclostyled, GDIC library

De Velde, A. and Morrissey O., (2002), Foreign Direct Investment: Who Gains, Oversee Development Institute, United Kingdom

Destino Cuba (2002), Number 24, EDITUR, Spain

Diaz Vasquez, L., (1997), *Cuba: Reforma Económica Dentro del Socialismo,* Centro de Investigaciones de Economía Internacional, University of Havana

Diaz-Briquets, S., (1994), "Cuba" in Greenfield G. M. (ed.), *Latin American Urbanisation. Historical Profile of Major Cities*, Greenwood Press, Westport Connecticut and London

Diaz-Briquets, S. and Pérez-López, J., (2000), *Conquering Nature: The environmental legacy of Socialism in Cuba*, Latin American series, University of Pittsburg Press

Doxey, G.V., (1975), *A causation theory of visitor-resident irritants, methodology and research inferences. The impact of tourism*. Sixth Annual conference proceedings of the travel research association, San Diego, 195-198

DPPF-CH, Dirección Provincial de Planificación Física Ciudad de la Habana, (1984), Havana's Master Plan of 1984, Havana

DPPF-CH, (1999), *Esquema de Ordenamiento Territorial Ciudad de La Habana*, unpublished, Havana

DPPF-CH, (2003a) *Montebarreto Development Plan*, unpublished, Havana

DPPF-CH, (2003b), Actualización del Plan General de Ordenamiento Territorial y Urbanismo, Redes Hidrosanitarias, Grupo Ingeniería Urbana, Havana

Eckstein, S., (1997), 'The Limits of Socialism in a Capitalist World Economy: Cuba Since the Collapse of the Soviet Bloc' in Centeno, M. A. and Font, M. (eds), *Toward a New Cuba? Legacy of a Revolution*, Lynne Rienner Publisher, London

ECLAC, United Nations Economic Commission For Latin America and The Caribbean, (2000), *La Economia Cubana: Reformas Estructurales y Desempeño en los Noventa*. Fondo de Cultura Economica, Mexico

EEA, European Environment Agency, (1999), *Environment in the European Union at the Turn of the Century*, European Union, Brussels

Elinson, H., (1999), *Cuba's Jineteros: Youth Culture and Revolutionary Ideology*, Cuba Briefing Paper Series 20, Washington D.C., Cuba Project, Center for Latin American Studies, Georgetown University

Espino, M.D., (1992), 'Environmental Deterioration and Protection in Socialist Cuba' in *Cuba in Transition* - Association for the Study of the Cuban Economy, ASCE, Miami, Florida International University, (2): 327-342

Espino, M.D., (2000), Cuban Tourism during the Special Period, in *Cuba in Transition* - Association for the Study of the Cuban Economy, ASCE, Miami, Florida International University, (10): 189-194

Esteva, G., (1992), 'Development', in Sachs W. (ed), *The Development Dictionary: A Guide to Knowledge and Power*, Zed Books, London

ETC, English Tourism Council (2002), Sustainability Indicators available at http://www.englishtourism.org.uk accessed on 14/02/03

European Commission (1997), *Employment and Tourism: Guidelines For Action*, Final Report, Brussels

EU, European Union, (2000), *Toward Quality Urban Tourism. Integrated Quality Management of Urban Tourism Destination*, European Commission, Brussels

EU, European Union, (2002), *Urban Audit*, available at http://www.inforegio.cec.eu.int/ urban/audit/src/results.html

Farrell, B.H. and Runyan, D. (1991), 'Ecology and tourism' in *Annals of Tourism Research*, 18 (1): 26-40

Fernandez, J.M., (1987), *Aspectos mas Relevantes del Desarrollo Urbano en La Ciudad de La Habana (1519-1987)*, Unpublished, DPPFA, Havana

Fernandez, J.M., (1998), *Regulaciones Urbanísticas de la Ciudad de La Habana*, Grupo para el Desarrollo Integral de la Capital, Havana

Ferradaz, I., (2002), Un Turismo de Calidad, *Cuba Foreign Trade*, (2): 6-15

Ferriol, A. and Carriazo, G., (1998), 'Efectos de Políticas Macroeconómicas y Sociales sobre los Niveles de Pobreza: El Caso de Cuba en los Años Noventa' in *Politicas Macro-economicas y Pobreza en America Latina y el Caribe*, Madrid, UNDP

Figueras, M.A., (2003), *International Tourism and the Formation of Productive*

Clusters in the Cuban Economy, World Tourism Organisation

Fisk, D., (2004), *Transition Assistance*, Paper presented to the Association for the Study of the Cuban Economy (ASCE) Conference, Miami, Florida

Flowerdew, R. and Martin, D., (1997), (eds), *Methods in Human Geography: A Guide For Students Doing Research Projects*, Longman

Font, M., (1997), 'Crisis and Reform in Cuba' in Centeno, M.A. and Font, M., (eds), *Toward a New Cuba? Legacy of a Revolution*, Lynne Rienner Publisher, London

Font, X. and Bendell, J., (2002), *Standards For Sustainable Tourism For The Purpose of Multilateral Trade Negotiations*, World Tourism Organisation

Foreign & Commonwealth Office, (1995), *Economic Reform in Cuba*, London

Forsyth, T., (1996) *Sustainable Tourism Moving from Theory to Practice*, Tourism Concern Published and WWF-UK, available at http://destinet.ewindows.eu.org/ aDefenition/D1/GENERIC_Tourism_Concern_Definition accessed on 08/06/03

Forsyth, T., (1997), 'Environmental responsibility and business regulation: the case of sustainable tourism', *The Geographical Journal*, 163 (3)

France, L., (1997), (ed), *The Earthscan Reader in Sustainable Tourism*, Earthscan Publications, London

Francisco, R.A., (1983), 'The Political Impact of Tourism Dependence in Latin America', *Annals Of Tourism Research*, (10): 363-376

Frank, A.G., (1969), *Capitalism and Underdevelopment in Latin America*, Monthly Review, New York

GDIC, Group for the Integral Development of the Capital, (2000), *Plan Estrategico de La Habana 2001-2003*, Havana

GDIC, (2002), '*La Habana del Futuro*' Proceeding of the conference 'Havana of the Future', 8 November 2002, Havana

Getz, D., (1993), 'Planning for tourism business district', *Annals of Tourism Research* 20 (3): 583-600

Gilbert, D and Clark, M., (1997), 'An Explanatory Examination of Urban Tourism Impact, with Reference to Residents Attitudes in the Cities of Canterbury and Guilford', *Cities*, 14 (6): 343-352

Gilderbloom, J., (1998), 'Viva Cuba. An enthusiastic look at our island neighbor', *Planning*, http://www.planning.org/pubs.cuba.htm accessed 15/02/00

Gollub, J. Hosier, A. and Woo, G., (2002), *Using Cluster-Based Economic Strategy to Minimize Tourism Leakages*, World Tourism Organisation

González M., (1995), *Sobre los Planos, Esquemas y Planes Directores de la Ciudad de la Habana*, Grupo para el Desarrollo Integral de la Capital, Havana

González Novo T. and Garcia Diaz I., (1998), *Cuba y su Medioambiente Despues de Medio Milenio*, Editorial Academia, Havana

González O., (2001), 'Inversiones en el Vedado', *Arquitectura y Urbanismo* (20): 4

González Rego, R., (2000), *Diferenciación Espacio-Territorial de Algunos Componentes del Ambiente Social en la Provincia Ciudad de la Habana*, PhD Thesis, Faculty of Geography, University of Havana

Goodall B., (1995), 'Environmental Auditing: a tool for assessing the environmental performances of tourism firm', *The geographical Journal*, 161 (1)

Gössling, S., Borgström Hansson, C., Hörstmeier, O. and Saggel, S., (2002), 'Ecological Footprint Analysis as a Tool To Assess Tourism Sustainability', *Ecological Economics* (43): 199- 211

Greenwood, J. and Lambie, G., (1999), 'Local Government in Cuba: Democracy through participation?', *Local Government Studies* 25 (1): 55-74

GTE Bahia Habana, (2003), *Situación de las Fuentes Contaminantes Indirectas le la Bahia De La Habana Para la Implementación De S.G.A*, Havana

Gunn, C., (2002), *Tourism planning: basics, concepts, cases*, with Turgut Var, Routledge

Gunn, G, (1995), *Cuba's NGOs: Government Puppets or Seeds of Civil Society*, Washington, D.C.: Cuba Briefing Papers Series, Georgetown University

Gutierrez Castillo, O. and Gancedo Gaspar, N., (2001), Tourism Development. Locomotive for the Cuban Economy, *Revista*, Harvard University available at http://www.fas.harvard.edu/~drclas/publications/revista/tourism/castillo.html

Hall, C.M., (1991), *Tourism in Australia: Impacts, Planning and Development*, Longman, Cheshire

Hall, C.M., (1994), *Tourism and Politics. Policy, Power and Place*, Wiley

Hall, D.R, (1984), 'Foreign Tourism under Socialism: the Albanian "Stalinist" model', *Annals of Tourism Research*, 11 (4): 539-555

Hall, D.R., (1990), 'Stalinism and Tourism. A Study of Albania and North Korea', *Annals of Tourism Research*, 17 (1): 36-50

Hall, D.R., (1991a), 'Introduction' in Hall D.R. (ed.), *Tourism and Economic Development in Eastern Europe and the Soviet Union*, Belhaven Press, London, 3-28

Hall, D.R., (1991b), 'Evolutionary Pattern of Tourism Development in Eastern Europe and the Soviet Union' in Hall D.R. (ed.), *Tourism and Economic Development in Eastern Europe and the Soviet Union*, Belhaven Press, London, 79-188

Hall, D.R, (2000), 'Evaluating the Tourism-Environment Relationship: Central and East European Experiences', *Environment and Planning B, Planning and Design*, 27 (3): 411-421

Hall, D.R., (2001), 'Tourism and Development in Communist and Post-communist Societies', in Harrison D. (ed.), *Tourism and the Less Developed Countries: Issues and Case Studies*, CABI, Wallingford

Hansen, M., (2002), 'Environmental Regulations of Transnational Corporations: Needs and Prospects' in Utting P. (ed.), *The Greening of Business in Developing Countries. Rhetoric, Reality and Prospect*, Zed Books and UNRISD, Zurich

Harloe, M., (1996), 'Cities in the Transition' in Andrusz G., Harloe M. and Szelenyi I. (eds) *Cities After Socialism. Urban and Regional Change and Conflict in Post-Socialist Societies*, Blackwell Publishers

Harrison, D., (1992), (ed.), *Tourism and the Less Developed Countries*, Belhaven Press, London

Healey, P., (1999), 'Institutionalist analysis, communicative planning, and shaping places', *Journal of Planning Education and Research*, 19 (2): 111-121

Heeley, J., (1981), 'Planning for Tourism in Britain', *Town Planning Review*, (52): 61-79

Hennessy, A., (1990), 'The Cuban Revolution: A Wider View' in Gillespie, R.O (ed.), *Cuba After Thirty Years. Rectification and the Revolution*, Frank Cass & Company Limited, London

Hernandez Padron, A. and Mercedes Guerra, E., (1997), 'Mi Barrio como un sol. Una Experiencia de Participación Comunitaria en el Consejo Popular Libertad' in Davalos Domínguez, R. and Basail Rodríguez A., (eds), *Desarrollo Urbano: Proyectos y Experiencias de Trabajo*, Universidad de La Habana, 113-122

Herod, A., (1999), 'Reflections on interviewing foreign elites: praxis, positionality validity and the cult of the insider', *Geoforum* 30:313-27

Hill, R.J., (1990), 'Cuba, Latin America, and the Communist Experience: A Comparative Note' in Gillespie, R. (ed.) *Cuba After Thirty Years. Rectification and the Revolution*, Frank Cass & Company Limited, London

Hinch, T., (1996), 'Urban tourism: perspective on sustainability', *Journal of Sustainable Tourism*, 4 (2): 95-110

Hoddinot, J. and Devereux, D. (eds) (1992), *Fieldwork in Developing Countries*, Harvester Wheatsheaf, Hemel Hempstead

Honey, M., (2001), 'Certification Programmes in the Tourism Industry' in Ecotourism and Sustainability, *Industry and Environment*, UNEP, (24): 3-4

Houck, O.A., (1999), 'Cuba's new law of the environment: an introduction' in Speir, J. (ed.), *Cuban Environmental Law. The Framework Environmental Law and Index of Cuban Environmental Legislation*, Tulane University and Center for Marine Conservation

Hughes, G., (2002), Environmental Indicators, *Annals of Tourism Research*, 29 (2): 457-477

Hultkrantz, L., (1998) 'Displacement Impact of a Mega Event: The World Championship in Athletics', Göteborg 1995'. *Festival Management and Event Tourism*, (5): 1-8

ICLEI, (1999), *Sustainable Tourism: A Local Authority Perspective*, background papers #3, http://www.iclei.org/la21/csd7_st.htm, accessed 21/6/00

INRH, Instituto Nacional de Recursos Hidráulicos, (1997a), *Estudio Sobre los Ciclos del Agua en La Habana*, EU and INRH, Havana

INRH, (1997b), Consumos y Perdidas de Agua de un Sector del Municipio Plaza de la Revolución, EU and INRH

Intur, Instituto para el Turismo, (1988), *Habana: Lineamientos Generales Para el Desarrollo Turístico. Estrategia Inversionista*, Internal Paper, DPPF, Havana

IPF, Instituto de Planificación Física, (1973), 'La Habana Metropolitana. Un Instrumento para el Desarrollo de Cuba Socialista', *Arquitectura Cuba* 341:(1)

IPF (1998), *Technical Potentialities and Service Capacities*, Havana.

IPF (2001), *Los Asentamientos Humanos, el Uso de La Tierra y los Cambios Globales En Cuba*, Havana

Jansen- Verbeke, M., (1986), 'Inner-city tourism: resources, tourist and promoters',

Annals of Tourism Research 19 (1): 79-100

Jones, K., (2000), Testimony Presented before the United States International Trade Commission at hearings on the Economic Impact of U.S. Sanctions with Respect to Cuba, Washington available at http://www.alamarcuba.com/testimony.html

Kilmister, A., (1992), 'Socialist Models of Development' in Allen, T. and Thomas, A., (eds), *Poverty and Development in the 1990s*, Oxford University Press

Kirby, P., (1999). *Involving young researchers. How to enable young people to design and conduct research*, York: Joseph Rowntree Foundation in association with Save the Children

Klak, T., (1998), 'Thirteen Theses on Globalisation and Neoliberalism' in Klak, T., (ed.), *Globalization and Neoliberalism. The Caribbean Context*, Rowman & Littlefield Publishers Inc.

Lanza, E., (1999), 'Planeamiento y diseño del turismo' in *El Planeamiento del Turismo a Las Puertas del Siglo XXI*, Havana

Law, C.M., (1992), 'Urban tourism and its contribution to economic regeneration', *Urban Studies*, 29 (3/4)

Law, C.M., (1993), *Urban Tourism: Attracting Visitors to Large Cities*, Mansell, New York

Laws, E., (1991), Tourism marketing, chap. 1, Cheltenham: Stanley Thornes

Laws, S., Harper, C. and Marcus, R., (2003), *Research for Development. A Practical Guide*, Sage. London

Ledo, T., (1999)., 'Aspectos generales del planeamiento territorial del turismo' in *El Planeamiento del Turismo a Las Puertas del Siglo XXI*, Havana

Leon, F., (1997), 'Socialism and Sociolismo: Social Actors and Economic Change in 1990s Cuba' in Centeno, M.A. and Font, M., (eds), *Toward a New Cuba? Legacy of a Revolution*, Lynne Rienner Publisher, London

Levett, R., (1997), 'Tools, techniques and processes for municipal environmental management', *Local Environment*, 2(2): 189-202

Lezcano, J.C., (1994), *Capital en Ruinas*, Paper presented at the Congreso Internacional de Derechos Humanos, Miami, Florida Internacional University

Li, X. and Yue-Man, Y., (1998), 'Transnational Corporations and Their Impact on Regional Economic Imbalance. Evidence From China', *Third World Planning Review*, 20 (4): 351-373

List J., and Co, C., (2000), 'The effects of Environmental Regulations on Foreign Direct Investment', *Journal of Environmental Economics and Management*, (40): 1-20

Liu, J and Var, T., (1986), 'Residents Attitudes Towards Tourism Impacts in Hawaii', *Annals of Tourism Research* (14): 14-37

Llanes Marrero, A, Bersagui Silva, W. and Oliver Gerardo, R., (1996), 'En Busca de Otra Vida. Proyecto de Transformacion Integral del Barrio La Corea' in Vàsquez-Penelas, A. and Davalos Domínguez, R., (eds), *Partecipacion Social. Desarrollo Urbano y Comunitario*, Universidad de La Habana, 119-132

Llloyd-Evans, S., (1994), *The Informal Sector in Trinidad: Space, Ethnicity and*

Gender, PhD Thesis, Royal Holloway, University of London

Marcuse, P., (1996), 'Privatization and its Discontents: Property Rights in Land and Housing in the Transition in Eastern Europe' in Andrusz G., Harloe M. and Szelenyi I. (eds) *Cities After Socialism. Urban and Regional Change and Conflict in Post-Socialist Societies*, Blackwell Publishers, Oxford, 119-191

Maribona, A., (1959), *Turismo en Cuba*, Lex, Havana

Marquetti Nodarse, H., (2001), Oferta Hecha en Cuba, *Negocios en Cuba* (25): 5-6

Mathéy, K., (1997), 'Self-Help Housing Strategies in Cuba: An Alternative to Conventional Wisdom?', in Potter, R. and Conway, D., (eds), *Self-Help Housing, the Poor, and the State in the Caribbean*, The University of Tennessee Press and The Press University of the West Indies

Mathieson, A. and Wall, G., (1982), *Tourism. Economic, Physical and Social Impacts*, Longman, Harlow

McIntosh. C and Nülle G., (2005), *Cuba's Dollar Ban*, Ludwig von Mises Institute, Alabama, USA

Mena, A.J., (2001), 'El Sector del Turismo en Cuba', *Planificación Fisica Cuba*, (2): 6-8

Mesa Lago, C., (1994), *Are Economic Reforms Propelling Cuba to the Market?*, Coral Gables: North South Center, University of Miami

Mesa Lago, C., (1998), *ECLAC's Report on the Cuban Economy in the 1990s*, Association for the Study of the Cuban Economy (ASCE), Miami, Florida International University, (8): 130-134

Mesa Lago, C., (2002), *Growing Economic and Social Disparities in Cuba: Impact and Recommendations for Change*, Cuba Transition Project, University of Miami

Metropolis-EU and INRH (Instituto Nacional de Recursos Hidraulicos), (1995), *Estudio Sobre los Ciclos del Agua en La Habana*, EU and INRH

Meurs, M., (1992), 'Popular Participation and Central Planning in Cuban Socialism-The Experience of Agriculture in the 1980s', *World Development* 20 (2): 229-240

Micons, Ministry of Construction, (1980), *La Arquitectura de Hoteles en la Revolucion Cubana*, Ministerio de la Construccion

Mintur, Ministry of Tourism, (1996), *Areas de La Politica de Desarrollo de la Actividad Turistica*, Havana

Mintur, (1998), *Turismo Nacional*, Tema 42, unpublished, Havana

Mintur, (2001a), *Informe a la Asamblea Nacional del Poder Popular,* Internal document, Havana

Mintur, (2001b), *Habana: 1995-2000*, cyclostyled, Havana City Library

Momsen, J.H., (1998), 'Caribbean Tourism and Agriculture: New Linkages in the Global Era?', in Klak, T., (ed), *Globalization and Neoliberalism. The Caribbean Context*, Rowman & Littlefield Publishers Inc.

Monreal, P., (1997), 'The Economics of the Present Moment' in Centeno, M.A. and Font, M. (eds), *Toward a New Cuba? Legacy of a Revolution*, Lynne Rienner

Publisher, London, 201-210

Montiel, S., (2001), Consideraciones Sobre el Turismo en Cuba en su Relacion con el Ordenamiento Territorial y el Desarrollo Sostenible, *Alquibla*, (7)

Mullins, P., (1991), 'Tourism Urbanization', *International Journal of Urban and Regional Research*, (15): 3, 326-342

Nuñez, R., (1995), 'El Suelo de la Habana: un nuevo recurso', *Carta de la Habana*, 8

Oliveros, M., (2002), *Turismo y Migracion en Moron*, unpublished paper, Geography Department, University of Havana

ONAT, (2003), *Total de Inscriptos Arrendamientos Habitaciones o Espacios*, Unpublished, Havana

ONE, Oficina Nacional de Estadísticas, (2002), *Anuario Estadistico de Cuba 2001*, Havana

OTE, Oficina Territorial de Estadísticas, (1997), *Informe de la Actividad Turística Hasta Diciembre de 1996*, Unpublished, Havana

OTE (2002), *Anuario Estadístico de Ciudad de la Habana*, Havana

OTE (2003), *Indicadores Seleccionados de la Actividad Turística en el Territorio*, Unpublished, Havana

OTH, Oficina de Turismo de La Habana, (2000), *Diagnostico Ambiental de la Habana*, Unpublished

OTH (2001), *Diagnostico de la Región Turística de la Habana*, Havana, Unpublished

OTH (2002a), *Encuesta*, unpublished, Havana

OTH (2002b), *Data sheet* provided by OTH on request, Unpublished, Havana

OTH (2003a)*, La Región Turística from OTH*, Havana

OTH (2003b), *Encuesta sobre el Nivel de Satisfacción de los Turistas*, Internal Document, Havana

OTH (2003c), *Indicadores Seleccionados de la Actividad Turística en el Territorio*, unpublished, Havana

Overton, J. and Van Diermen M., (2003), Using Quantitative Techniques in *Development Fieldwork. A Practical Guide*, (eds) Scheyvens R. and Storey D., Sage Publications, London

Page, S., (1995), *Urban Tourism*, Routledge, London

Page, S. and Hall C.M., (2003), *Managing Urban Tourism*, Prentice Hall

Parfitt, J., (1997) 'Questionnaire design and sampling', in *Methods in human geography*, Flowerdew, R. and Martin, D. (eds), Longman, Essex, 76-109

Pearce, D., (1989), *Tourism Development*, Longman, London

Pearce, D., (1995), *Tourism Today. A geographical Review*, Longman, London

Pearce, D., (1999), Introduction in *Contemporary Issues in Tourism Development*, Routledge, London and New York

Pearce, D. (2001), 'An Integrative Framework For Urban Tourism Research', *Annals Of Tourism Research*, 28 (4): 926-946

Pearce, P.L. and Moscardo, G., (1999), 'Tourism Community Analysis' in *Contemporary Issues in Tourism Development*, (eds) Pearce, D.G. and Butler,

R.W., Routledge

Pérez Fernandez, P. and Garcia Zamora, A., (1999) 'El Planemiento Integral de La infraestructura Vial y de Parqueo Como Solucion a Algunos Problemas del Desarrollo Turistico' in *El Planeamiento del Turismo a Las Puertas del Siglo XXI*, internal document, DPPF-CH, Havana.

Pérez Hernandez, L. and Prieto Valdes, M., (1996), 'Cuba, las Relaciones Estado-individuo: garantias de los derechos, Municipios y Legitimidad' in Vàsquez-Penelas, A. and Davalos Domínguez, R. (eds), *Partecipacion Social. Desarrollo Urbano y Comunitario*, Universidad de La Habana, 28-34

Pérez López, J., (1995), 'Cuba's Socialist Economy Toward the Mid-1990s', *The Journal of Communist Studies and Transition Politics* (11): 5

Pérez López, J., (1998), 'The Cuban Economic Crisis of the 1990s and the External Economic Sector' in *Cuba in Transition*-Volume 8, Association for the Study of the Cuban Economy, Washington

Pérez, M., (1999), 'Local Policy Approach with Community Participation for Environmental Improvement', *Sustain Magazine*

Pérez Mók, M. and Garcia, A., (2000), *Reformas Economicas en Cuba: Retos, Posibilidades y Perspectivas*, paper presented at the XXII International congreso of the Latin American Studies Association (LASA), Miami, Florida

Pérez Rodríguez, N., (1995), *Diferenciación del Ambiente Urbano en Ciudad de la Habana. Potencialidades para la Gestion Comunitaria*, PhD Thesis, Faculty of Geography, Unpublished, University of Havana

Pérez Villanueva, O.E., (2002), 'La Inversion Extranjera Directa en Cuba: Evolucion y Perspectivas', in *Cuba. Reflexiones Sobre su Economia*, Centro de Estudios de la Economia Cubana, University of Havana

Pérez-Stable, M., (1997), 'The Invisible Crisis: The Exhaustion of Politics in 1990s Cuba' in Centeno, M.A. and Font, M. (eds), *Toward a New Cuba? Legacy of a Revolution*, Lynne Rienner Publisher, London, 25-38

Pérez-Stable, M., (1999), 'Caught in a contradiction - Cuban socialism between mobilization and normalization', *Comparative Politics*, October: 63-79

Peters, P., (1997), *Cuba's Emerging Small Business Sector*, The Alexis de Tocqueville Institution, Virginia, USA

Peters, P. and Scarpaci, J., (1998), 'Cuba's New Entrepreneurs: Five Years of Small-Scale Capitalism', available at http://www.adti.net/html_files/cuba/TCPSAVE.htm, accessed on 04-2003

Phelps, N.A. and Tewdwr-Jones, M., (2000), 'Scratching the surface of collaborative and associative governance: identifying the diversity of social action in institutional capacity building', Environment and Planning A. (32):111-130

Pickvance, C.G., (1996), 'Environmental and Housing Movements in Cities after Socialism: The Case of Budapest and Moscow' in Andrusz G., Harloe M. and Szelenyi I. (eds), *Cities After Socialism. Urban and Regional Change and Conflict in Post-Socialist Societies*, Blackwell Publishers, Oxford, 232-267

Ponce de Leon, E., (1997), *La Capital para el Turismo o el Turismo para la Capital?*,

Unpublished, DPPF, Habana

Potter, R.B., (1985), *Urbanisation and Planning in the Third World: Spatial Perception and Public Participation*, New York, St Martins Press

Potter, R.B., (2000), *The Urban Caribbean in an Era of Global Change*, Ashgate, Aldershot and Burlington

Potter, R.B., and Dann G., (2000), 'Tourism, Post-Modernity and the Caribbean Urban Imperative' in Potter R.B., *The Urban Caribbean in an Era of Global Change*, Ashgate, Aldershot and Burlington, 77-102

Potter, R.B., Binns T., Elliott J., and Smith D., (2004a), *Geographies of Development* (Second Edition), Prentice-Hall, London and New York

Potter, R.B., Barker, D., Conway D. and Klak T., (2004b), *The Contemporary Caribbean*, Pearson Prentice Hall, London and New York

Prebish, R., (1950), *The Economic Development of Latin America*, United Nations, New York

Quiroz Lodoli, T., (2001), Los Emisarios del Litoral Habanero, *Aguas de la Habana*, (1): 19-20.

Rees, W., (1995), 'Achieving Sustainability: Reform or Transformation?', *Journal of Planning Literature*, 9 (4): 343-361

Rees, W.E. and Wackernagel, M., (1996), *Our Ecological Footprints. Reducing Human Impact on the Earth*, New Society Publishers, Canada

Rey Santos, O., (1999), 'Reflections on the legislative process of the new environmental law' in Speir J. (ed.) *Cuban Environmental Law. The Framework Environmental Law and Index of Cuban Environmental Legislation*, Tulane University and Center for Marine Conservation

Roberts, W.A., (1953), *Havana: The Portrait of a City*, Coward-McCann, New York

Rodríguez Garcia, L.J., (2000), *Informe Sobre Los Resultados Economicos del 2000 y Plan Economico y Social para el Año 2001*, Havana, 23 December 2000.

Rodríguez, Cruz F., (1997), Se volverá a pescar en la Bahia de la Habana?, *Habanera*, (3): 33-36

Ryan, C., (1991), *Recreational Tourism*, Routledge, London

Rydin, Y. and Pennington, M., (2000), 'Public Participation and Local Environmental Planning: The Collective Action Problem and the Potential of Social Capital', *Local Environment*, 5 (2): 153-169

Salinas Chavez, E., (1998), *El Turismo en Cuba: Desarrollo, Retos y Perspectivas*, Horizontes Hotels, Havana

Santamarina, V., (1944), *El Turismo, Industria Nacional*, Patronato del Balneario de San Diego de los Baños, Havana

Satterthwaite, D., (1997), 'Sustainable Cities or Cities that Contribute to Sustainable Development?', *Urban Studies*, 34 (10) : 1667-1691

Satterthwaite, D., (1999), 'The Key Issues and the Works Included' in Satterthwaite D. (ed.) *The Earthscan Reader in Sustainable Cities*, Earthscan Publications Ltd, London

Scarpaci, J., (2000a), 'On the transformation of socialist cities', *Urban Geography*,

21 (8): 659-669

Scarpaci, J., (2000b), 'Reshaping Habana Vieja: Revitalization, historic preservation, and restructuring in the socialist city', *Urban Geography*, 21 (8): 724-744

Scarpaci, J., (2002), 'Havana: The Dynamics of Local Executive Power', in Myers D. and Dietz H. (eds), *Capital City Politics in Latin America. Democratization and Empowerment*, Lynne Rienner Publisher, London

Scarpaci, J., Segre, R., Coyula, M., (2002), *Havana Two Faces of the Antillean Metropolis*, The University of North Carolina Press, Chapel Hill and London

Scheyvens, R. and Storey, D., (2003), Introduction in *Development Fieldwork. A Practical Guide*, (eds) Scheyvens R. and Storey D., Sage Publications, London

Scheyvens, R., Nowak, B. and Sheyvens, H., (2003) Ethical Issues in *Development Fieldwork. A Practical Guide*, (eds) Scheyvens R. and Storey D., Sage Publications, London

Scheyvens, R., Sheyvens, H. and Murray, W. E., (2003), Working with Marginalised, Vulnerable or Priviledged Groups in *Development Fieldwork. A Practical Guide*, (eds) Scheyvens, R. and Storey, D., Sage Publications, London

Schmidt, H.W., (2002), *Tourism and the Environment*, Statistics in Focus, Industry Trade and Services, Theme 4 (40), European Union

Schwartz, R., (1997), *Pleasure Island: tourism and temptation in Cuba*, Lincoln and London, University of Nebraska Press

Segre, R., (1995), *Arquitectura y Urbanismo de la Revolucion Cubana*, Editorial Pueblo y Educación

Segre, R., Cardenas, E. and Aruca, L., (1981), *Historia de la Arquitectura y del Urbanismo: America Latina y Cuba*, Editorial Pueblo y Educación

Segre, R., Coyula, M., Scarpaci, J., (1997), *Havana Two Faces of the Antillean Metropolis*, World cities series, Wiley

Shaw, G. and Williams, A., (1994), *Critical issues in Tourism*, Blackwell

Shaw, G., Greenwood, J. and Williams, A.M., (1988), The United Kingdom: Market Responses and Public Policy, in Williams A.M. and Shaw G. (eds), *Tourism and Economic Development: Western European Experiences*, Belhaven Press, London

Sidaway, J. D., (1992), 'In other worlds: On the Politics of research by "First World" geographers in the "Third World"', Area 24 (4): 403-8

Solano, R., (1995), Catastrofe del Ecosistema Cubano, *El Nuevo Herald* (22 April), Miami

Souty, F., (2002), *Passport To Progress: Competition Challenges For World Tourism And Global Anti-Competitive Practices In The Tourism Industry*, World Tourism Organisation

Spadoni, P., (2002), 'Foreign Investment in Cuba: Recent Developments and Role in the Economy' in *Cuba in Transition*, Association for the Study of the Cuban Economy (ASCE), Miami, Florida International University, (12): 158-170

Stark, D., (1992), 'Path Dependence and Privatization Strategies in East Central

Europe' *East European Politics and Societies* 6 (1): 17-54

Stone, O., (2000), *El Comandante*, Film-Documentary, New York

Stonich, S.C., (1998) Political Ecology of Tourism, *Annals Of Tourism Research*, 25 (1): 25-54

Szelenyi, I., (1996), 'Cities under Socialism- and After' in Andrusz G., Harloe M. and Szelenyi I. (eds) *Cities After Socialism. Urban and Regional Change and Conflict in Post-Socialist Societies*, Blackwell Publishers, 286-317

Tosun, C., (2002), Host Perceptions Of Impacts. A Comparative Tourism Study, *Annals of Tourism Research*, 29 (1): 231–253

Travieso Diaz, M., and Trumbull, C., (2002), Foreign Investment in Cuba: Prospects and Perils, in *Cuba in Transition*, Association for the Study of the Cuban Economy (ASCE), Miami, Florida International University, (12): 179- 188

UN, (1997), *Monitoring Human Settlements with Urban Indicators*, United Nations Centre for Human Settlements (Habitat), Nairobi, Kenya

UNAIC, Unión Nacional de Arquitectos y Ingenieros Cubanos, (2003), *Havana del Futuro*, Conference proceedings, Havana

UNCSD (2001), *Sustainable development of tourism*, United Nations available at www.un.org accessed on 28/02/03

UNCTAD (1998), *International Trade In Tourism-Related Services: Issues And Options For Developing Countries*, UNCTAD

UNCTAD (2001), *World Investment Report, Promoting Linkages*, UNCTAD

UNEP (2000), Urban Environmental Management, *Industry and Environment,* 23 (1-2), UNEP

Urry, J., (1990), *The Tourist Gaze: Leisure and Travel in Contemporary Societies*, Sage Publications, London

Van der Borg, J., (1991), *Tourism and Urban Development. The impact of tourism on urban environment: towards a theory of urban tourism and its application to the case of Venice, Italy*, Thesis Publishers, Amsterdam

Vàsquez-Penelas, A., and Davalos Domínguez, R., (1996) 'Partecipacion, Cultura y Comunidad' in Vàsquez-Penelas A. and Davalos Dominguez R. (eds) *Partecipacion Social. Desarrollo Urbano y Comunitario*, Universidad de La Habana, 132-146

Villalba, E., (1993), *Cuba y el Turismo*, Ciencias Sociales, Cuba.

Vourc'h, A., (2001), 'Tourism and Local Agenda 21s', in Ecotourism and Sustainability, *Industry and Environment*, 24 (3-4), UNEP

Weaver, D.B., (1993), 'Model of urban tourism for small Caribbean island', *Geographical Review*, 82 (3): 134-140

Werlau, M., (2001), 'A Commentary on Foreign Investment in Cuba' in *Cuba in Transition*, Association for the Study of the Cuban Economy (ASCE), Miami, Florida International University, (11): 290 -292

Williams, A.M. and Baláž V., (2000), *Tourism in Transition. Economic Change in*

Central Europe, Tauris, London

Wilson, J., (1988), *Politics and Leisure*, Unwin Hyman, Boston

World Bank, (2001), *Global Development Finance*, (CD ROM)

WTO, World Tourism Organisation, (1993), *Yearbook of Tourism Statistics*, World Tourism Organisation, Madrid

WTO (2003), *Tourism Market Trends 2003 - World Overview & Tourism Topics*, available on line at http://www.world-tourism.org/isroot/wto/pdf/1353-1.pdf accessed on 03/06/04

WTO, World Tourism Organisation (2004), *Tourism Highlights 2003*, Madrid

WTO, World Tourism Organisation (1990-2004) *World Tourism Statistics*, Various years

Yuksel, F., Bramwell, B. and Yuksel, A., (1999), 'Stakeholder Interviews and Tourism Planning at Pamukkale, Turkey', Tourism Management (20): 351-360.

Index